NOTES FOR FLUTISTS

Notes for Performers

Series Editor
Kyle J. Dzapo

Notes for Flutists

A GUIDE TO THE REPERTOIRE

Kyle J. Dzapo

OXFORD UNIVERSITY PRESS

Oxford University Press is a department of the University of Oxford. It furthers the University's objective of excellence in research, scholarship, and education by publishing worldwide. Oxford is a registered trade mark of Oxford University Press in the UK and certain other countries.

Published in the United States of America by Oxford University Press
198 Madison Avenue, New York, NY 10016, United States of America.

Library of Congress Cataloging-in-Publication Data
Name: Dzapo, Kyle J.
Title: Notes for flutists : a guide to the repertoire/Kyle J. Dzapo.
Description: New York: Oxford University Press, [2016] | Series: Notes for performers |
Includes bibliographical references and index.
Identifiers: LCCN 2015037966| ISBN 9780199857074 (pbk. : alk. paper) |
ISBN 9780199857050 (hardcover : alk. paper)
Subjects: LCSH: Flute music—History and criticism.
Classification: LCC ML937 .D93 2015 | DDC 788.3/2—dc23
LC record available at http://lccn.loc.gov/2015037966

9 8 7 6 5 4 3 2 1

Printed by Sheridan Books, Inc., United States of America

To William

Contents

Preface

I HAVE LONG been interested in connecting musical performance with pertinent aspects of scholarship. My favorite theory professor, John Buccheri (Northwestern University), used to say that to know a piece intuitively, technically, and intellectually is to really know a piece. While some may argue that one should simply "play from the heart," knowledge can be a powerful tool in strengthening or refining a performer's instincts.

My interest in connecting performance with ancillary studies began during my first lessons with Wally Mayhall when I was fifteen. This Cleveland-born-and-bred flutist captivated me not only with the beauty of his sound and the brilliance of his technique but also with his wide-ranging interests, his curiosity, and his unique way of looking at almost everything. My interest blossomed as I worked with Tom Nyfenger, the quintessential "complete musician." When he sat at the piano to perform pieces with me—whether with written or improvised accompaniments—his sensitive phrasing fueled my interpretation. While his ear may have led him to inflect passages in different ways at different times, his fundamental understanding of harmony, rhythm, meter, and structure guided him in bringing the music to life.

Later, I benefited from a music history assistantship as a master's student in flute performance at New England Conservatory. My approach coalesced when, in 1993, I accepted an offer to teach flute and music history at Bradley University. Three years later I began serving as a preconcert lecturer for the Chicago Symphony Orchestra. The satisfaction I've experienced from enhancing the CSO concertgoers' understanding of specific pieces of music, including several flute concertos, led me to the thought of pursuing a similar endeavor for flutists and their audiences.

While there are helpful resources for learning about chamber, orchestral, and operatic works, there are, in most cases, no in-depth resources to guide one's understanding of a given orchestral instrument's solo repertoire. In 2010, I proposed a book—and later a series—to Oxford University Press. My goal was to contribute to the intellectual understanding necessary, as Dr. Buccheri would suggest, for a flutist to *really* know a piece. Now, six years later, I am pleased to offer the first volume in Oxford's Notes for Performers series.

The selection of pieces is admittedly a subjective one. I began by trying to identify the best-known compositions written for unaccompanied flute, flute with keyboard, and flute with orchestra. To gain the broadest selection, I chose only one work of each composer. While J. S. Bach's E minor sonata and A minor partita are certainly worthy of inclusion, for example, I chose the B minor sonata and then went on to compositions of others. Walfrid Kujala, Bonita Boyd, Mary Stolper, and John Bailey were a great help, reviewing my lists and offering suggestions. My conversations with John were particularly stimulating: he is a model scholar and musician whom I have long admired.

It is my hope that flutists will view this book as a starting point for connecting performance studies with scholarship, that it will help them to gain a more complete picture of the works and the context in which they were written, and that it will encourage them to explore other works in a similar fashion. Many more works are worthy of inclusion in this book, and in time, perhaps a second volume may be added with additional compositions, as well as more recent works that are seen to have stood the test of time and to have become part of the core flute repertoire.

While I hope that all flutists will gain insights from this book, the writing is geared to undergraduate flutists: students who may have begun to study sonata form, for example, but who may not yet have the knowledge to apply it to the Reinecke sonata; students who may have encountered Johann Strauss's *Emperor Waltzes* but not realized that Godard, too, put together a string of waltzes in the third piece of his op. 116; students who may not yet have studied the time, place, and conditions under which Hindemith or Prokofiev composed their flute sonatas.

I couldn't have completed this book without the skillful analysis and valuable editing of William Wilsen. Friends describe him as "scary bright," and I am lucky to have had him offer his expertise and broad knowledge as I studied both the composers' lives and their music. James Ludwig and Oxford editors Suzanne Ryan and Todd Waldman helped me launch the idea, and the librarians at Bradley University, most notably Daniel Fuertges, obtained every resource I requested. My mom has continually encouraged my journey . . . as has my dad. I wish only that he could have lived longer to see how the journey has unfolded.

NOTES FOR FLUTISTS

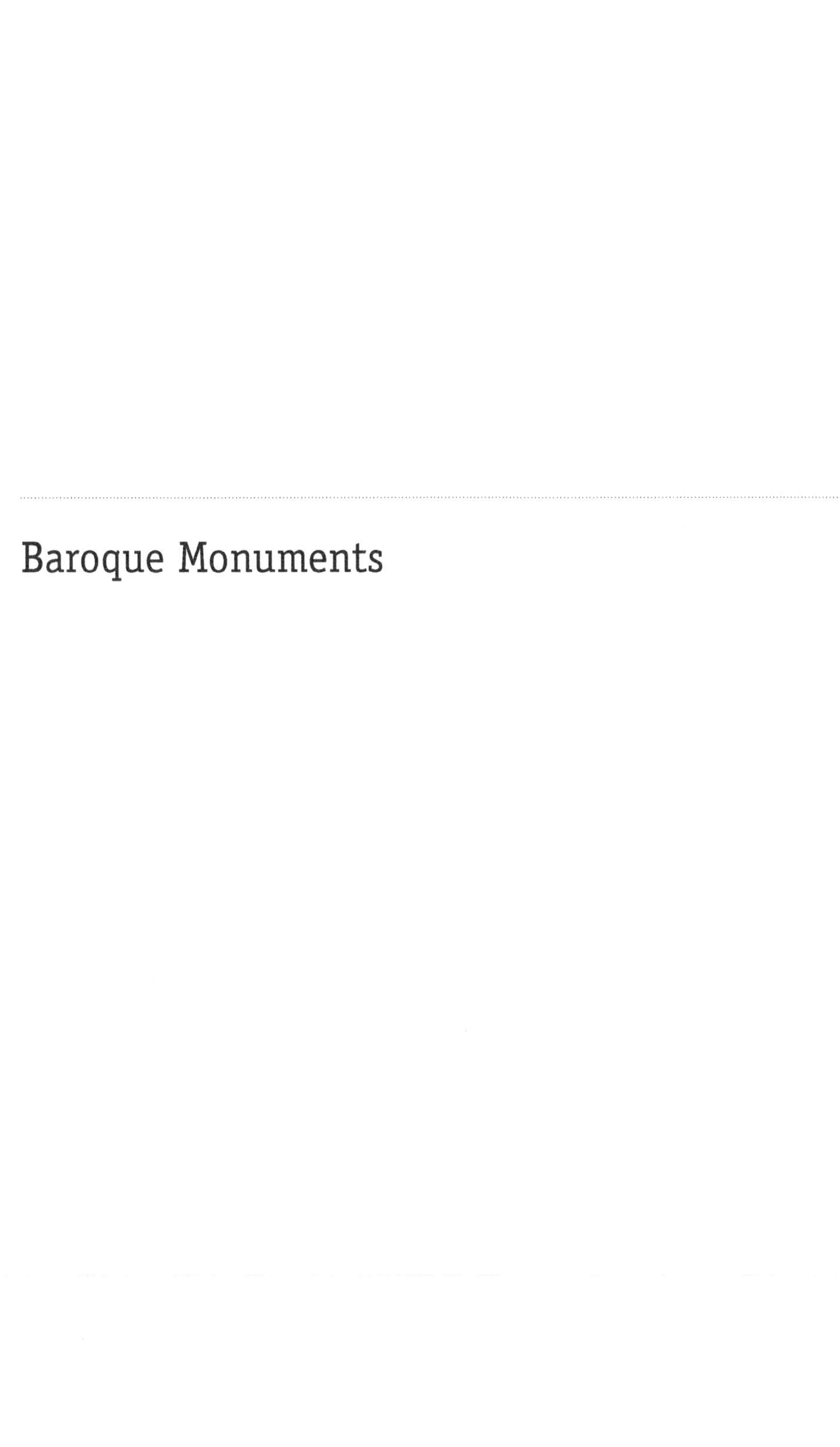

Baroque Monuments

1 Georg Philipp Telemann—Suite in A Minor

GEORG PHILIPP TELEMANN (1681–1767), who excelled in an age that demanded the constant production of new works, became the Baroque's most prolific and fashionable composer. Handel once remarked that Telemann "wrote a cantata in the time it took most people to write a letter," and although biographer Richard Petzoldt suggests that Handel made the comment "somewhat disdainfully,"[1] there is no doubt that Telemann's contemporaries admired him as a progressive and versatile composer.

Telemann was born in Magdeburg, then a provincial Prussian town situated in the center of a triangle formed by Leipzig, Berlin, and Hanover. His father died when Georg Philipp was but four, leaving his mother to oversee the education of her two young sons. Georg Philipp was drawn to music at an early age, participating in singing lessons, teaching himself to play several instruments, and learning to compose by copying the scores of others. He wrote his first opera at the age of twelve. Wishing to guide him toward a respectable and lucrative career, his mother forbade him to continue studying music and sent him at age thirteen to school in Zellerfeld and then, in 1697, on to the famous Gymnasium Andreanum, an academic high school in Hildesheim dating back to before 1225. He continued musical pursuits, however, and according to the composer's 1718 autobiography, his mother wrote from Magdeburg demanding that he "leave music" and pursue the study of law.[2]

Perhaps this was his plan as he set off for Leipzig in the fall of 1701, stopping along the way at Halle. Here he met Handel, an encounter that led to a lifelong friendship. Arriving in Leipzig, Telemann acquired a roommate, who happened to discover in the young composer's luggage his setting of Psalm 6. The work was soon performed at St. Thomas Church, after which Leipzig's mayor sent for Telemann and commissioned him to compose works for the St. Thomas choir to perform twice a month. Telemann plunged into these compositions and others and never looked back.

After founding the Collegium Musicum, which Bach would later direct, and working as music director of the Leipzig Opera and organist at the Neue Kirche, Telemann left Leipzig in the spring of 1705 to accept a court position in Sorau (present-day Zary, in Poland). It was during his brief tenure as kapellmeister to Count Erdmann von Promnitz that his travels introduced him to Polish folk music, and it was here that he began to compose suites like the famous one in A minor for recorder and strings. "Indeed, here I really began to be prolific for the first time, and that which I had done in Leipzig with vocal works I set out to do here with instrumental music, especially with *Ouvertüren*, for his Highness the Count had recently returned from France and therefore loved them."[3]

During the early eighteenth century, the suite was a favorite genre, and Telemann wrote hundreds of them: usually a two-part French overture followed by a series of dances, all in the same key. Like Bach, he sometimes incorporated a solo instrument; their efforts resulted in two of the most-often performed works in the genre: Telemann's Suite in A Minor and Bach's Second Orchestral Suite, in B Minor, featuring solo recorder and flute, respectively. The creation of this suite-concerto hybrid, while seen as incompatible with the true French style,[4] became one of the most important German contributions to Baroque music. Telemann led the cultivation of the German "mixed taste," which blended German counterpoint with French, Italian, and Polish elements. His Suite in A Minor is a good example.

Telemann had developed an interest in the French style during his teens, when he visited the courts of Hanover and Brunswick-Wolfenbüttel.[5] Dance was a spectacular feature of French opera, and Jean-Baptiste Lully, knowing that the public adored them, created collections of dances for performance at balls and festivals. To introduce this series of dances, he would add the overture of one of his operas. "The title 'Ouverture' (from 'ouvrir,' to open) was eventually applied to the entire suite."[6] Gradually, Lully's practice was taken up by musicians outside France, and as part of the mixed taste, German composers would write a "suite" including a French overture and some French as well as non-French dances.[7]

The Suite in A Minor's French overture opens with a majestic homophonic section featuring double-dotted rhythms that, since the time of Lully's operas (1660s–1680s), have evoked the image of the king's entrance into the royal loge of the theater.

Here, the Grave consists of two periods, the first moving from A minor (mm. 1–5) by means of a sequence to C major (mm. 7–11). The second period modulates back to A minor (m. 15), then on to E minor, ending with a Picardy third, a chord that doubles as the dominant of A minor.

It was typical for the Grave of a French overture to end on the dominant, leading to a resolution at the start of the livelier second section where a change of meter and of texture—from homophonic to contrapuntal—would also occur. Not so typical, and indeed rather refreshing, is Telemann's fusion of aspects of two genres: he casts the Allegro of this French overture, with all the aforementioned customary traits, in ritornello structure, a form typical of the outer movements of a concerto. The tutti sections, each based on the same theme, create pillars. The intervening solo sections provide contrast, the essence of a concerto.

The ritornello theme, tutti, is in two parts, "a" and "b," the second beginning in m. 33 with staccato sixteenth notes over a circle of fifths. When the soloist enters, it is with material from "a" as its point of departure. Following the second pillar ("a" and "b"), the recorder presents a long sequential passage (mm. 80–87) with tonicizations occurring by root movements down a third, then up a fourth: d (minor)–B♭ (major)–e (diminished)–C–F–D–G–E (= V/a). Following one more lengthy solo section, the ritornello makes its final appearance. Then, as expected, this French overture ends with a return to the style of the grand opening section.

French influence continues in the second movement, "Les Plaisirs" ("Pleasures"), the suite's first dance. French composers would often attach descriptive titles suggesting the affect, that is, the characteristic emotion of the music. The well-known Baroque theorist Johann Mattheson boldly declared in his book *Der vollkommene Capellmeister*:

> Anything which proceeds without these praiseworthy affections amounts to nothing, does nothing, and is worth nothing. . . . [I]n the case of plain instrumental music which hath no words . . . one's purpose should be to imagine and incorporate the reigning passion of the moment, so that the instruments, by means of their tone, immediately present an eloquent and understandable address.[8]

This movement, a bourrée,[9] is constructed in a large-scale ternary design with each section following the traditional binary form used for Baroque dances. The solo recorder is featured in the middle section, where Telemann introduces a different texture (as he had in the solo episodes of the overture), writing here a duet for recorder and bass.

The third movement, "Air à l'Italien," is the only movement except for the overture that is not dance-inspired. Instead, its mood and form suggest a da capo aria, so popular in Italian opera of the Baroque. Thus, it is this movement and the ritornello structure in the overture that constitute the Italian elements of the mixed taste. In spite of frequent short rests, the "A" section's lines are long and sinuous. The sprightly "B" section, by contrast, is clearly conceived for a virtuoso instrumentalist rather than a singer. After modulating from C major to G major, then back to C major and on to E minor, it is followed by a reprise of the opening section, which features improvised embellishments in the Baroque vocal tradition.

According to Mattheson, a minuet implied "moderate merriment" and a passepied, "giddiness, unrest, and vacillating spirits."[10] These movements each follow the same form as "Les Plaisirs," with the solo recorder featured in the second part of the ternary design. In a departure from the more closely related keys of the other movements, Telemann writes the second passepied in the key of the parallel major. Between Minuet and Passepied, he inserts a festive "Réjouissance" ("Rejoicing"). Breaking out of its accompanimental role, the orchestra participates in the festivity by engaging in dialogue with the soloist.

Concluding the suite is a Polonaise and Trio, introducing the Polish aspect of the mixed taste. This stately national dance in a moderate triple meter usually featured dotted eighth–sixteenth figures and phrases with feminine cadences. Telemann's triplets and contrasting rhythms within the span of a few beats also contribute to the movement's Polish character.[11]

In addition to this suite, Telemann wrote sonatas, unaccompanied *fantaisies*, duets, and concertos for the flute. And although Philipp Spitta and Albert Schweitzer denigrated some of Telemann's cantatas in favor of those attributed to Bach, the latter works have since been shown to be Telemann's,[12] and the largely negative reception of his compositions in the nineteenth century has changed decidedly.

After leaving Sorau, Telemann went on to positions in Eisenach, Frankfurt, and Hamburg. But he never forgot Leipzig, and people there never forgot him. When Cantor Johann Kuhnau died in June 1722, twenty years after the young Telemann had first met him, the town council unanimously selected Telemann for the position. In the end, however, the council in Hamburg acquiesced to the composer's demands for higher wages, he stayed in Hamburg, and the Leipzig council ended up hiring its third choice, Johann Sebastian Bach.

Notes

1. Richard Petzoldt, *Georg Philipp Telemann*, trans. Horace Fitzpatrick (New York: Oxford University Press, 1974), 186.

2. Petzoldt, 14.

3. Georg Philipp Telemann, "Lebens-Lauff mein Georg Philipp Telemanns; Entworffen In Frankfurth am Mayn d.10[-14] Sept. A. 1718." In Johann Mattheson, *Grosse General Baß-Schule. Oder: Der exemplarischen Organisten-Probe* (Hamburg: Johann Christoph Kißner, 1731), quoted in Steven Zohn, *Music for Mixed Taste* (New York: Oxford University Press, 2008), 20.

4. Zohn, 42.

5. Zohn, 14.

6. Petzoldt, 70.

7. Petzoldt, 70.

8. Johann Mattheson, *Der vollkommene Capellmeister*, 1739, quoted in Petzoldt, 75–76.

9. A bourrée is a lively duple-meter dance with a single upbeat that often appeared as one of the optional dances in a Baroque suite.

10. Johann Mattheson, *Kern melodischer Wissenschaft*, 1737, quoted in Petzoldt, 76.

11. Hans Werner Unger, "Volksliedhafte Melodik in Triosonaten Georg Philipp Telemanns" (diss., Leipzig University, 1967), quoted in Petzoldt, 194.

12. *Grove Music Online*, s.v. "Telemann, Georg Philipp," by Steven Zohn, accessed December 31, 2011, http://www.oxfordmusiconline.com.ezproxy.bradley.edu/.

2 Georg Frideric Handel—Sonata in E Minor, HWV 379

IN AN AGE when most musicians were employed as skilled servants for churches or wealthy courts, Georg Frideric Handel (1685–1759) was the Baroque's great entrepreneur. During his youth in Halle, his friend Telemann introduced him to opera, and he remained forever attracted to it. In the course of his career, he won and lost fortunes as he devoted himself to the composition and production of one opera (and later oratorio) after another. He penned his charming solo sonatas for recorder, flute, oboe, and violin at various times between 1707 and 1750, fitting their composition in among his larger works.

At the age of eighteen, Handel left his native Halle for Hamburg, one of the busiest and most famous opera centers in northern Europe. When the dissolute director had to leave town to escape his creditors, Handel got his chance to compose an opera. By the time he was twenty-one, he knew that he wanted a career in the theater, wanted to see more of the world, and most definitely did not want the life of a servant-composer at a provincial German court. So while Bach, who was the same age, had already settled down as a church organist in Arnstadt, only a few miles from where he had been born and brought up, Handel took off for Italy to learn about opera in the land where it had been born. It was also at this time that he wrote his first three solo sonatas, one for oboe, one for violin, and the D major flute sonata, HWV 378.

Handel spent four years in Italy, a decision that conveys a sense of his cosmopolitan and independent nature, especially when one considers that he could hardly speak Italian at the time of his arrival. He was in Venice in 1709 when the second opera he wrote in Italy, *Agrippina,* opened the carnival season there with enormous success. Carnival was the most popular time for visitors, and Handel's triumph before an international audience immediately established his reputation and provided influential contacts. Fortunately for him, no one at the time realized that only five of the opera's fifty-five musical numbers were specifically composed for this opera.[1] Clearly, he saw no reason to write everything anew when he could simply adapt music he had written previously. As we shall see, the same is true of the E minor flute sonata.

The elector of Hanover (later George I of England) had permanent boxes at the Venice opera, and it is likely that the ruler's brother attended a performance of *Agrippina* and, like everyone else, was carried away. Perhaps this is what led to Handel's appointment as the elector's kapellmeister.[2]

Handel was reluctant but accepted the appointment because he was permitted a twelve-month leave to go wherever he pleased. Within weeks, he was off to London because of its Italian opera company at the new Queen's Theatre, named for reigning Queen Anne (subsequently, the King's Theatre for George I) and sometimes known informally as the Haymarket Opera House. This was the primary opera house in England and, for over twenty-five years, the home of Handel's operatic career.

Arriving in London in 1710, the year Christopher Wren completed St. Paul's Cathedral, Handel made a stunning impact on the city. He made enemies, too, notably Joseph Addison and Richard Steele, who had tried to establish a school of English opera but failed. Before long, Handel was producing one Italian opera after another and making the genre all the rage. He did, however, have to return to his job in Hanover for fifteen months.

Then, in 1712, with the elector's acquiescence, Handel returned to London "for a reasonable time" and never turned back. He later struck a deal with Hanover's ambassador in London, who secured him an honorable severance from the court—in exchange, it seems, for confidential information about Queen Anne's health. The queen had not been well, and because of questions of succession, it was important to know if her death were imminent. It was actually two years later that Queen Anne died and the elector of Hanover, great-grandson of the Stuart king James I and Anne's closest Protestant relative, became George I of England.

In time, there came plans for a new company, which would become the Royal Academy of Music. Not to be outdone by the French, the English no doubt drew their name from Louis XIV's Académie Royale de Musique, which had been established fifty years earlier. In spite of strong movements to develop English opera, in the end the Royal Academy employed Handel to produce Italian opera, which was fine with King George, who never learned to speak or understand English well.

While Handel probably composed two oboe sonatas (HWV 363 and HWV 366) between 1712 and 1716, it was during the 1720s, while fully occupied with the academy, that he wrote most of his solo sonatas—three for violin, four for recorder, and two others without specified instruments. He also assembled the Sonata in E Minor, HWV 379.

Handel put together this five-movement "sonata a travers. e basso" by borrowing movements he had previously composed, changing aspects (key, tempo, rhythm, articulation) as he saw fit. The first and fourth movements were adapted from the D minor violin sonata, HWV 359a, while the second and fifth were borrowed from the G minor recorder sonata, HWV 360. The only newly composed movement was the third, and even that begins with a motive that appeared in the D major flute sonata, HWV 378 (and would later be incorporated into the D major violin sonata, HWV 371).

The dotted rhythms, broad tempo, and simple duple meter of the first movement immediately remind the listener of the stately French overtures with which Handel opened his operas, oratorios, and concerti grossi. Here he spins out long phrases, setting up cadences and then thwarting their resolutions both harmonically and melodically. Beats 2 and 3 of mm. 4 and 5 offer examples. In the first instance, Handel resolves the V chord of E minor deceptively to iv^6. Over the V, the flute plays an E, an anticipation of the resolution, but as the harmony changes, the melody drops an octave, further foiling expectations. One measure later, Handel again leads toward an authentic cadence, this time in A minor. A ii^6_5 chord on the second eighth note of the measure is followed by V on the second beat. The flute's sixteenth-note A at the end of that beat anticipates resolution. Handel surprises the listener again, first by dropping the flute to C♯ instead of remaining on A, but especially by substituting A major for the expected A minor (à la "tierce de Picardie") and then, on the second half of the beat, introducing G♮s to turn the cadential A major into A^7 (V^7/iv), which quickly becomes vii^7/iv, resolving not to D minor but D major (Picardy third again), which is then revealed to be functioning as the dominant of G major. The first authentic cadence of the piece, on G, is thus postponed until m. 6. This is one of many examples of the composer's ingenuity.

The second phrase is built on a two-beat motive that is repeated sequentially, forming a large-scale descending melodic line in the flute, mm. 7–10: D♯–C♯–B–A♯–G♯–F♯–E. The opening melody returns in m. 12 over the same bass line that accompanied it in m. 1. Beginning at the end of m. 13, one hears another sequence, this time with an ascending scalar pattern on the first and third beats of m. 14 and the downbeat of m. 15. Again, a cadence is postponed until m. 20. Even here, after a "final" cadence in the tonic key of E minor, Handel adds a one-and-a-half-measure extension, ending with a Phrygian cadence (iv^6–V) whose dominant triad resolves on the downbeat of the second movement.

Though Baroque sonatas were often labeled "da chiesa" (church) or "da camera" (chamber), the distinction soon became blurred, and the sonata, as exemplified here, was often a mix of the two. The second, fourth, and fifth movements of the Sonata in E Minor are stylized dances in binary form. The second and fifth share versions of the same opening melodic line. In the second, that opening phrase, over a walking bass, is answered by a two-measure motive accompanied by a lively sixteenth-note figure; much of the rest of the movement is spun out of sequences based on that motive. In the fifth movement, by contrast, the "A" section consists of rhythmic imitations of the opening phrase. The "B" section begins with a playful two-measure eighth-note gesture that is repeated and then spun out, after which the "A" material returns. It is interesting to note that when Handel concluded the G minor recorder sonata, HWV 360, with this movement, it began on a downbeat; here, though, Handel begins on the third quarter note, creating a gavotte, though the movement is simply labeled "Presto."

The central movement of the sonata is a through-composed Largo, the only one in a different key, the relative major. The homophonic style and broad tempo create a simple, expansive aura. As in the first movement, Handel concludes with a Phrygian cadence leading directly to the next movement. In this Allegro, one measure after the flute begins the melody, the bass line imitates it two octaves lower, creating a canonic relationship unlike the texture of any of the other movements. The canon breaks off after three measures, but the same construction recurs each time the principal melody is presented (mm. 17, 32, 58). Unusual is the fact that the "B" section begins identically to the second half of "A" (at m. 17), though the first tonal goal of "B" is A minor, not the confirmation of G major that occurs in "A." The flute's virtuoso passagework adds to the rollicking spirit of this passepied.

Handel's autograph of this sonata is housed at the British Library. Though sometimes erroneously labeled op. 1, no. 1a, the piece never appeared in early publications of opus 1 and, in fact, was not published at all until after the composer's death.

The labeling of this work is but one area of confusion among many that have long plagued Handel's sonatas. The questions date back to mistakes in the first eighteenth-century publications. John Walsh was the first to publish Handel's sonatas, in the days when "the enforceable border between legitimate publication and piracy was virtually non-existent."[3] Walsh, it seems, was anxious to capitalize on the composer's (and the transverse flute's) popularity, but he did not have Handel's authorization to publish the sonatas. So as not to get into trouble, he used the imprint of the deceased publisher Jeanne Roger of Amsterdam for his first edition. Walsh published the sonatas with many errors, the D minor violin sonata (from which the first and fourth movements of the E minor sonata are derived), for example, appearing as "Traversa solo #1 in E minor." It was a "disgracefully botched edition . . . faked title-page, two sonatas by another composer, four of the genuine sonatas assigned to the wrong instrument, and, in places, a wildly corrupt text."[4] Some corrections were made a short time later when Walsh republished the works, but many mistakes persisted. This was "compounded by the unfortunate tendency of later editors, among them [nineteenth-century music historian Friedrich] Chrysander, to base their editions on the Walsh prints rather than the autographs."[5] In recent years, Handel scholars have gone back to the autographs, have studied the paper on which they were written, and have published articles and new editions that correct the mismatched movements and the other bumbled aspects of Handel's great contribution to the flute repertoire.

Notes

1. John E. Sawyer, "Irony and Borrowing in Handel's 'Agrippina,'" *Music & Letters* 80 (Nov. 1999): 531.
2. Wendy Thompson, *Handel* (London: Omnibus, 1994), 45.
3. Donald Burrows, *Handel* (New York: Schirmer, 1994), 190.
4. Terence Best, "Handel's Chamber Music: Sources, Chronology, and Authenticity," *Early Music* 13 (Nov. 1985): 482.
5. Best, 478–479.

3 Antonio Vivaldi—Concerto in D Major (*Il Gardellino*)

AS THE OLDEST SON born of a poor family, Antonio Vivaldi (1678–1741) was destined for the priesthood. But in September 1703, only months after having been ordained, the twenty-five-year-old was appointed to the respected position of *maestro di violino* at Venice's Ospedale della Pietà. From this time on, the "Red [i.e., redheaded] Priest" would devote his life to music, rarely ever celebrating Mass again.

Venice's four *ospedali* were state-supported charitable institutions. Pietà took in, fed, clothed, and educated orphaned, illegitimate, and abandoned girls. A small group of the students was selected to receive first-rate musical training and to perform choral and orchestral programs in the institution's chapel every Sunday and holiday. These programs, which raised money to assist with financing the *ospedali*, were renowned throughout Europe. Contemporary reports boasted that the quality of music was equaled by only a few large European courts, and in fact, the eighteenth-century French scholar and politician Charles de Brosses declared that the Pietà strings surpassed even those of the Paris Opera.[1]

In addition to teaching the violin students, Vivaldi was responsible for the acquisition and maintenance of instruments and the composition of new works to be added to the Pietà's repertoire.[2] Concertos were the order of the day, and early on he gained fame as the master of this genre. With the publication of *L'Estro Armonico*, op. 3, a collection of twelve concertos published by Estienne Roger of Amsterdam in 1711, Vivaldi's name spread throughout Europe. (Johann Sebastian Bach later arranged six of these works.) Concertos continued to pour from Vivaldi's pen, including "chamber concertos," a genre he developed.[3]

These new compositions were created for ensembles of three or four solo wind and string instruments with continuo, but they incorporated musical characteristics of the orchestral concerto. In other words, they are concertos without orchestra. *Il Gardellino*, RV 90, in D major, is an example.

Scholars don't know why the young composer created this first version of *Il Gardellino*. It may have been for a performance at the Pietà or perhaps for the court in Mantua, where he served as *maestro di cappella da camera* between 1718 and 1720. Of course, we know that Baroque musicians often reworked and reused compositions, and Federico Maria Sardelli, author of *Vivaldi's Music for Flute and Recorder*, tells the story of the second incarnation of *Il Gardellino*:

> Two of Vivaldi's chamber concertos [*Il Gardellino*, RV 90, and *La Pastorella*, RV 95] are linked to commissions from Cardinal Pietro Ottoboni, the Venetian prelate who from his court at Rome exercised an energetic and free-spending patronage of the arts. Vivaldi was in Rome for the Carnival seasons 1722–23 and 1723–24 in connection with the production there of his operas and the display of his talents as a violinist. On one of these occasions he travelled with a large quantity of instrumental compositions that were performed by Ottoboni's orchestra and taken into its repertory. After the cardinal's death in 1740, by which time he had spent his way to complete bankruptcy, all his art collections, including his collection of music, were sold off cheaply. An English traveller, Edward Holdsworth, bought (by weight!) a good part of this music on behalf of his friend Charles Jennens and took it back to England, where, after passing through various hands, it eventually arrived at its present home in the Henry Watson Music Library, Manchester.[4]

The Ottoboni-Manchester version of *Il Gardellino*, catalogued as RV 90b, is an adaptation of the earlier source (RV 90a) in the composer's personal archive. In the later arrangement, in addition to some purely musical changes, Vivaldi changed the scoring from "Flauto Trav.[ersier]" to "flauto [dritto (straight)] ó viol[in]o p[ri]mo,"[5] thereby sanctioning the transverse flute part to be performed on recorder or violin. He also added alternatives for the oboe and bassoon parts, suggesting a string ensemble in which a violin could substitute for the oboe and a cello for the bassoon[6] (thus, cello, continuo, and three violins: the original solo violin plus two more on the original flute and oboe parts).

Vivaldi lived most of his life in Venice, with long periods of employment at the Pietà. There were, however, protracted periods spent away from his native city—carnival seasons in Rome, for example—and there were times when the Pietà's governing board did not approve renewal of his contract. The reasons for the governors' actions remain one of the mysteries of Vivaldi's biography.

In February 1709, for example, the composer did not receive the two-thirds majority required for reappointment. He was then rehired in 1711. Between 1717 and 1722, his name again does not appear on the payroll, but in 1723 he received a new appointment. Michael Talbot, a leading Vivaldi scholar, relates that

> In July 1723 the Pietà governors agreed to ask Vivaldi to supply the orchestra with two concertos every month (at one sequin each), sending them by post if necessary, and to direct three or four rehearsals of them when in Venice. The institution's accounts confirm payment to him for over 140 concertos between 1723 and 1729. As a composer Vivaldi was evidently a major asset to the Pietà, notwithstanding his frequent travels, which ruled out a teaching post.[7]

It was during the late 1720s, when Vivaldi would have been about fifty, that Michel-Charles Le Cène, Estienne Roger's son-in-law and successor, published three sets of Vivaldi's concertos in rapid succession. One set, Vivaldi's op. 10, a collection of six concertos for solo flute and strings, has the distinction of being the first set of concertos ever published for solo flute. Given the era, it is perhaps not too surprising that five of the six, including op. 10, no. 3, the version of *Il Gardellino* analyzed below, were adaptations of earlier works.

Vivaldi composed approximately thirty pieces with a programmatic element (or at least an extramusical title). *Il Gardellino* ("The Goldfinch") is one of many that includes birdsong. When Vivaldi adapted the piece from chamber concerto to solo concerto, he rewrote the opening so that the flute introduces the distinct voice of the goldfinch from the first measure instead of having the instrument participate in the melody of the ritornello and wait until the solo section to introduce its song.

As had become Vivaldi's custom, the concerto's outer movements use ritornello structure, the orchestra opening with music that will recur in abbreviated form between the soloist's utterances and at the movement's conclusion. The opening movement's first solo section (mm. 13–20) is unaccompanied, a delightful cadenza for the goldfinch. Its indication "*a piacimento*" ("at will," "as you please"), varied rhythms, and melodic flourishes vitiate the propulsive rhythmic drive one expects of Vivaldi's allegros. Following an abridged presentation of the ritornello (mm. 21–26), the solo flute begins another passage without orchestra, but this time the solo first and second violins join in. This solo section effects a modulation to B minor, which is confirmed by the subsequent ritornello. A longer final solo section (mm. 53ff.) features even more interplay among all of the solo instruments (solo viola and cello, in addition to the aforementioned flute and violins), effectively drawn sequential passages, and a sparkling virtuosity that demonstrates why Vivaldi was not only the most popular composer of his day but was esteemed as the most original.

The Larghetto cantabile is a quiet movement in D major for solo flute with continuo. Marked throughout by the dotted rhythm of a siciliano in 12/8 meter, the movement is a lovely pastoral interlude between the irrepressible exuberance of the outer movements. As is customary in a binary-form movement, the first section moves to the dominant key. The second section begins in E minor and returns to D major by way of a vii^{o7} chord of the parallel minor.

The finale, an allegro in triple meter, returns to ritornello structure, this time with four solo sections between five recurring pillars. Like the first movement, the goldfinch interjects its voice into the opening orchestral section, this time in thirds with a solo first violin. As demonstrated here and in the solo sections, when Vivaldi adapted this concerto from its original chamber setting to a solo concerto, he wanted to retain the interplay between solo voices instead of featuring only the flute. In the final solo section (mm. 94–111), however, just as in the first one of the opening movement, he dispenses with dialogue and features a florid goldfinch accompanied minimally by solo strings. A final sequence (mm. 105ff.) leads to a cadence that flutists often embellish with a cadenza, thereby ending the bird's song with even more freedom than it had when it was presented in the first movement's opening solo.

Following the burst of concerto publications in the late 1720s and widespread travels in the ensuing years, Vivaldi's last decade was spent largely in Venice, when his popularity as a composer of concertos and operas was in decline. He continued to compose for the Pietà, though he lost his official position again with the governors' vote of 1738. As summarized by Charles de Brosses, who visited the city frequently:

> To my great amazement, I have found that he is not as appreciated here as he deserves, for fashion is everything in Venice, where his works have been heard for too long and where last year's music makes no money. The current man of the day is the famous 'Sassone' [Saxon] (Hasse).[8]

While demand for new concertos and operas continued unabated, the public's taste was indeed changing. The man who claimed that he could complete an opera in five days and compose a concerto faster than a scribe could copy it could still produce works quickly, but he could no longer draw large audiences to hear them.

Some speculate that his waning popularity prompted his departure from Venice in 1740 and that perhaps he went to Vienna hoping for royal patronage and the production of an opera at the Kärntnertortheater.[9] When Emperor Charles VI died in October 1740, however, the theaters closed—and Vivaldi's dreams were dashed. Nine months later, on July 28, 1741, the once-famous composer died impoverished in a foreign city that knew nothing of him. A simple service was held prior to burial at his new parish church, St. Stephen's Cathedral, where the nine-year-old Franz Joseph Haydn served as one of six choirboys.[10] Ironically, the burial account book listed Vivaldi only as "secular priest"; no mention was made of his being the foremost Italian composer of his day.

Notes

1. Karl Heller, *Antonio Vivaldi: The Red Priest of Venice* (Portland, OR: Amadeus Press, 1997), 29.

2. Michael Talbot, *Vivaldi* (London: British Broadcasting Corporation, 1979), 15.

3. Federico Maria Sardelli, *Vivaldi's Music for Flute and Recorder*, trans. Michael Talbot (Aldershot, UK: Ashgate, 2007), 91–92.

4. Sardelli, 113–114.

5. Sardelli, 114.

6. Sardelli, 114.

7. *Grove Music Online*, s.v. "Vivaldi, Antonio," by Michael Talbot, accessed August 2, 2014, http://www.oxfordmusiconline.com.ezproxy.bradley.edu/.

8. Charles de Brosses, *Lettres historiques et critiques sur l'Italie* (Paris: Pointhien, 1799), quoted in Heller, 259.

9. Heller, 261.

10. H. C. Robbins Landon, *Vivaldi: Voice of the Baroque* (New York: Thames and Hudson, 1993), 166.

4 Johann Sebastian Bach—Sonata in B Minor, BWV 1030

JOHANN SEBASTIAN BACH (1685–1750) penned the extant autograph of his Sonata in B Minor, arguably the finest of his flute and keyboard works, while living in Leipzig during the mid-1730s. He was in his early fifties and had for thirteen years shaped the city's musical life through prodigious composition and the supervision of innumerable performances. This was his final position and the culmination of a career spent diligently working for the churches and courts in what is today central Germany.

Bach and his family moved to Leipzig in May 1723, where he took on the twofold position of cantor and *director musices*:

> As "Cantor zu St. Thomae" he was responsible for the musical education of the pupils of the school at St. Thomas's (he was later exempted from giving them Latin lessons) and for the musical supervision of the four principal churches of Leipzig; and as "Director musices" he was the senior musician of the city and answerable for the musical organization of official occasions like council elections and homage ceremonies.[1]

In those, the days of the great cantors, almost every Sunday would bring a new church composition of major proportions, most often a cantata. And so with his new position, Bach embarked on a huge artistic undertaking. In the next years, in addition to other responsibilities, he wrote a cantata for almost every Sunday and church holiday. There were interruptions in this immense production only on occasions when he repeated compositions or performed the works of others.[2]

In 1729, Bach added a new position: he became director of Leipzig's Collegium Musicum, an association of professional musicians, university students, and Bach children; they performed weekly two-hour concerts at Zimmermann's, Leipzig's largest and best-known coffeehouse.[3] The Sonata in B Minor may well have been prepared for a Collegium performance. A posthumous copy of the harpsichord part suggests that Bach may have originally composed this sonata in G minor between 1729 and 1731. He returned to the piece in 1736 or 1737, at which time he prepared a fair copy, now in the more suitable key of B minor.[4] Studies reveal that the paper Bach used for the autograph was made by N. Michael and used by the composer only in 1736 and 1737,[5] years when he was fully engaged with the Collegium concert series.

Also during this period, Bach strengthened his connection to the Saxon royal court in Dresden. His acquaintance with Dresden's master flutist Pierre-Gabriel Buffardin (1689–1768) no doubt inspired and influenced his writing of the B minor sonata. Bach had undertaken his first trip to the brilliant court in 1717, and he made the daylong journey to perform organ recitals and enjoy virtuoso orchestral and operatic performances at least four more times during his tenure in Cöthen and Leipzig.[6] In 1733, frustrated that he had "innocently had to suffer one injury or another" in Leipzig, he applied for a position in the Saxon capital. He believed that the "injuries would disappear altogether" if he were appointed Dresden's composer of the royal court *Capelle* (chapel). After three years of inaction, he applied again; happily for Bach, he received the title on November 19, 1736. While it is not known if the appointment, which he held concurrently with his Leipzig position, resulted in any commissions, the distinction did seem to ease tensions in Leipzig.[7]

While most Baroque flute sonatas include skeletal keyboard accompaniments—a bass line with figures for realizing the right hand—Bach, in the Sonata in B Minor, composed a complete harpsichord part, engaging the two instruments (three lines) as equal partners in the contrapuntal texture. In his day, the ear was conditioned to hear simultaneous melodic lines that in their synchronicity defined the chords, the harmonic progression. The delightful interplay of these voices is a testament to Bach's genius.

The first movement is an unusually lengthy and complex one in which Bach moves skillfully among three textures:

1. counterpoint among equally important voices engaged in different lines
2. counterpoint among equally important voices in imitation
3. melody with accompaniment

Changes between textures help delineate the form.

Rich contrapuntal writing (texture 1) dominates the opening B minor section, all three voices engaged in the conversation. With the entrance of a new ornate theme in the flute in m. 21, the texture changes as the keyboard steps back to an accompanimental role. The melody then moves to the keyboard in m. 27, when for the first time the flute becomes accompanimental ever so briefly before dropping out altogether. With the flute's return to the principal theme in m. 33, the opening texture is taken up again as the keyboard also returns to its opening lines. All three voices then engage in a falling-fifth sequence (F♯–B–E) built on the fragmented line that the bass first states in m. 35. In m. 38, Bach inverts the counterpoint, the right hand of the keyboard now playing the principal theme while the flute takes over the opening keyboard line.

Following the half cadence at m. 44, one hears a new texture, the imitative one (texture 2), again built on sequences. Here, for thirteen measures (mid-44 through mid-57), the flute and right hand of the keyboard pass their lines back and forth, imitating at the octave or the fifth, at rhythmic intervals ranging from one to two to four beats. Measures 55 and 56 feature not only imitation at the interval of two beats but another falling-fifth sequence (A–D–G–C) leading to a full cadence in F♯ minor in m. 58.

The flute dominates (texture 3) the next section (mm. 59–64) until counterpoint (texture 1) reasserts itself as the keyboard's right hand sounds the principal theme (m. 63). Harmonically, this passage accomplishes a modulation to G major by means of a ten-beat circle of fifths beginning at the end of m. 60. Measures 65 through 70 present the same material as the preceding six measures: textures 3 and 1, with the top two voices' roles reversed, modulating from G major to E minor. At m. 71, imitative texture returns over a twenty-five-note descending scale in the bass, an emphatic full cadence in E minor, and a modulation back to B minor with a half cadence that sets up the reprise. From m. 87 to the end of the movement, the imitative texture predominates.

The Largo e dolce is a richly harmonized binary-form movement in D major. Like the Air of Bach's Third Orchestral Suite, it is a beautiful "song without words," whose point of departure may have been the siciliana. It is a perfectly balanced movement unified by affect and by Bach's inclusion of the opening melody and a syncopated repeated-note figure in both halves. As one would expect of the form, the first half moves from the tonic to the dominant key. The second half begins in the dominant and moves through B minor (mm. 10–12) before concluding in D major.

Like other composers of his day, Bach was fluent in all contemporary genres, and he frequently merged aspects of one with another: suite and concerto movements sometimes include elements of fugue, while cantata movements and suites may

Fugue section	Exposition							Episode			Middle Entry			
theme	subject	answer	transition			subject					answer			
starts m#	1	9	16			20		27			34			
			elision			elision		elision			elision			
# of mm	8	7+	1	+2	1+	1	+6+	1	+5	+1+	1	+6+		
key	**b**	**f#**		**mod**	**b**				**mod**	**f#**				
starts m#	1	9		17	19				28	33				
section	Episode			Middle Entry		Episode			Middle Entry		Coda			
theme				subject					subject					
starts m#	41			52		59			66		73			
	elision			elision		elision			elision		elision			
# of mm	1	+7	3+	1	+6+	1	+5	1+	1	+6+	1	+4	5	1
key/chord	**(f#)**	**mod**	**e**				**mod**	**b**				**mod**	**b**	**V**
starts m#		42	49				60	65				74	78	83

CHART 4.1 Bach, Sonata in B Minor, BWV 1030: Analysis of the third movement.

Gigue														
themes in flute*	a	b									a	b		
themes in keybd rh*			a	b					a	b			$b^{aug\dagger}$	
starts m#	84	86	88	90					102	104	106	108	112	
key	**(b)**				**mod**	**D**	**mod**	**f#**						
starts m#	84				93	94	98	101						
*Themes "a" and "b" and sequences (including cadential melodic patterns) prevail in the gigue.														
†aug = augmented														
themes in flute*	c			b^{aug}	a	a						a	b^2	
themes in keybd rh*	c			a	b^{aug}		a		b^1		a			
starts m#	114			116	118	120	122		124		126	128	130	
key	**(f#)**			**b**	**e**			**mod**		**G**				**mod**
starts m#		115		116	118			123		125				131
		i V^7 $I^{\#3!}$ (Picardy 3rd) ($I^{\#3}$/f# = V/b)												
themes, flute	a	b^{aug}	x				a		b^{aug}	c				
themes, keybd rh	b^{aug}	a			x			a		c				
starts m#	132	134	138½ (→140)		139½ (→141)		142	143	144	146	147			
key	**e**	**b**												
starts m#	132	134	139 (→142) circle of 5ths		140½ (→143) basso ostinato						i V^7 $i^{(b3!)}$ (no Picardy 3rd)			

CHART 4.1 Continued

incorporate characteristics of the French overture. Some would argue that the recurring themes alternating with episodic passages in the first movement of the B minor sonata suggest the ritornello structure of the Baroque concerto. Certainly the form and character of the second movement are typical of the suite as is the finale's gigue. The finale's first section is a fugue.

This fugue, in B minor and simple duple meter (¢), is in three-part counterpoint, reminding one of what Bach elsewhere called "invention." The exposition comprises an eight-measure subject in the flute, an answer in F♯ minor in the keyboard's right hand, and a third statement, back in B minor, in the bass. As can be seen in Chart 4.1, episodic material then alternates with additional presentations of the subject, each episode including a modulation to a related minor key. The fugue ends in B minor on a V–iv–V half cadence.

The resolution occurs with the start of the second part of the movement, now in a highly syncopated compound duple meter, with the character of a gigue. Characteristic of dance music, the gigue is in binary form. It begins in B minor with a two-part theme presented by the flute: "a," mm. 84 and 85; "b," pickups to m. 86 through the downbeat of m. 88. The theme is immediately repeated in the right hand of the keyboard. A sort of episode (mm. 92–101) includes sequences (beginning at mm. 92 and 98) and modulates first to D major, then (mm. 98–101) to F♯ minor, the goal of the first half. Upon arrival in that key, the two-part theme returns for two additional presentations. A Picardy third ends the section.

Bach unifies the two parts of the gigue by returning to "a" for the start of the second section, once again in B minor. Now, however, it is transferred to the right hand of the keyboard and coupled with a varied, augmented version of "b," emphasizing the stepwise descending melodic pattern. The chart denotes presentations of the principal thematic material and the harmonic scheme. It's a contrapuntal tour de force exemplifying once again the formidable skill of the great Baroque master.

Notes

1. Christoph Wolff, *Bach: Essays on His Life and Music* (Cambridge, MA: Harvard University Press, 1991), 30.

2. Wolff, 30.

3. Christoph Wolff, *Johann Sebastian Bach: The Learned Musician* (New York: Norton, 2000), 352.

4. Robert L. Marshall, *The Music of Johann Sebastian Bach* (New York: Schirmer Books, 1989), 216.

5. Wisso Weiss, "Papier- und Wasserzeichen der Notenhandschriften von Johann Sebastian Bach" (unpublished manuscript, Johann-Sebastian-Bach Institut, Göttingen, 1962), quoted in Richard David Claypool, "J. S. Bach's Sonatas for Melody Instrument and Cembalo Concertato: An Evaluation of All Related Manuscript Sources," vol. 1 (PhD diss, Northwestern University, 1975.)

6. Wolff, *The Learned Musician*, 208.

7. Wolff, *The Learned Musician*, 372.

Enlightenment Gems

5 Carl Philipp Emanuel Bach—Sonata in A Minor, Wq. 132

CARL PHILIPP EMANUEL BACH (1714–1788), third surviving child of Johann Sebastian and his first wife Maria Barbara, was born in Weimar just after his father's promotion to concertmaster at the court of Duke Wilhelm Ernst. The young Emanuel received musical training from his father and was further shaped through his immersion "from an earliest age in a phenomenally active musical family environment . . . [in which he] lived, breathed, and ate music as no one today ever did or could."[1] During the course of his long career, Emanuel emerged not only as the most prolific and best known of Bach's sons but also as the most innovative German composer of his generation.

The family moved to Cöthen when Emanuel was three, then on to Leipzig when he was nine. One of the reasons cited for the family's second move was the intellectual stimulation the larger city would afford. Johann Sebastian cared deeply about the education of his children and wanted his sons to have the university education that had not been possible for him. In 1731, after studies at the Thomasschule, Emanuel matriculated as a law student at the University of Leipzig. At the same time, he served "as a most important musical assistant"[2] to his father and created the first of his surviving musical compositions. Emanuel and his older brother Wilhelm Friedemann "had the best of both worlds: liberal education and constant musical activity in a household full of music."[3] Three years after entering law school, Emanuel moved to Frankfurt an der Oder, a city in eastern Prussia near Poland, where he continued law studies and took a leading role in the musical life of the city. He supported himself by giving keyboard lessons, composing, and directing public concerts and ceremonies.[4]

In 1738, just as he was about to embark on a tour of Austria, Italy, France, and England with Count Hermann Keyserlingk, son of the Russian ambassador to Dresden (for whom Sebastian had composed his *Goldberg* Variations), Emanuel received "an unexpected and gracious summons to Ruppin [a Prussian garrison town about forty miles northwest of Berlin] from the then crown prince of Prussia."[5] The young keyboardist and composer canceled plans for the tour, knowing that he couldn't refuse the future king. The position of harpsichordist, Emanuel's first major post, began informally with payments from Frederick's private purse and continued formally after Frederick's accession to the throne. Emanuel would continue in the same position for nearly thirty years. During this time he composed approximately three hundred works, including keyboard and chamber music compositions, symphonies, keyboard concertos, an Easter cantata, a Magnificat, and the Sonata in A Minor for solo flute.

When Emanuel entered the service of Crown Prince Frederick, he found a patron enthralled by music. Ten years earlier (1728), Frederick's father, King Friedrich Wilhelm I of Prussia, had taken his son to Dresden. While there, the sixteen-year-old crown prince was introduced to the Saxon court's artistic splendor. Already devoted to music, he was overwhelmed by the virtuoso flute playing of J. J. Quantz and by the experience of hearing his first opera (Hasse's *Cleofide*). While his father demanded that his son become a skilled soldier and railed against his musical and literary interests, Frederick held steadfast in his pursuits. He began flute studies with Quantz (author of a valuable treatise on flute playing, *Versuch einer Anweisung die Flöte traversiere zu spielen*, 1752), and when he was allowed to reside in Ruppin, away from his father, in 1732, he began to assemble the coterie of orchestral musicians who served as the nucleus of the large musical establishment over which he would preside as sovereign.

"When Frederick finally acceded to the throne on 31 May 1740 he plunged into social and political reforms, military conquest and the rehabilitation of Prussian arts and letters, all at once. . . . Indeed, in the first years of his reign Frederick enlarged both Prussia's geographical and cultural boundaries, with equal verve."[6] A devotee of the *galant* style, he made Berlin the center of musical life in northern Germany, launching the Berlin Opera and overseeing some fifty musicians (including Quantz, Franz and Joseph Benda, Johann Friedrich Agricola, and the Graun brothers). The greatest of his musicians—though Frederick never realized it—was Carl Philipp Emanuel Bach.

In 1747, the year that Sebastian made the second of his visits to Frederick's court and the year in which Frederick began residing in his newly completed summer retreat, Sanssouci ("Without a Care"), in Potsdam, Emanuel composed his solo flute sonata in A minor. At this time of transition in music, when both Emanuel and Friedemann "admitted to Forkel that they were 'driven to adopt a style of their own by the wish to avoid comparison with their incomparable father,'"[7] Emanuel succeeded masterfully in blending stylistic elements he had learned from his father with aspects of the new, expressive *Empfindsamer Stil* (literally, sensitive or sentimental style). Influenced by his friend, the writer, dramatist, and philosopher Gotthold Lessing, Emanuel adopted principles of drama and rhetoric "to achieve an intimate, sensitive, and subjective expression; gentle tears of melancholy were one of its most desired responses."[8] His use of harmonic surprises, suspense-filled pauses, and abrupt changes of rhythmic motion contributed to the new musical expression, making his sonata far different from his father's solo flute work in the same key. This is especially apparent in the opening slow movement of Emanuel's sonata.

The opening phrase, in the tonic key of A minor, establishes both melody and bass, the upper voice's ornamentation contributing to the expressivity of its lyrical line. Following a half cadence in m. 8, Bach immediately establishes the relative major, leaving the mournful affect of the first phrase behind, if only for a moment. In m. 15, the interval of an augmented second followed by a descending stepwise line introduces a turn toward the supertonic before another authentic cadence in C, mm. 22–24. A sequential passage (mm. 25ff.) leads away from and back to C major, but its expected arrival in C is thwarted by a deceptive cadence to a diminished-seventh chord (mm. 30–31) that outlines the opening melody. The lower voice now progresses chromatically from F♯ to G to A♭ to G and resolves to C in mm. 36–37. A surprise moment of silence on the downbeat of m. 34 is followed by an equally surprising augmented-sixth chord in an open position that spans A♭^{1} to E♭^{3}. This "German" augmented-sixth resolves conventionally to V^7 of C major in m. 35, where the drive to the cadence is interrupted by a questioning ascending minor seventh and rest before the cadential passage resumes, finally resolving to the tonic chord of the relative major in m. 37.

The "B" section of the movement begins dramatically in D minor with a plunging four-note gesture, *forte* suddenly to *piano*, begun three times. The gesture then appears in E minor, its third iteration spun out leading to a return of the opening theme of the movement (mm. 50ff.). A driving *forte* passage in sixteenth notes, beginning in m. 56, leads forcefully to a cadence in E minor, followed in m. 62 by a return to the tonic key and a change of affect. Halfway through m. 66, a *subito forte* begins a drive to a half cadence. After a brief pause, "A" returns. Here, Bach varies the opening material, spinning out a long passage, the latter part of which includes a large-scale chromatic descent. Moving from A (m. 80) to G♯, G, F♯, F, E, and finally to D as the third of a B♭ major Neapolitan chord leading to V^7/a in m. 85, the tension is further prolonged by a deceptive melodic move to F in m. 87, on to E, the dominant, in m. 89, a full-measure's pause, and then, at the performer's discretion, an improvised cadenza over the dominant chord of the final cadence.

The sonata's three-movement sequence, slow-fast-fast, with each movement in the tonic key, may strike listeners as unusual, but in fact this structure was standard during Frederick's reign.[9] The latter two movements, both allegro and in rounded binary form, achieve contrast through their differences in meter and affect. The first section of each movement moves from A minor to the relative major and includes virtuoso sixteenth-note passagework. Most interesting and unexpected in the third movement are the abrupt changes from *forte* to *piano* and vice versa and a quick succession of other contrasts: the turn from C major to E minor in m. 27; the diminished (instead of minor) triad used as the harmonic basis of a restatement of the principal theme in m. 33, now suddenly and ominously *piano*; the unexpected eighth rest in m. 37 followed by an outburst of vigorous sixteenths suddenly suppressed by eighth notes *subito piano* (mm. 41–44); and the jagged two-voice counterpoint leading to a cadence in E minor to conclude the first half. This twenty-six-measure passage is a brilliant example of Emanuel Bach's new rhetoric.

The "B" sections of both movements begin in the relative major, but it is in the second movement that one experiences excursions into many keys: D minor, C major, E minor, a languid passage in D minor (beginning with the pickup to m. 77), and then a sequential statement in E minor. A new sequence begins with the pickup to m. 85, now back in the movement's tonic, A minor. The third iteration of this sequence is a devilishly difficult, extended elaboration of the dominant chord preparing the return of "A" at m. 95. Contributing to the quixotic character of this movement are irregular phrase lengths and accent patterns that result in "mixed meters" (emphases occurring on the second beat of mm. 66, 68, and 72, for example).

Frederick the Great assembled and presided over one of the largest musical courts in Germany. He himself composed flute sonatas and concertos and enjoyed performing in private chamber music concerts several nights each week with his gifted musical servants, Quantz and Emanuel among them. When the Seven Years War (the third war between Prussia and Austria for control of Silesia) began in 1756, however, Frederick was forced to turn his attention away from his musical endeavors. The opera house closed, and musicians had to accept reduced pay or, during certain periods, none at all. While he had "exerted considerable influence on the lively development of music in the city [Berlin/Potsdam] . . . his taste [at this time] ceased to develop, and he eventually contributed to the stultification of musical life at court."[10] After the war ended in 1763, Frederick continued to perform music in the *galant* style and was uninterested in more progressive works, including those of the *Empfindsamer Stil.* It was time for the innovative fifty-three-year-old Emanuel to move on.

He had applied for other positions over the years, but it was not until the death of his godfather, Georg Philipp Telemann, in 1767, that Emanuel won a major post—succeeding Telemann as *Kantor* of Hamburg's Johanneum Lateinschule and music director of the city's five principal Protestant churches. He requested a release from the king, which was finally awarded after much prodding and perhaps a less-than-honest complaint of poor health.[11] This allowed the gifted harpsichordist, whose treatise (*Versuch über die wahre Art das Clavier zu spielen*, Teil I, 1753; Teil II, 1762) had brought much acclaim to the court, to accept the Hamburg post. Emanuel spent the final twenty years of his life in a position much like the one his father had held in Leipzig years earlier. And like his father, he immediately negotiated handing off the teaching responsibilities associated with the position. Emanuel composed prolifically to satisfy the enormous demands of his new job but wrote only one more flute sonata, the well-known "Hamburg."

Notes

1. Peter Williams, "Towards a Close Reading of Carl Philipp Emanuel Bach," in *Eighteenth-Century Music in Theory and Practice: Essays in Honor of Alfred Mann*, ed. Mary Ann Parker (Stuyvesant, NY: Pendragon, 1994), 143.

2. Eugene Helm, "Carl Philipp Emanuel Bach," in *New Grove Bach Family* (New York: Norton, 1983), 252.

3. Williams, 144.

4. Helm, *New Grove Bach Family*, 252–253.

5. C. P. E. Bach, quoted in Helm, *New Grove Bach Family*, 255.

6. *Grove Music Online*, s.v. "Frederick II, King of Prussia," by E. Eugene Helm and Derek McCulloch, accessed October 5, 2013, www.oxfordmusiconline.com.ezproxy.bradley.edu/.

7. J. N. Forkel, *Johann Sebastian Bach: His Life, Art, and Work*, trans. and ed. C. S. Terry (London, 1920), 105, cited in Hans-Günter Ottenberg, *C. P. E. Bach*, trans. Philip J. Whitmore (Oxford: Oxford University Press, 1987), 20.

8. *Grove Music Online*, s.v. "Empfindsamkeit," by E. Daniel Heartz / Bruce Alan Brown, accessed April 25, 2015, www.oxfordmusiconline.com.ezproxy.bradley.edu/.

9. Mary Oleskiewicz, "The Flutist of Sanssouci: King Frederick 'the Great' as Performer and Composer," *Flutist Quarterly* 38 (Fall 2012): 24.

10. *Grove Music Online*, s.v. "Bach, III (9) Carl Philipp Emanuel Bach," by Christoph Wolff, accessed October 5, 2013, http://www.oxfordmusiconline.com.ezproxy.bradley.edu/.

11. Helm, *New Grove Bach Family*, 264.

6 Wolfgang Amadeus Mozart—Concerto in G Major, K. 313

MOZART DASHED OFF the most famous of flute concertos—in fact, most of his works for flute—as a love-struck twenty-two-year-old. It was September 1777 when the composer and his mother set out for Paris on what would become a sixteen-month trip, spending time in Munich, Augsburg, and Mannheim on the way. As with many earlier travels, the primary goal of this journey was the attainment of a lucrative position for Wolfgang, one that would allow the family to leave provincial Salzburg and enjoy the luster of a more prestigious court and locale. Leopold, Wolfgang's fifty-seven-year-old father, had to remain behind in Salzburg. The prince archbishop would not allow a leave of absence, and Leopold's pragmatic character and familial responsibilities wouldn't permit him to consider resigning his position as Wolfgang had done. This was the first time father and son had been separated. Just after the departure, Leopold wrote a poignant letter: "After you both had left, I walked up our stairs very wearily and threw myself down on a chair." He went on to describe his first agonizing day, alone with his daughter, concluding, "This is how we spent that sad day which I never thought I should have to face."[1]

It was a difficult time for both parents, but Wolfgang was delighted to be away from Salzburg. During his first stop, he applied for a court appointment from the elector of Bavaria, Maximilian III, in Munich. This would have been a plum for the young composer because, in 1777, except for "emperor," "elector" was the most prestigious title in Europe. Maximilian was one of nine rulers (two kings, including George III of England; two dukes; a marquis; a count; and three archbishops) who had the right to elect the Holy Roman emperor. Mozart did not obtain the desired appointment, and after three weeks in Munich, Leopold insisted that mother and son be off to Mannheim, capital of another important electorate, the Palatinate. In 1720 Mannheim had succeeded Heidelberg as capital; by the 1770s, it was at the height of its glory. Elector Karl Theodor had made the city a leading center for music and theater, the crown jewel of which was the finest orchestra in Europe. Wolfgang and his mother arrived there in late October 1777 with high hopes.

For a time it seemed that Wolfgang might receive an appointment at this illustrious court. As he waited for word, he earned small amounts of money teaching keyboard and composition lessons and enjoyed the hospitality of various court musicians, most notably the flutist Johann Baptist Wendling. Wendling also helped to secure a commission for him: a wealthy Dutch amateur flutist, Ferdinand Dejean, wanted Mozart to compose three "short, simple" concertos and several quartets for flute and string trio. Dejean offered the fine sum of two hundred gulden, nearly half-a-year's salary for Mozart.

At the same time, Mozart fell madly in love with a seventeen-year-old beauty, Aloysia Weber. Daughter of a poor Mannheim copyist and theater prompter whose annual earnings were less than half of what Wolfgang had been making in Salzburg, she was a stunning soprano with an exceptionally high range. While Wolfgang had originally planned to complete the Dejean commission within two months, he was now more interested in Aloysia, and a worried Leopold wrote on December 18: "Set to and carry out his commission."[2]

By the end of January, however, Wolfgang had still not completed the job. Instead, he was concocting a plan to take Aloysia to Italy and to compose an opera for her debut there. Leopold was furious, but on February 12, after a sleepless night, he managed to sit down and write a long letter, which Bernhard Paumgartner considers "the most admirable he ever wrote: 'My dear son! I have read through your letter of the 4th [February] with amazement and shock.... Thank God I have always been in good health. I wouldn't have recognized my son in your letter except for the flaw that he takes everyone at face value, that he opens his soft heart to everyone who flatters and says pretty words to him, that he allows himself to be manipulated into the position of sacrificing his own reputation and fortune, and even the help he owes his worthy old parents, in order to assist strangers.'"[3] There follow several paragraphs in which Leopold recapitulates the purposes of the trip and offers wise, heartfelt advice, probably not for the first time. Then he continues: "I can hardly put pen to paper when I think about your proposal to travel around with Herr Weber and, *nota bene*, two daughters, a proposal which almost made me lose my mind.—Dearest son! How can you allow yourself to be taken in for even an hour by such a hideous suggestion?"[4]

On February 14, Wolfgang had to confess to his father that Dejean, who was about to depart for Paris, would pay only ninety-six gulden because Mozart had finished only three quartets and two concertos. Even this was an exaggeration. While we do not know exactly what Mozart gave Dejean, it was probably two quartets and two concertos, one of which was, in fact, only a transcription of his oboe concerto. He had composed this work the previous year in Salzburg, and it had already been performed five times in Mannheim.[5] Mozart never fulfilled the rest of the commission.

Undoubtedly, the finest work initiated by Dejean was the G major flute concerto. Cast in the standard three-movement structure of the classical concerto, it typifies the elegance of early classicism but also reveals Mozart's dramatic genius in his imaginative treatment of harmonic and large-scale tonal relationships and his adroit handling of the contrasting sonorities of soloist and orchestra. The first movement, outlined in Chart 6.1, opens with a bright, assertive orchestral exposition, establishing the tonic key and creating anticipation for the soloist's entrance.

As is typical of a classical concerto, the solo exposition introduces the polarity of a principal theme, "a¹," in the tonic key (mm. 31ff.) and a subordinate theme, "b1," in the dominant (mm. 72ff.), though Mozart tantalizes the listener by

section	**Orch Exposition**			**Solo Exposition**						**Development**			
starts m#	1			31						106			
# of mm	30			75						43			
%	14%			34%						20%			
themes	a	b1	b2	a¹	c	d	b1	b2¹	a²	various + passagework			
# of mm	15	7	8	15	15	11	7	12	15				
keys	**G**			**G**	**e**	**D**				**d**	**a**	**e**	**G**
# of mm	30			15	4	50				3	11	15	14
section				**Reprise**									
starts m#				149									
# of mm				71									
%				32%									
themes				a¹	c	d	b1	b2	a³				
# of mm				15	15	11	7	12	11				
keys				**G**									
# of mm				71									

CHART 6.1 Mozart, Concerto in G Major, K. 313: Analysis of the first movement. Superscript characters (a¹, a²) indicate different versions of a theme; other numbers (b1, b2) show segments of a theme.

modulating to E minor (m. 46) before moving on to D major four measures later. In another twist, instead of introducing the subordinate theme with the arrival at the dominant key, he postpones it for twenty-two measures. Mozart intensifies the tonal conflict in the virtuosic development section, which boils through a series of minor keys, its dramatic leaps characteristic of *Sturm und Drang*. Here, instead of manipulating thematic material from the expositions, he exploits the flute's dexterous capabilities, creating vibrant, ever-changing figurations. A dominant pedal (mm. 142–148) ushers in the reprise, which provides the customary resolution of the tonal conflict by presenting the material of the solo exposition in the home key of G major.

Mozart turned to sonata form for the second movement as well (See Chart 6.2) and showed that he could achieve remarkable expressiveness and variety within its framework. This movement, the most eloquent he ever wrote for the flute, is a lovely aria with beguiling three-measure phrases and, again, the poignancy of the minor mode (E minor and B minor) in the development section as opposed to the D major–A major polarity of the solo exposition. The genius and beauty are in the detail: the expressive appoggiaturas and syncopations, the large leaps in the soloist's line in the first three measures of the secondary theme, "b1" (mm. 17–19, 45–47), the delicate new theme, "c," in the development section (mm. 29–32). The reprise and coda, almost perfectly balanced with the expositions in terms of number of measures (25 and 26, respectively), reaffirm the tonic key.

section	**Orch Exposition**	**Solo Exposition**		**"Development"**		
starts m#	1	10		27		
# of mm	9	17		11		
%	15%	27%		18%		
themes	A	A	B	(A)	C	
motives	x, a1, a2, a3, a4	x, a1, a5	b1, b2, b2^1, b3	a2	c	d
keys	**D**	**D**	**A**	**A**	**e**	**b**
# of mm	9	7	10	5	2	4
section		**Reprise**		**Coda**		
starts m#		38		57		
# of mm		19		6		
%		30%		10%		
themes		A	B	A		
motives		x, a1, a2, a3	b1, b2, b2^2, a4, cadenza	a2, x, a1		
keys		**D**		**D**		
# of mm		19		6		

CHART 6.2 Mozart, Concerto in G Major, K. 313: Analysis of the second movement.

The dichotomy of major mode contrasting with emotionally charged sections in minor mode continues in the rondo finale, a delightful minuet back in G major. The form is A–B–A–C–A–B–A (See Chart 6.3), the sections connected by transitions that drive the movement forward, mostly with sixteenth-note scalar passages. The beautiful theme introduced by the flute at the start of the "C" section is the movement's most memorable moment. This deeply moving passage in E minor presages the impassioned utterances of Mozart's final years in Vienna.

Mozart was surrounded by spectacular musicians and madly in love as he completed this concerto. He would have been content to stay in Mannheim, but his father was distressed that the liaison with Aloysia Weber would be disastrous. Because no

section	**A**				**trans**	**B**		**trans**	
starts m#	1				36	46		74	
# of mm	35				10	28		12	
%	A + transition = 16%					B + transition = 14%			
themes	a1	a2	a3		transition	b1	b2	transition	
# of mm	15	6	14		6+4	14	14	8+4	
keys	**G**				**G→D**	**D**			
section	**A**					**C**		**trans & cadenza**	
starts m#	86					107		138	
# of mm	21					31		27	
%	7%					C + transition & cadenza = 20%			
themes	a1				$a2^1$	c1	c2	transition	
# of mm	15				6	16	15	12	15
keys	**G**				**G→e**	**e**	**C**		**G**
section	**A**				**trans**	**B**		**trans**	
starts m#	165				190	194		222	
# of mm	25				4	28		19	
%	A + transition = 10%					B + transition = 16%			
themes	a1	$a2^2$			transition	b1	b2	transition	
# of mm	15	10			4	14	14	8+4+2+3+2	
keys	**(G)**								
section	**A**								
starts m#	241								
# of mm	50								
%	17%								
themes	a1	a4	passagework	a3					
# of mm	15	14	7	14					
keys	**(G)**								

CHART 6.3 Mozart, Concerto in G Major, K. 313: Analysis of the third movement.

major commission or court appointment had come through, he commanded, "Off with you to Paris."[6] He insisted that Wolfgang's mother accompany him, though she had been ailing and had planned to return to Salzburg. On March 23, 1778, exactly six months after setting out on their journey, the two arrived in Paris.

Within a week of their arrival, there was hope: Mozart was commissioned to write a sinfonia concertante for winds which was to have its premiere at *Le Concert spirituel*, the first private concert series in France. Wendling, Friedrich Ramm, and Georg Wenzel Ritter, the flute, oboe, and bassoon players whom he had gotten to know in Mannheim, were now in Paris and were to perform the piece along with Giovanni Punto, a splendid horn player.

That hope was soon crushed, however. As Mozart wrote to his father on May 1, 1778: "I think that something is going on behind the scenes, and that doubtless here, too, I have enemies. . . . I had to write the sinfonia in a great hurry and I worked very hard at it. . . . I believe, however, that [Giuseppe] Cambini, an Italian maestro here, is at the bottom of the business."[7] Indeed, as Robert Levin explains, "In writing a *sinfonia concertante* for performance at the *Concert spirituel*, Mozart could not help challenging Cambini on his own ground."[8] Cambini succeeded in getting his own sinfonia concertante programmed for an April 12 performance and exerted pressure on the director of the series to "forget" to have the Mozart parts copied. In this way, Cambini, who had previously been humiliated by Mozart's improvisational skills, ensured that he would not again be embarrassed by having audiences compare Mozart's sinfonia concertante to one of his own.[9]

Mozart's disappointment was compounded by his increasing debts. Though he had written the now-famous Concerto for Flute and Harp on commission from the French nobleman Adrien-Louis de Bonnières de Souastre in April, he was never paid for the work. Then, on July 2, he suffered "the saddest day of my life. . . . My mother, my dear mother is no more."[10] Leopold demanded that he return forthwith to detested Salzburg, but he postponed his departure until September 26. Taking a roundabout way home and sojourning for days and weeks en route in Strasbourg, Mannheim, and Munich, where Aloysia, now a celebrated court singer with a salary more than three times Mozart's, rudely rejected him, he did not arrive at the place of his birth until the middle of January 1779.

Notes

1. Leopold Mozart to his wife and son, September 25, 1777, *The Letters of Mozart and His Family*, trans. and ed. Emily Anderson (London: Macmillan, 1938), vol. 1, 395–396.

2. Leopold Mozart to his son, December 18, 1777, Anderson, vol. 2, 627.

3. Bernhard Paumgartner, *Mozart* (Zurich: Atlantis, 1973), trans. William Wilsen, 212–213.

4. Paumgartner, 214.

5. Konrad Küster, *Mozart: A Musical Biography* (Oxford: Clarendon, 1996), 78.

6. Leopold to his son, February 11–12, 1778, Anderson, vol. 2, 706.

7. Wolfgang to his father, May 1, 1778, Anderson, vol. 2, 786–787.

8. Robert D. Levin, *Who Wrote the Mozart Four-Wind Concertante?* (Stuyvesant, NY: Pendragon, 1988), 6.

9. Barry S. Brook, "The *Symphonie Concertante*: An Interim Report," *Musical Quarterly* 47 (1961): 501–502, quoted in Robert D. Levin, *Who Wrote the Mozart Four-Wind Concertante?*, 6–7.

10. Paumgartner, 227.

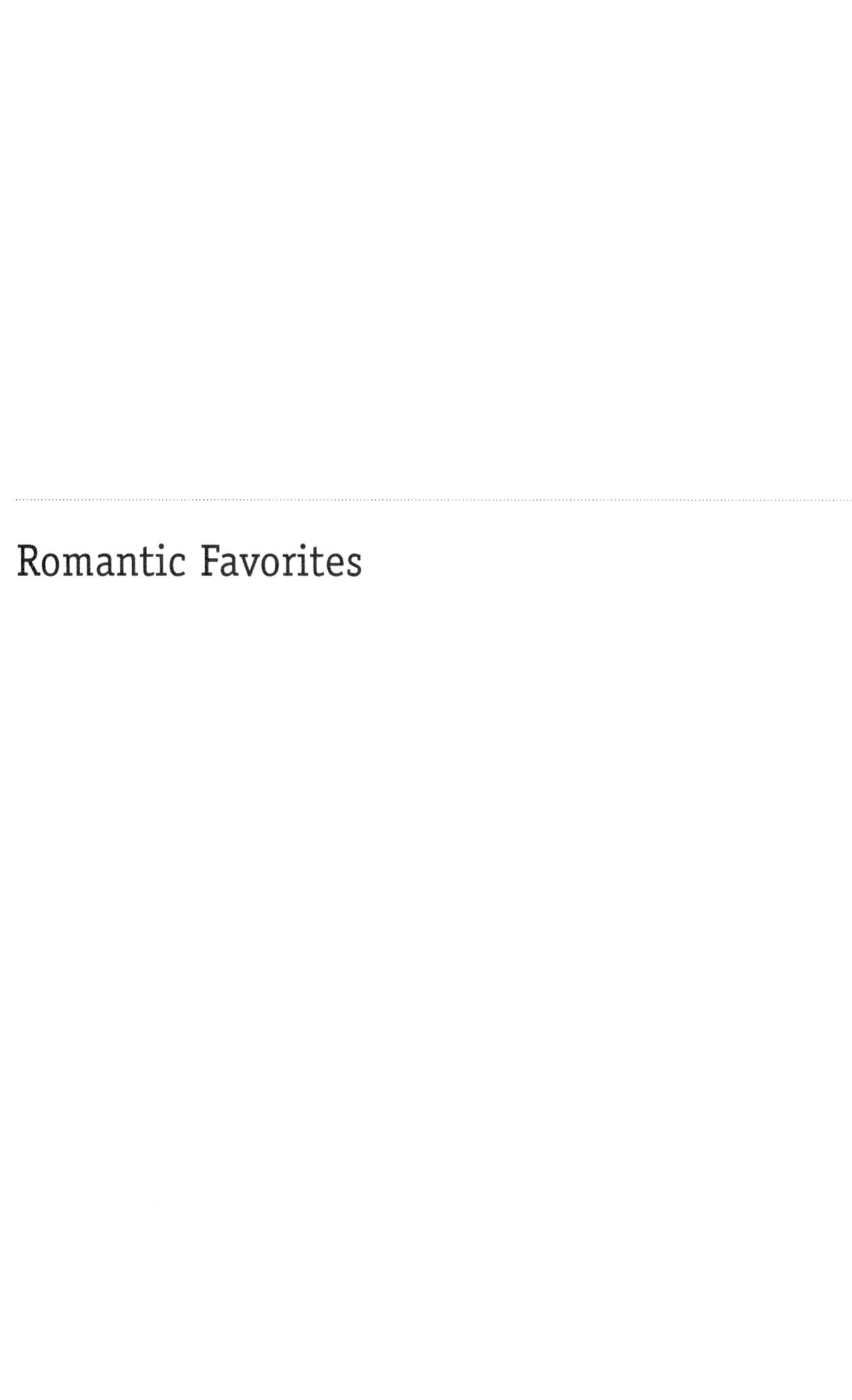

Romantic Favorites

7 Franz Schubert—Introduction and Variations, op. posthumous 160

FRANZ SCHUBERT (1797–1828), the son of a humble, hardworking schoolmaster and amateur musician and his loving wife, grew up in Vienna at a pivotal time. These were the years of the Napoleonic Wars, the industrialization and urbanization of the city and its environs,[1] and, musically, the years when Beethoven—who had arrived in Vienna five years before Schubert's birth—was making his indelible mark and leading the way toward romanticism. Schubert's father recognized his son's talents early on; he gave the boy his first violin lessons and, in 1807, took him to Antonio Salieri, kapellmeister to Austrian Emperor Franz I, for recommendations regarding his musical future. The ten-year-old Schubert arrived for the meeting ready to sing, play the violin and piano, and share his latest compositions. Salieri, impressed, advised that as soon as Schubert reached the age of eleven, he should audition for a position in the court chapel choir.[2]

Sailing through the highly competitive audition, Schubert won the position, which entitled him to free tuition at the highly regarded Academic-Grammar School and free room and board at the Stadtkonvikt. Associated with the University of Vienna, the Academic-Grammar School was "the principal boarding school for non-aristocrats [and assured Schubert] the kind of education usually reserved for titled Viennese."[3] In November 1808, the eleven-year-old entered his new world and quickly established himself as a good student, an able pianist and violinist, and a gifted composer. It was during his years spent living at the Stadtkonvikt that Schubert began composition lessons with Salieri and made his first important and lasting friendships, most notably with Josef von Spaun, a law student and the Stadtkonvikt's student music director.

After five years, Schubert was anxious to terminate his general academic studies and devote himself wholly to music. He struck an agreement with his pragmatic father allowing him to leave the school if he would enter a ten-month training course at the Imperial Normalhauptschule to become an assistant elementary teacher.[4] In November 1813, three months shy of his seventeenth birthday, Schubert entered the program. The following year he began serving as his father's sixth assistant. He completed two years (1814–1816) as teacher of the youngest students—six-year-olds—enduring a job he loathed and for which he was paid only a pittance. In spite of (or perhaps because of) this, Schubert exploded into a burst of creative activity "virtually unrivaled in the history of Western music,"[5] writing, among other compositions, 145 songs in 1815 alone.

Already by the fall of 1816, he could stand his teaching position no more: he left home and job and moved into the apartment owned by the mother of his friend Franz von Schober. A year later, when Schober's brother returned and needed the room,[6] Schubert went back to his family and job, only to give up teaching permanently a year later (1818). He lived only ten more years, years enriched (and degraded) by a circle of musicians, artists, and literary friends. While Beethoven associated with Viennese nobility, Schubert lived among the bourgeoisie. "It may justly be said that the two composers, who met only once, lived at the same time in different Viennas."[7]

Schubert's circle included poet Johann Mayrhofer; playwright Eduard von Bauernfeld; painters Leopold Kupelwieser and Moritz von Schwind, the latter of whom illustrated Schubert's songs for publication and in the 1860s painted murals for the entrance of the *Hofoper*, the future Vienna State Opera House; baritone Johann Michael Vogl, who enjoyed a successful career with the *Hofoper* and often performed Schubert's lieder with the composer at the piano; and his most controversial friend, the aforementioned poet Franz von Schober.

With this group, the "Schubertiads" began: middle-class salon gatherings at the homes of Schober, Spaun (Schubert's old friend from boarding school days), and others. Motivated by the intellectual, aesthetic, and social environment, Schubert made artistic strides. At the same time, because he was no longer teaching, he had no substantial source of income. He lived with friends and, with their encouragement and financial assistance, continued composing lieder as well as chamber and orchestral music and works for the theater.

Schubert's remarkable productivity continued in the 1820s. His new compositions were performed at the Schubertiads, his music was published and reviewed, and he was accepted as a member of the Gesellschaft der Musikfreunde, leading to contact with Vienna's foremost musicians.[8] Meanwhile, Schober had left Vienna for a year; when he returned, in early 1821, he led Schubert into debauchery. As Schubert's friend Josef Kenner later recalled:

> Anyone who knew Schubert knows how he was made of two natures, foreign to each other, how powerfully the craving for pleasure dragged his soul down to the slough of moral degradation, and how highly he valued the utterances of friends he respected, and so will find his surrender to the false prophet [Schober], who embellished sensuality in such a flattering manner, all the more understandable. But more hardened characters than he were seduced, for longer or shorter periods, by the devilish attraction of associating with that apparently warm but inwardly merely vain being into worshipping him as an idol.[9]

Schubert's irresponsible behavior ended abruptly at the end of 1822, when he developed the first devastating symptoms of syphilis. For the remainder of his life, he

> was affected in one way or another by the illness. . . . Physically, it was a story of severe pain and socially embarrassing visible symptoms, interspersed with periods of remission; artistically, of expressions of acute anguish mingled with paeans of joy, sometimes in the selfsame work; socially, of withdrawal, to home or hospital, alternating with returns to something like the former pattern of contacts with society.[10]

In the fall of 1823, having grappled for nearly a year with the disease, Schubert began work on his first song cycle, *Die schöne Müllerin* ("The Miller's Beautiful Daughter"), a setting of poems of the Prussian poet Wilhelm Müller. Omitting Müller's prologue and epilogue and three other poems, Schubert set twenty; together they tell the story of a young journeyman who goes to work at a mill, where he falls in love with the miller's daughter. Just as he thinks he has won her heart, she rejects him in favor of (what else?) the rakish hunter so beloved of German romanticism. Broken-hearted, the young man drowns himself in a stream.

In January 1824, two months after finishing the song cycle, Schubert began work on a theme-and-variations piece for flute and piano. He based this piece on "Trock'ne Blumen," the climactic eighteenth song of *Die schöne Müllerin*, where the young man asserts that the maiden will appreciate and return his love when she chances upon his grave with its "wilted flowers," which will then burst into bloom: "Winter is over, May will have come."

Kreissle von Hellborn, Schubert's first biographer, suggested that the piece was composed for Ferdinand Bogner (1786–1846), a well-known Viennese flutist who performed in major Gesellschaft concerts and taught at the Vienna Conservatory, but there is no evidence beyond his statement.[11] The story behind the composer's rewriting of the fifth variation is also unknown.[12]

Unlike Beethoven, who invented thirty-three variations to turn a fifty-five-second theme of Diabelli into a fifty-five-minute work, Schubert, in only seven variations, makes of his own ninety-second theme a twenty-minute work. However, Schubert's is not just a theme and variations but an extended work in ten sections with a well-developed introduction and coda and two substantial transitional passages: introduction, theme (|: A:| B |: C:|), variation 1, variation 2, variation 3, variation 4, variation 5, variation 6 with a transition to variation 7 that begins after the repetition of "C," variation 7 with a transition that likewise begins after the repetition of "C," and a coda beginning after twelve measures of that transition.

The substantial introduction is tightly woven thematically but expansive harmonically. After four measures in E minor, Schubert turns to the parallel major, then back to the minor in the middle of m. 8. Some serious meandering begins in m. 12: A minor, D minor, G minor, and E♭ major in the middle of mm. 12, 14, 16, and 18, respectively, then B minor and G major at mm. 21 and 23 before the tonic is reattained at m. 24. For the last fourteen measures, the bass alternates between the fifth and sixth scale degrees, B and C, and the French-sixth chord, first employed in m. 29, plays a prominent role: mm. 32–34 rock back and forth between it and the dominant triad. The introduction comes to an anticipatory close on the dominant ninth and, finally, seventh.

Five motives dominate the introduction and ensure its cohesiveness:

- Δ (piano, right hand, middle and lower voices, mm. 1–2: four half notes) recurs in mm. 3–4, 10–11 (flute), 12–13, 14–15, 16–17, 24–25, 26–27;
- π (flute m. 5½: double-dotted quarter, sixteenth, quarter) recurring in several guises at mm. 6½, 7½, 8½ (piano), 9½, 18½, 19½, 21, 22½, 23½, 29½ (4 notes from here on), 32, 32½, 33, 33½, 34, 34½, 35;
- μ (flute, m. 12¼ to end of m. 13) recurring at mm. 14¼, 16¼, 24¼, 26¼;
- Σ (piano, right hand, lower voice, m. 18: 4 beats) recurring at mm. 19, 20 (6 beats), 21½ (6 beats), 23 (5 beats);
- Ω (piano, left hand, lower voice, m. 27¾: 4 beats) recurring imitatively at mm. 28¼ and 28¾ and again at mm. 30¼, 30¾, and 31¼.

The transition from variation 6 to variation 7 (starting at m. 54 of the former) is a modulating tour de force, beginning in E minor and touching on C major, F minor,

A♭ major, C♯ minor, E major, A minor, C major, and A minor (m. 78), where, by means of an Italian-sixth chord, Schubert leads us onto an eight-measure dominant pedal in E, the key of variation 7.

In contrast, the transition from variation 7 (starting at m. 33) to the coda remains rooted in E major/minor, though here, too, Schubert struts his harmonic stuff. Consider, for example, (1) the rich chords supported by the marvelous bass line in octaves, dropping ten times in half steps (except for B to A) from D in m. 33 to D♯ at m. 38, or (2) the unorthodox deceptive cadences leading to B-seventh instead of B major at m. 39 and to E-seventh at m. 45, where the coda begins, not triumphantly in E major, but heading for the subdominant, A major.

After four measures' flirtation with the subdominant, a ii–V^7–I cadence in E (mm. 5–6 of the coda) leads listeners to believe they are finally home, only to hear Schubert bound off into G major for three measures before settling back into the tonic for four measures featuring another great bass line, this time supporting the French-sixth chord alternating with subdominant and dominant chords: V^7–Fr^6–(V/IV)–IV–Fr^6–V–Fr^6–V. The coda "begins again" at m. 16 and this time wanders off into F major (beginning in m. 23) before returning to E for the final sixteen measures. The form of the coda may be construed as w (8 mm.), x (7), w^1 (8), x^1 (5), y (4), y (4), z (6).

Chart 7.1 illustrates the structure of the heart of "Trock'ne Blumen," the theme and seven variations. As shown, the second iteration of "b" is always written out, thereby allowing for melodic changes ("b^1") from the first iteration. The second iteration of "C/c" is always indicated by a repeat sign and is thus always literal (except for the replacement of some connecting notes at the end of the first ending by a full stop at the end of the second ending). The case of "a" is slightly more complicated: whereas in the theme and variation 7, all four "a's" are written out, variations 1–6 employ repeat signs (|: a a^1:|). Thus, performers who wish to play the piece without observing the repeat signs and yet maintain the work's proportions would have to (1) play the theme and variation 7 starting at the ninth measure of each or effect a cut from

Theme and Variation 7	A (8 measures)		A (8)		B (8)		C (8)	C repeated (8)
	a (4)	a^1 (4)	a (4)	a^1 (4)	b (4)	b^1 (4)	c (8)	c repeated (8)
Variations 1–5	A (8)		A repeated (8)		B (8)		C (8)	C repeated (8)
	a (4)	a^1 (4)	a/a^1 repeated (8)		b (4)	b^1 (4)	c (8)	c repeated (8)
Variation 6	A (20)		A (21)		B (16)		C (16)	C repeated (16)
	a (10)	a^1 (10)	a (10)	a^1 (11)	b (8)	b^1 (8)	c (16)	c repeated (16)

CHART 7.1 Schubert, Introduction and Variations, Op. 160: Form of the Theme and Variations 1–7.

the end of the eighth measure to the beginning of the seventeenth and (2) omit the first four measures of "B" in variations 1–6.

The structure of variation 6 is not four-square like the others. Even taking into account that, generally, two measures of this variation correspond to one of the theme, its structure isn't even 8–8–8–8–8–8–16–16. Its asymmetry is due to imitative counterpoint and the tricky structure of "A" (a pickup measure before the initial repeat sign and first and second endings before and after the second repeat sign): a (10), a^1 (11, including elision), a (10), a^2 (11), b (8), b (8), c (16), c (16). The last phrase of "A" the first time through (piano, beginning m. 17) ends with an elision (the first ending), in which the final measure of "a^1" is simultaneously the first measure of the repeat of "a." Upon arrival at m. 17 the second time, the last phrase of "a^1" features a terminal fifth measure (the second ending).

In the theme and variation 1, a notable difference between "a" and "a^1" is that the antecedent phrase "a" ends with a stronger perfect authentic cadence (full stop in the middle of the period) than the consequent "a^1," which ends with an imperfect authentic cadence in which the top voice is not the root of the chord, propelling harmonic motion forward into the next phrase. All the other variations except the sixth feature perfect authentic cadences at the ends of both "a" and "a^1." In no. 6, "a" ends with a deceptive cadence in tonicized B major (V^7 to V^7/IV), "a^1" with a perfect authentic cadence in tonicized C♯ minor.

Harmonic progressions that differ between the theme and sundry variations (e.g., no. 4, as shown in Chart 7.2) or among variations testify to Schubert's harmonic genius, which in this work has often been overlooked amidst carping about how the nobility of the theme and its straightforward harmonization are defiled by the ostentation of the figuration, the boisterous dynamics, and the lush harmony of the variations.

Chart 7.3 offers a harmonic analysis of the first and final chords of the theme's and variations' six four-bar phrases: a, a^1, b, b^1, c (mm. 1–4) and c (mm. 5–8). These data invite any number of observations concerning harmonic progressions that are common to the theme and most variations and those that vary considerably among them. For example, the tonicization in the fourth measure of "c" is a constant, as is the unbroken drive from the following A♯ diminished-seventh chord (vii^{o7} of B, the dominant of E) in the fifth measure of "c" to the final cadence in E major in the eighth measure.

The "B" section ("b" and "b^1") begins and ends on the dominant, whether on B in E minor (theme, variations 1, 2, 4, 5) or on G♯ in C♯ minor (variation 6). Exceptions are variation 3, in which the final B major triad functions as a (temporary) tonic, and variation 7, in which "B" begins on the dominant of G♯ minor (D♯ major) but then in the last two measures modulates to F♯ major and cadences on its tonic, which

Chord inversions not indicated except for V$^{6/4}$. **Chords at mid-measure in boldface.** RM indicates relative major.

a	m#	1	2	3	4
		9	10	11	12
Theme	key	**e**			
	chord	i	i	RM	V/RM V^7/RM **RM**
Variation 4	key	**e**			
	chord	V V^7 **i**	V^7/iv iv **V**	vii/VI vii^7/VI **V/VI** V^7/VI	iv^{b3}/RM V^7/RM **RM**
a^1	m#	5	6	7	8
		13	14	15	16
Theme	key	**(e)**			
	chord	i	i	RM	V/RM V^7/RM **RM**
Variation 4	key	**(e)**		**E**	
	chord	V V^7 **i**	V^7/iv iv **V**	V iii/iii **iii**	iv/iii V/iii **iii**
b	m#	17	18	19	20
Theme	key	**(e)**			
	chord	V **i**	V/RM **RM**	V **i**	vii/V **V**
Variation 4	key	**e**			
	chord	V^7 **RM**	ii^7/RM V^7/RM **RM**	V^7 **RM**	vii^7/RM V^7/V **V**
b^1	m#	21	22	23	24
Theme	key	**(e)**			
	chord	V **i**	V/RM **RM**	V **i**	vii/V **V**
Variation 4	key	**(e)**			
	chord	V^7 **RM**	ii^7/RM V^7/RM **RM**	V^7 **RM**	vii^7/RM V^7/V **V**
c	m#	25	26	27	28
		33	34	35	36
Theme	key	**E**			
	chord	V^7 **V$^{6/4}$**	V^7 **V$^{6/4}$**	V/vi **vi**	V/vi **vi**
Variation 4	key	**E**			
	chord	V IV **V/vi**	iii V^7 **I**	vii^{o7}/vi **V^7/vi** vi	I vi V^7/IV **IV**
c (cont'd)	m#	29	30	31	32
		37	38	39	40
Theme	key	**(E)**			
	chord	vii^{o7}/V **V$^{6/4}$**	vii^{o7}/V **V$^{6/4}$**	vi vii/V **V$^{6/4}$**	V^7 **I**
Variation 4	key	**(E)**			
	chord	vii^{o7}/V **I**	V^7/ii **ii^7** V^7/V vii^{o7}/iii	I V^7/V **I** V^7 V$^{6/4}$	V^7 I V^7 **I**

CHART 7.2 Schubert, Introduction and Variations, Op. 160: Harmonic analysis comparing "Trock'ne Blumen" Theme and Variation 4.

Note: RM indicates relative major.

PERIOD	**a**	**a¹**		**b**	**b¹**	**c**	
Theme	mm 1→4 & 9→12	mm 5→8 & 13→16		mm 17→20	mm 21→24	mm 25→28	mm 29→32
key	**e**					**E**	
1st → last chord	i → RM	i → RM		V → V	V → V	V^7 → vi	vii^{o7}/V → I
Variation 1	mm 1→4	mm 5→8		mm 9→12	mm 13→16	mm 17→20	mm 21→24
key	**e**					**E**	
1st → last chord	i → RM	i → RM		V^7 → V	V^7 → V	V^7 → vi	vii^{o7}/V → I
Variation 2							
key	**e → b**	**[b] e**				**E**	
1st → last chord	i → i	[VI] RM → RM		V → V	V → V	V^7 → IV	vii^{o7}/V → I
Variation 3							
key	**E**			**B**	**E B**	**E**	
1st → last chord	I → iii	I → V^7		V^7 → I	V^7 → I	V^7 → vi	vii^{o7}/V → I
Variation 4							
key	**e**	**E**		**e**		**E**	
1st → last chord	V → RM	V → iii		V^7 → V	V^7 → V	V → IV	vii^{o7}/V → I
Variation 5							
key	**e**					**E**	
1st → last chord	i → RM	i → RM		V → V	V^7 → V	V^7 → vi	vii^{o7}/V → I
Variation 6	mm 1→10	mm 11→21		mm 22→29	mm 30→37	mm 38→45	mm 46→53
key	**c# → [B] E**	**e → c#**				**E**	
1st → last chord	i → [V^7/IV] V^7	i → i		V^7 → V	V^7 → V	V^7 → vi	vii^{o7}/V → I
Variation 7	mm 1→4 & 9→12	mm 5→8	mm 13→16	mm 17→20	mm 21→24	mm 25→28	mm 29→32
key	**E**		**g#**		**F#**	**E**	
1st → last chord	I → V I → iii	I → V^7	I → i	V → V	V → I	V^7 → vi	vii^{o7}/V → I

CHART 7.3 Schubert, Introduction and Variations, Op. 160: Harmonic analysis of first and final chords of "a," "a¹," "b," "b¹," "c" mm. 1–4, and "c" mm. 5–8.

happens to be (1) the dominant of the relative major of the key in which "b" began (G♯ minor) and also (2) the dominant of the dominant (V/V) in E major, the key in which the next section ("c") begins.

An overview of Chart 7.3 reveals use of the following keys (in addition to the many touched on in the introduction and coda): E minor and major, B minor and major, C♯ minor, G♯ minor, and F♯ major—in short, keys on all the steps of the E major scale except the fourth and seventh.

This piece was the first of four chamber works that Schubert composed early in 1824. He had always been an incredibly fast composer, and the completion of the "Trock'ne Blumen" variations, the A minor (*Rosamunde*) and D minor (*Death and the Maiden*) string quartets, and the Octet in F Major for strings and winds typifies this facility.

Sadly, he lived only six more years, dying on November 19, 1828, at the age of thirty-one. His brother reported that in a conversation with Franz just before his death, the composer intimated his desire to be buried near Beethoven in the Währing cemetery. Whether the story is true or the tale of a loving brother who wanted the world eternally to associate the two composers, Schubert was indeed buried there two days after his death. In 1888, the remains of both men were transferred to section 32A, Ehrengräber der Musiker (Musicians' Graves of Honor) of Vienna's Central Cemetery.

Notes

1. Waltraud Heindl, "People, Class Structure, and Society," in *Schubert's Vienna*, ed. Raymond Erickson (New Haven, CT: Yale University Press, 1997), 38.

2. Elizabeth Norman McKay, *Franz Schubert: A Biography* (Oxford: Clarendon Press, 1996), 12.

3. *Grove Music Online*, s.v. "Schubert, Franz," by Robert Winter, accessed August 2, 2014, http://www.oxfordmusiconline.com.ezproxy.bradley.edu/.

4. McKay, 33.

5. Winter, 658.

6. Stephen Jackson, *Franz Schubert: An Essential Guide to His Life and Works* (London: Pavilion, 1996), 26.

7. Raymond Erickson, "Vienna in Its European Context," in *Schubert's Vienna*, 26.

8. McKay, 122.

9. Josef Kenner [1858], quoted in Charles Osborne, *Schubert and His Vienna* (New York: Knopf, 1985), 96.

10. Brian Newbould, *Schubert: The Music and the Man* (Berkeley: University of California Press, 1997), 210.

11. Gretchen Rowe Clements, "Situating Schubert: Early Nineteenth-Century Flute Culture and the 'Trockne Blumen' Variations, D. 802" (PhD diss., State University of New York at Buffalo, 2007), 9.

12. The first version of the fifth variation, which Schubert scratched out in the manuscript, is included in Schubert, Franz, *Variationen für Flöte und Klavier über "Trockne Blumen" aus "Die schöne Müllerin," D. 802*. Urtext of the New Schubert Edition (Kassel: Bärenreiter, 1986).

8 Franz Doppler—*Fantaisie Pastorale Hongroise*, op. 26

LIKE JOACHIM ANDERSEN and his brother of Copenhagen, the Dopplers, Franz (1821–1883) and Karl (1825–1900), were trained by their musician father and became renowned flutists, composers, and (excepting Vigo Andersen) conductors during the mid- to late nineteenth century. The Doppler brothers toured together and sometimes composed together, but as in the case of the Andersens, it was the elder, Franz, composer of *Fantaisie Pastorale Hongroise*, op. 26, who became the more acclaimed.

The second of three children, Franz Doppler was born on October 16, 1821, in Lemberg, Galicia (now Lviv in western Ukraine), in the northeastern corner of the Austrian Empire. His father, a military bandmaster, was stationed with the Austrian garrison there, and Franz later recalled that the Hungarian melodies intoned by the soldiers in the barracks formed his first musical impressions.[1] A precocious child, he surprised his father when, at the age of four and a half, he used two sticks on a wooden table to play with absolute precision all the band's drum cadences. In September 1830, at the age of eight, he was given the gift of a *Terzflöte,* a small flute that sounds a minor third higher than the written pitches. After only seven months of study, he performed a set of variations for flute and orchestra during an intermission at the Theatre Rozmaitosci, in Warsaw. His family had moved to that city in 1828 after his father left the military to become principal oboist of the Polish National Theatre.[2]

The family fled Warsaw during the revolution of 1830/31 and returned to Lemberg before embarking on a concert tour to Vienna. There, Franz performed his debut concert with great success on December 28, 1834, at the hall of the Gesellschaft der Musikfreunde.[3] He was thirteen years old. In August of the following year, the Dopplers moved to Bucharest, where three family members accepted positions with the opera: Joseph, the father, as principal bassoonist; Franz as principal flutist, his first permanent position; and Elizabeth, Franz's older sister, as a singer of youthful roles.[4]

Within a couple of years, the family was on to Pest (the larger part of Budapest on the eastern bank of the Danube), where the family's four musicians gained employment at the Royal City Theatre. (Karl, now age twelve, there won his first position: second flutist.) It was at this time that Franz began composition studies and, within a short time, was composing overtures and entr'actes for the Hungarian National Theatre.[5]

After an extensive concert trip to Russia in 1840, Franz, in 1841, left the Royal City Theatre to accept the position of principal flute at the National Theatre. The influential Hungarian composer Franz (Ferenc) Erkel served as kapellmeister of the theater and promised a performance of Doppler's first opera, *Beniowsky*. The successful premiere in 1847 encouraged Doppler to compose additional operas, as well as ballets and smaller works. Though he was Austrian, not Hungarian, by birth, his operas earned him a reputation as a Hungarian nationalist composer. His brother Karl, following in their father's footsteps, served as a military bandmaster—but unlike his Austrian father, on the Hungarian side.[6]

With Karl, Erkel, and other members of the National Theatre, Franz participated in the establishment of the Hungarian Symphony Orchestra in 1853. Successful tours followed: between October and December 1854, the brothers performed in Linz, Salzburg, Dresden, Leipzig, Berlin, Weimar, and Hamburg, among many other cities, getting to know Liszt and Meyerbeer along the way. Later tours included performances in Stuttgart, Brussels, Paris, London, and cities in Turkey. Their Hungarian Fantasy, op. 35, written jointly, was among the many pieces the brothers performed.[7]

In 1858, while in Vienna, Franz was offered the positions of principal flutist and ballet conductor at the *Hofoper* there. Known in English as the Imperial and Royal Court Opera, and after World War I, as the Vienna State Opera, the prestigious *Hofoper* served Franz Joseph in his dual roles as Emperor of Austria and King of Hungary. Doppler found it difficult to leave Pest, but the promise of the performance of one of his operas led him to accept Vienna's offer. However, a few years later, when the *Hofoper*'s kapellmeister left Vienna and his agreements were not honored, Doppler decided to return to Pest and the National Theatre. To retain him, the Viennese offered a lifelong position as principal flutist and a new commitment to perform his operas.[8] With that, Franz decided to stay in Vienna, where in 1865 he was named professor of flute at the conservatory. In 1870, he became music director of the Imperial and Royal Ballet and six years later was appointed kapellmeister of the *Hofoper* itself. During these, his final years, Franz Doppler composed his most famous work, the *Hungarian Pastoral Fantasy*, op. 26.

Like the Hungarian operas, the Dopplers' flute works drew on nationalistic themes, which they brought together and embellished to create appealing compositions that showcased their virtuosity. The *Hungarian Pastoral Fantasy* strings together four sections,

no. 1: Molto andante (mm. 1–47)
no. 2: Andantino moderato (mm. 48–102)
no. 3: Andantino moderato, continued (mm. 103–115)
no. 4: Moderato. Allegro (mm. 116–194)

then concludes with an accompanied cadenza and coda.

The brooding, *pianissimo* introduction in D minor leads to the flute's entrance and the florid spinning of the first tale over punctuating chords in the accompaniment. The two phrases of the middle section in A minor, poco animato, gain momentum and lead into a cadenza over a sustained C♯ diminished-seventh chord, resolving to D minor with the return of "A" at m. 30. A codetta meanders above a rhythmically strict accompaniment and concludes with soft harmonics (an unusual effect for flutists in 1874) and a final accented punch.

Section 2 opens with a bright, rhythmic introduction in D major. The flute enters trippingly with a syncopated line, rife with offbeat accents and unexpected dynamic contrasts that introduce an air of delightful coquettishness. Presentations of the principal theme (mm. 58ff.) and its variations (mm. 75ff. and mm. 94ff.) in D major alternate with a contrasting passage in A major (mm. 66ff.) and its variation (mm. 83ff.), extended by another dazzling cadenza over an A dominant-seventh chord (mm. 92–93).

Section 3 is surprisingly short, but its character suggests neither interlude nor, until m. 114, introduction. The first seven measures and the following four, where the flute presents a suave, chromatically inflected melody, cry out for fuller development along the lines of the previous two sections. But then, in the second half of m. 114, in the treble of the accompaniment, an energetic motive is subtly interjected. Repeated in m. 115, this motive continues (in mm. 116, 117, and, in augmentation, 118–119), and becomes the introduction to the final section, allegro. Here the flute expands the motive into the main theme (in two identical halves) of a rhythmic dance in 2/4 (mm. 120–127). Variants of this theme, "x," and a complementary theme, "y" (mm. 128–135), comprise the "A" section and are followed by an eight-measure transition, più lento, to a contrasting "B" section ("z" and "z[1]") back at tempo primo. In D major and playful in its contrasting dynamics, this short section leads to a transition (mm. 184–194) followed by a *cadenza accompagnata* and a final spirited coda, assuring thunderous applause for Doppler's virtuoso performance.

It was only four years after writing this piece that Franz Doppler's flute-playing career came to an end. Having contracted an asthmatic illness, he was forced to leave his position with the *Hofoper* and three years later to step down from his position as professor.[9] His health steadily declined, and he died on July 27, 1883, at the age of sixty-one. Three years later, Albert Klautzsch arranged the *Fantaisie Pastorale Hongroise* for flute with orchestral accompaniment.[10] Now, over 130 years later, the composition remains among the most popular pieces in the flute repertoire.

Notes

1. Gernot Stepper, "Die Gebrüder Franz und Karl Doppler," *Tibia* 7, no. 2 (1982): 88, trans. William Wilsen.
2. Stepper, 88.
3. Stepper, 88–89.
4. Stepper, 89.
5. Stepper, 90.
6. Stepper, 91.
7. Stepper, 93.
8. Stepper, 93–94.
9. Stepper, 94.
10. András Adorján, "Doppler, Franz," *Lexikon der Flöte*, ed. András Adorján and Lenz Meierott (Laaber, Germany: Laaber, 2009), 233.

9 Carl Reinecke—Sonata, op. 167, *Undine*

LIKE SO MANY of the gifted musicians who admired his work—Mendelssohn, Schumann, and Liszt among them—Carl Reinecke (1824–1910) was a versatile artist. Though remembered primarily as a composer and conductor, he was also a teacher, administrator, writer, editor, and extraordinary pianist. He was born in Altona, now part of the city of Hamburg, and raised by his father, his mother having died when he was barely four. Rudolf Reinecke, a conductor and teacher of music theory, raised his two children strictly and conscientiously and provided the whole of Carl's early musical training in piano, violin, and theory.[1]

By the age of nineteen, Carl Reinecke, already highly esteemed as a pianist, embarked on his first concert tour, traveling to Copenhagen, Sweden, and Norway as accompanist for Moravian violinist Heinrich Wilhelm Ernst, the great rival of and successor to Paganini. Altona was under Danish rule at the time, and Ernst's introduction of Reinecke to King Christian VIII led to a stipend that allowed Reinecke to continue his musical studies.[2]

Fascinated by the idea of studying in the vibrant musical city of Leipzig, he moved there forthwith. Leipzig was, with Vienna, the co-capital of Western music: it was the site of music publisher Breitkopf and Härtel, the famed Gewandhaus concerts, and the two leading music periodicals, the *Allgemeine Musikalische Zeitung* and the *Neue Zeitschrift für Musik*. It was also the home of Mendelssohn, Ferdinand David, and at the time, the Schumanns—Robert, age thirty-three, believing that nowhere in Germany, perhaps the world, was there a better place for young musicians.[3]

During his early years in the city, Reinecke performed as piano soloist in Gewandhaus concerts at the invitation of its music director, Felix Mendelssohn, and toured extensively as a soloist and chamber musician. He held a series of positions, first as court pianist to King Christian VIII (1846–1848), then, after some time in Bremen and Paris, as a teacher at the conservatory of Cologne (1851–1854), music director in Barmen (1854–1859), and conductor and academic director of the Singakademie in Breslau (1859). Returning to Leipzig whenever he could, his ties to the city remained strong. In 1860, his appointment to positions as music director of the Gewandhaus concerts (which he held for thirty-five years) and professor of piano and composition at the Leipzig Conservatory, of which he became director in 1897, enabled him to settle permanently in his favorite city.

Reinecke was a prolific composer who, from an early age, incorporated composition into his daily schedule. "Should you look into his study early in the day, you will find him at his desk, busy with some new composition, while on each knee would be sitting one of his 'little ones' with their arms locked around their father's neck."[4] With seven children at the time and his jobs at the Gewandhaus and conservatory, it must have been quite a feat to find private moments every day.

Reinecke was a seasoned composer when, in 1882, at the age of fifty-eight, he began work on the *Undine* Sonata, the first of his three compositions for flute. (Twenty-six years later, he contributed both a flute concerto and the *Ballade* for Flute and Orchestra, which bears his last opus number, 288.) At a time when flutist-composers were writing lighthearted, virtuoso theme-and-variation pieces and opera fantasies and other composers were ignoring the flute as a solo instrument, Reinecke created a full-scale, masterful romantic sonata. He dedicated the piece to Wilhelm Barge, the Gewandhaus's principal flutist and flute professor at the conservatory, though it was probably Paul Taffanel who premiered the work at a concert of his Société des instruments à vent in Paris on February 15, 1883.

On its own, the sonata could be a well-crafted, formally convincing piece of absolute music, but Reinecke included the subtitle *Undine*, a reference to a well-known German novella of the time. Friedrich Heinrich Karl, Baron de la Motte Fouqué, had penned this literary work, his only enduring success, in 1811, and early listeners of Reinecke's sonata would have appreciated the composer's musical allusions to the story. Reinecke had long been interested in fantasy and fairy tales, having written texts using his middle names Heinrich Carsten as a pseudonym,[5] so it is not surprising that he was attracted to the Undine legend.

Fouqué's story tells of a fisherman and his wife, their long-lost daughter Bertalda, now a noblewoman, and their playful, adopted daughter, Undine. A water spirit,

Undine is a lovely girl who looks human but does not have a soul. The only way for her to acquire one is to earn the love of a mortal. When the knight Huldbrand is stranded in the haunted forest on the peninsula inhabited by Undine and her parents, he takes shelter in their cottage. Though he had been on a quest to gain the love of the beautiful Bertalda, he and Undine begin to fall in love as they converse, and he tells her stories of the great world beyond the peninsula.

The first movement of the sonata, perhaps inspired by images of Undine as a water nymph (her name derives from the Latin word for "wave"), opens with a melody consisting of arpeggiated chords in 6/8 meter. Reinecke, a master of classical structure, cast this movement in well-proportioned sonata form in the key of E minor. A short, turbulent transition, ignited by virtuoso sixteenth-note cascades in the piano's right hand, ushers in the second theme, a plaintive cry in B minor played by the flute, followed by a sweeter consequent phrase in G major, the whole of which is then presented in the piano. A short closing theme, accompanied by material from the principal theme, ends the exposition in the relative major.

The development, the longest section of the movement, deftly demonstrates Reinecke's ability to exploit the potential for tonal conflict implied in an exposition. The rich harmonic language, rapidly changing keys (including the remote C♯ major and E♭ minor), and stormy sixteenth-note passages contribute to tension that is sustained even as Reinecke reintroduces the principal theme in m. 145, a "false reprise" in the key of A minor. The real reprise, in E minor, begins at m. 177. As in the exposition, the spinning out of the principal theme occurs over a dominant pedal (mm. 185ff.). The tonal stress intensifies until m. 197, where it is finally relieved by an authentic cadence. In the transition to the second theme, Reinecke's use of a dominant pedal point drives the tonality to E major for the consequent phrase of theme 2. The lovely little closing theme in E major turns to E minor, where, over a tonic pedal point, a codetta based on the principal theme brings the movement to a quiet close.

The recurring scherzando of the sonata's second movement, a scherzo with two trios,[6] suggests a mischievous and impetuous Undine. The first trio (mm. 33ff.) stands in sharp contrast, perhaps representing the knight, Huldbrand. (Since the time of Lully's French overtures in the seventeenth century, strong, recurring dotted rhythms have been associated with nobility.) The slower second trio (mm. 98ff.), in B major, can be interpreted only as a tender love theme. Here the essence of the story begins to unfold: Huldbrand and Undine have fallen in love.

The beautiful third movement, grounded in G major, opens with a dialogue between flute and piano, suggesting the bliss of the newly married young couple. Most interesting in the "A" section (mm. 1–35) is the six-measure chromatic passage, based in the remote key of A♭ major, that begins in m. 21. While the modulation is short lived and the key returns to G major in m. 27, the slithering chromaticism intimates trouble to come.

Two programmatic descriptions have been suggested for the sharply contrasting "B" section. Could it be the appearance of Undine's uncle, Kühleborn, warning that the water spirits (portrayed here with rapid triplets) will tolerate no insult by a mortal and will exact revenge should Huldbrand ever insult or harm Undine?[7] Or could it be, as Mary Ann Smart suggests, that this short, tumultuous section portrays the agitated scene in which Undine reveals her origins to Huldbrand, after which, with the return of "A" at m. 54, he reassures her of his love and fidelity?[8] Either scenario leads to a climactic moment, musically represented by a diminished-seventh chord on C♯, *sforzato* (m. 53). Through reiterations of the common tone "G," a resolution is effected, and the calm and beauty of the "A" section return in the tonic key of G major.

As multimovement genres moved from the classical era to the romantic, composers changed the relative weight of the first and last movements. Whereas the finale had previously provided a lighthearted, often dance-inspired conclusion, the romantics transformed the structure by closing with an emotionally profound movement. For Reinecke, this structure supported Undine's story. As the drama progresses, Bertalda, Huldbrand's former love, comes to live with the knight and the nymph. Huldbrand's attention strays from Undine as he struggles with her absorption in her supernatural world and begins to focus on the all-too-human charms of Bertalda. As he loses Undine, Huldbrand, desolate, agrees to marry Bertalda. Undine returns to the sea, as had been prescribed by the water spirits if she were to be hurt by a mortal, but then reappears, delivering a final kiss to Huldbrand, which she knows will end his life. In her grief, she transforms herself into a brook that will eternally encircle the grave of her mortal beloved.[9]

The turbulence of the finale asserts itself in the flute's first disjunct interval, a descending tritone, the piano's first chord, a German sixth, and the piano's rapid arpeggios, suggesting rough waters. The emotionally charged sonata-form movement continues unabated through the exposition of two strikingly similar themes (mm. 1–11 and 54–69) and a development that treats the first theme to virtuosic manipulation in several keys. Though the reprise begins in the tonic key, E minor, its subsequent modulations defeat the goal of tonal resolution, most unexpected being the passage in A♭ major (mm. 213–228), which leads to yet another turbulent section in distant keys that finally find their way back to E minor. The sonata's ending, a coda in E major that poignantly reprises the love theme from the second movement, marks Reinecke's most audacious departure from classical practice. This epilogue, recalling the love of Undine for her knight, brings an end to the tragedy and a sublime conclusion to the work.

Reinecke's conducting, teaching, composition, and piano performance brought him into contact with leading musicians of his day, from Brahms and Berlioz, whom he got to know in Cologne and Paris, to Liszt, with whom he played duo concerts and to whose daughter he gave piano lessons for a short time. Other students included Max Bruch, Edvard Grieg, Leoš Janáček, and Johan Svendsen. He conducted the premieres of Schumann's Violin Concerto and Brahms's German Requiem, and his strong, effective leadership of the Leipzig Conservatory transformed it into one of the most respected in Europe. In the end, however, it is his *Undine* Sonata, the most frequently performed of his compositions, for which he is chiefly remembered today.

Notes

1. Stephanie Bethea, "The Flute Music of Carl Reinecke" (DMA diss., University of Washington, 2008), 2–3.

2. Bethea, 9.

3. Myrna Brown, "Programmatic Elements in Carl Reinecke's Sonata, Opus 167, 'Undine,'" *National Flute Association Newsletter* 7 (Winter 1982): 9.

4. Edwin J. Butler, "A Biographical Sketch of Carl Reinecke," *Dwight's Journal of Music* 31 (1871): 102.

5. Adeline Tomasone, "A Fresh Look at Reinecke's Undine," *Flute Talk* 26 (Nov. 2006): 10.

6. Such duple-meter scherzos are to be found among composers as diverse as Bach (Third Keyboard Partita scherzo; Second Orchestral Suite *Badinerie*), Beethoven (Piano Sonata no. 18), Mendelssohn (String Octet), Schumann (Second Symphony), Tchaikovsky (Fourth Symphony), and Brahms (Second String Sextet).

7. Brown, 11–12.

8. Mary Ann Smart, "A Critical Comparison of Three Settings of the Undine Myth in Works by Hoffman, Lortzing and Reinecke" (MA thesis, McMaster University, 1989), 157.

9. Tomasone, 11.

Belle Époque Legacies of the Conservatoire

10 Benjamin Godard—*Suite de trois morceaux,* op. 116

BENJAMIN GODARD'S *Suite de trois morceaux* exemplifies the salon music of "la belle époque," roughly defined as the period between the Franco-Prussian and First World Wars that the French, who later endured the horrors of World War I, came to think of as peaceful and prosperous, idyllic. Godard (1849–1895) lived during the golden years of this period and was forever attracted to its precepts.

A child prodigy, he studied the violin with Richard Hammer and later with Henri Vieuxtemps at the Paris Conservatory while also studying composition with Henri Reber. Though he won no prizes at the school, he was sometimes compared to the young Mozart because of his tremendous facility as both performer and composer. After leaving the conservatory, he worked as a violinist and violist in Parisian string quartets and, in 1878, won the Prix de la ville de Paris with *Le Tasso,* a three-part dramatic symphony for soloists, chorus, and orchestra.

Godard composed prodigiously throughout his life, completing concertos for violin and for piano, string quartets, four symphonies, violin sonatas, solo piano pieces, a cello sonata, two piano trios, four operas, and over one hundred songs. In 1887 he became a professor of chamber music and composition at the conservatory and just over two years later, at the age of forty, composed the *Suite de trois morceaux* for Paul Taffanel, the conservatory's renowned flute professor. Taffanel performed the suite with the Leipzig Gewandhaus Orchestra in February 1890 and again the following month in Paris with the Société des instruments à vent.[1]

Each of the movements in the suite is a character piece, an immensely popular genre among the romantics. Composed in ternary form, each suggests one mood, often with a programmatic association. Godard's contributions are elegant ones that no doubt charmed audiences in both intimate settings, with piano accompaniment, and in more imposing venues, as when Taffanel played them with orchestra alongside performances of Mozart's G major concerto.

The Allegretto opens in B♭ major with a jaunty melody over a syncopated accompaniment. While the melody sounds as though it begins on a downbeat, in fact it begins on the second beat of the measure, a situation rectified by the three beats beginning in the middle of m. 5. A tonic pedal point (mm. 1–6) leads to dominant harmony (mm. 9–14), which resolves in m. 15 for the start of a varied repeat of the opening section, "a." While beginning just as "a" had, the final measure of the first phrase of "a^1" leads to a C♯ over a diminished-seventh chord, signaling a modulation that leads to D minor in m. 21. This proves to be a short-lived tonicization, however: the C♮ in m. 24 and the authentic cadence in mm. 26 and 27 confirm C major.

With the beginning of "B" (m. 28), E♮ changes to E♭, a harbinger of the increased chromaticism that will pervade this section, the first five measures of which are in B♭ major. The rising chromatic line in the flute is accompanied by restless chords that resolve to the tonic in m. 32. The diatonicism at the end of this first phrase gives way to a second chromatic melody, a minor seventh higher than the first, over the same harmonic progression but now in the key of A♭ major, resolving to the new tonic in m. 40.

Another chromatic passage begins in the flute in m. 44 over a chromatically ascending bass line. The harmony changes with every measure of this modulating passage (mm. 44–49) as the dynamic level increases from *piano* to *forte*. An eight-measure retransition begins in G minor over a five-measure dominant pedal point then progresses through a series of chords common to both that key and its relative major. The final four measures (54–57) accompany a chromatically ascending melody, similar to mm. 28–30, 36–38, and 44–48, as the harmony leads to the V^7 of B♭ major, which, as expected, resolves to the tonic for the return of "A."

Here Godard repeats the opening material through the V^7 chord in m. 69, at which point one anticipates a resolution. To the expected tonic triad, however, the composer adds an A♭, a deception that sets up a move toward E♭ major, the subdominant key. Godard here borrows a construct of classical composers, who often turned to the subdominant in the coda of a sonata-form movement. Godard serves up another harmonic deception when in m. 73 the V^7 of E♭ leads not to the tonic but to a V^7/vi in m. 74 and tonicizations of C minor and G minor before returning to B♭ major for the codetta.

The first and third measures of the codetta (mm. 82 and 84) color the tonic harmony with subdominant chords borrowed from B♭ minor. Then, as the bass line descends the octave from B♭, the flute moves in contrary motion through arpeggiations of the tonic chord, the two instruments arriving on widely spaced tonic pitches for the last note of the piece.

After the vibrant, playful opening movement, Godard offers a sensitive, lyrical Idylle in G major. Again in ternary form, the piece opens with an "A" section in two parts. Following a four-measure introduction, one hears two symmetrical four-measure phrases, each beginning the same way but diverging in the third bar. The second part, in D major, has the same structure ("b," "b^1"), with the final three measures (18–20) effecting a modulation to F major.

Much of the middle section (mm. 21–43) is devoted to sequence: four presentations of a two-measure phrase beginning with the three pickups to m. 28. Each phrase consists of a measure of dominant harmony followed by a measure of tonic. The passage begins on the dominant chord of F major (colored by an augmented fifth), then modulates in two-measure segments through E major and A♭ minor (again with the dominant chord colored by an augmented fifth) to E♭ major. A long E♭ pedal point underpins the highly chromatic conclusion to this section, with a hemiola in mm. 39–40 adding rhythmic tension. A German-sixth chord in m. 43 leads back to G major and the return of "A," this time over a nine-measure dominant pedal. Godard's inventiveness is displayed through the melodic variations of "a" (at mm. 44 and 57) and "b," (at m. 48) leading to the coda (mm. 62ff.), which introduces new melodic material over a tonic pedal that began in m. 53 and extends through the final twenty-six measures of the piece.

Though its title, Valse, implies a single waltz, the final movement of the suite is actually a chain of waltzes, similar to Johann Strauss Jr.'s *Emperor Waltzes*. The repetition scheme creates a large-scale ternary design, each section offering three waltzes and opportunities for dazzling virtuosic display.

An introduction in B♭ major leads to "A," which contains a sixteen-bar "a," two "b" sections (of sixteen and fourteen measures), and a cantabile sixteen-bar "c" whose repetition is in G minor. The minor mode continues into the middle section of the work with its three new waltzes. The first, "d" (sixteen measures in D minor, repeated), includes rhythmic game playing as the flute participates on the offbeats of hemiolas in the third and fourth and seventh and eighth measures of the phrase. The legato "e" (mm. 114ff.) continues in D minor until its final measures (128–129) where it modulates to C major and leads seamlessly to a more virtuosic "f." Here, the flute's ascending line (a^1 in m. 130, leading to b^1 in 134, c^2 in 138, and e^2 in 142) builds momentum before pulling back to begin a varied presentation of the same material (mm. 146ff.) which this time ends with a whirlwind of scales for solo flute *ff* over a dominant-seventh chord. Comically, the emphatic two-chord cadence that firmly stamps the end of this section is a deceptive one that drives the music into C minor for the beginning of the retransition.

A sequential passage, over chromatically moving tremolos in the bass reinforced in the middle voice of the piano, begins the long, suspenseful return to "A." Time and again, Godard uses the effective combination of modulation (laced with augmented-sixth chords), chromatically ascending motion, and increasing dynamic levels to build up anticipation. A sixteen-measure dominant pedal (mm. 194ff.) supports a flute line that becomes more fervent and aggressive until it finally arrives on the tonic at the return of the brilliant opening melody, now accompanied by a fervid countermelody. Following reprises of the first three waltzes at mm. 210, 226, and 256, a coda rips through chromatically inflected scales to burst forth in a rousing and jubilant conclusion.

Godard's career began when virtuoso performer-composers like Liszt and Sarasate and Godard's own teacher, Vieuxtemps, were all the rage, and he continued to create music in the style of the early romantics throughout his life. Coinciding with the development of the Boehm flute and writing alongside composer-flutists who wished to dazzle audiences with its new mechanism, Godard created the suite in this vein, and the success of the endeavor is demonstrated by the tremendous popularity that the piece continues to enjoy. Historians, however, often cite the composer's reluctance to change with the times as a reason that his music largely disappeared after la belle époque. Indeed, while the suite remains popular, it is one of only a couple of Godard works ever heard today.

Note

1. Edward Blakeman, *Taffanel: Genius of the Flute* (New York: Oxford University Press, 2005), 144.

11 Gabriel Fauré—*Fantaisie*, op. 79

GABRIEL FAURÉ'S LONG LIFE (1845–1924) extended across a rich and rapidly changing period in music. He was active at the time of Wagner, Brahms, and Dvořák, but also at the time of Schoenberg, Bartók, and Stravinsky. Amidst all the strong influences that surrounded him, however, he remained independent and ever fresh in his approach to composition.

Gabriel's musical talent was nurtured after his father asked the representative of their *département* (Ariège, in southern France) in the French national assembly to hear the eight-year-old play the piano and then to offer advice about his musical prospects. The legislator recommended that Toussaint Fauré send his youngest son to the École de musique classique et religieuse (later known as École Niedermeyer), a Parisian school that had just been established to prepare students for careers as church musicians. Gabriel Fauré entered this boarding school—five hundred miles from his home—a year later (October 1854) and studied there for eleven years. His education included literary studies and intensive training in organ, harmony, counterpoint and fugue, solfège, piano, and composition. Here Fauré was introduced to the whole of the repertoire, including plainsong, Renaissance church music, the masterpieces of J. S. Bach, and contemporary music.

When Louis Niedermeyer, the school's founder and director and Fauré's piano teacher, died in March 1861, Camille Saint-Saëns took over the piano class. Under his tutelage, Fauré began to compose, and the two forged a profound lifelong relationship. Fauré later said that he "owed everything" to his older colleague.[1] Saint-Saëns introduced him to renowned composers and performers, advised him with regard to publishers, and helped him into and out of sometimes prickly employment situations. They also worked together as members of the Société nationale de musique, an organization founded by Saint-Saëns and Romain Bussine in 1871 to sponsor performances of contemporary French music, especially by young composers.

Because of the fame and positions that Fauré eventually achieved, it is easy to forget that he spent forty years as a work-a-day church musician. Leaving the Niedermeyer School at the age of twenty with honors in all the musical subjects he studied, he began a long string of church jobs interrupted by seven months' service as a soldier in the Franco-Prussian War: organist at St. Sauveur in Rennes; then, in Paris, assistant organist at Notre-Dame de Clignancourt, organist at St. Honoré d'Eylau, and assistant organist at St. Sulpice.

In 1877 Saint-Saëns resigned as organist at l'église de la Madeleine. This was a desirable position because the Madeleine was the parish church of the Elysée, one of Napoleon III's palaces, and since 1873 the official residence of the presidents of France. In order to succeed Saint-Saëns as organist, Théodore Dubois vacated his position as the church's choirmaster, at which time Fauré obtained the post. The thirty-two-year-old Fauré continued at the Madeleine for twenty-eight years (becoming chief organist in 1896) until 1905, when he became director of the Paris Conservatory.

Just after his appointment as choirmaster, Fauré suffered the breakup of his engagement to the younger daughter of the renowned Pauline Viardot, at whose salon Fauré's music was frequently performed. He had been in love with Marianne Viardot for five years and was devastated when she ended their relationship. Six years later, a friend "essentially negotiated" his marriage to the daughter of sculptor Emmanuel Fremiet.[2] Fauré endured this disappointing union only with difficulty and infidelity. He supported his wife and two sons largely through his work at the Madeleine. The job was demanding, including collaborating with the clergy to determine the music for each service, rehearsing with the choir and its accompanying instrumentalists, and worrying constantly about recruiting singers.[3]

Work at the Madeleine consumed each morning, after which Fauré would travel by streetcar and train through Paris and its suburbs to accompany singing classes for young ladies and give piano and theory lessons. Evenings were often spent attending salon concerts where his music was being performed. While time-consuming, these events offered encouragement to the unsure composer and valuable opportunities to promote his music. He could sometimes squeeze in time for composing, but he was a slow, painstaking worker,[4] and much of his creative production had to be relegated to summer holidays. His biographer Jean-Michel Nectoux writes: "Too many occupations prevented him from concentrating on composition; he was disturbed about writing too slowly and dreamt of vast works—concertos, symphonies, and innumerable operatic projects in collaboration with Verlaine, Bouchor, Samain, Maeterlinck, Mendès, and others. As the years passed he despaired of ever reaching the public."[5]

The musical demands became even greater when, in 1896, Fauré was appointed to the composition faculty of the Paris Conservatory, replacing Jules Massenet. He oversaw a brilliant group of young musicians, including Maurice Ravel, Charles Koechlin, Jean Roger-Ducasse, Florent Schmitt, George Enescu, and Nadia Boulanger. Boulanger later recalled their lunches together, "during which sometimes he would not speak a word, then would disappear at the end of the meal and come back in some embarrassment saying, 'Forgive me, I've just been writing down what I composed during lunch.' "[6] Such was the life of the busy musician.

There was perhaps no busier time than the early summer months of 1898, when Fauré composed his *Fantaisie* for flute and piano. He spent March and early April of that year in London, during which time the English actress, Mrs. Patrick Campbell, asked him to write incidental music for a production of Maeterlinck's *Pelléas et Mélisande*. She was completely taken by this play and was convinced that Fauré was the composer to write music for it. He agreed to the project, returned briefly to Paris, then left two weeks later to fulfill obligations related to his position as inspector of the national conservatories outside Paris. Writing to his wife on April 25, he offered, "All I know is that I'll really have to get down to *Mélisande* as soon as I get back. The whole score has to be written in a month and a half, though it's true some of it is already lying around in this old head of mine!"[7]

Fauré's work on *Pelléas* moved along with unusual dispatch, and he completed it by the end of May. At the same time, he received an urgent commission from Professor Paul Taffanel to compose pieces for the conservatory's flute examination, to be held July 28. The primary piece, meant to demonstrate the aspirants' skill and artistry, had to be completed before he left for the June 21 première of *Pelléas* in London. The second would be a short, less complex one for the sight-reading exam. Having never had much interest in orchestration, he delegated the task of orchestrating Mrs. Campbell's incidental music to his student Charles Koechlin and set about composing the flute piece. He later wrote to Saint-Saëns that he could not recall any other composition that he had found so demanding to write.[8]

The *Fantaisie* opens with an intimate, delicate sensibility characteristic of the great master of French song. The accompaniment of this berceuse or barcarolle is rhythmically simple but features a rich harmonic language. In this idyll, Fauré leads the listener through a long series of deceptive cadences, each one providing a subtle surprise. Together they propel the music from the first measure to the first authentic cadence in m. 33. The melodic presentation becomes increasingly elaborate. Note, for example, the embellishments of the opening theme when it appears in mm. 25–29.

Though the *Fantaisie* was written at the turn of the twentieth century, when many composers were rejecting traditional form and harmony, Fauré believed that

> In whatever realm of thought one takes—literature, science, art—an education which is not based in the study of the classics can be neither complete nor fundamental. . . . In the wide reaches of the human spirit, all those who have seemed to create ideas and styles hitherto unknown have only been expressing, through the medium of their own individualism, what others have already thought and said before them.[9]

Indeed, the Allegro section of the *Fantaisie* may be seen as a sonata-form movement that draws on Fauré's "study of the classics" while at the Niedermeyer School. (See Chart 11.1) The introduction establishes the tonic key of C major. Then, in m. 88, Fauré returns to E minor, the key of the Andantino, for a reminiscence of that movement's opening phrase. Measure 97 initiates a sequential repetition of the same phrase a whole step lower, in D minor. The immediately following and technically challenging transition again begins with a sequence and leads to the expressive "B" theme, which will dominate the development section. While at work on the piece, Fauré wrote to Koechlin, saying, "I am drowned in the Taffanel and plunged up to my neck in scales, arpeggios, and staccati!"[10] One can envision the composer writing hundreds of sixteenth notes, knowing that a demonstration of facile technique was required of a conservatory examination piece, yet also working to create a cohesive and musically satisfying work of art.

One aspect of Fauré's handling of sonata form in the *Fantaisie* is not characteristic of his revered classical models (though not unheard of there either). Opening the coda with a version of the movement's main theme lends the whole a feeling of recurring returns—that is, of rondo: "A" (in the exposition), "B" (in the exposition [second part] and development), "A" (in the reprise), "B" (in the reprise [second part]), "A" + coda (in the sonata-form coda).

Keys support sonata rather than rondo, where one might expect the second "B" section to be in a different key from the preceding "A" section: C, G, C, X, C rather than C, G, C, C, C. The movement's proportions aren't typical of either sonata (introduction, 20 mm.; exposition, 73 mm.; development, 31 mm.; reprise, 43 mm.; coda, 44 mm.) or rondo (introduction, 20 mm.; "A," 57 mm.; "B," 47 mm.; "A," 19 mm.; "B," 24 mm.; "A," 25 mm; coda, 19 mm.). Maybe it's just a fantasy.

Fauré's *Fantaisie*, as well as the *Morceau de concours*, which he wrote on Bastille Day to serve as the sight-reading piece, were first performed at the conservatory

Andantino											
theme	Intro	a	a^1	b		a^2	Codetta				
starts m#	1	2	11	19		25	33				
key	**e**			**F**	**G**	**e**					
			or	**e: II^b** Neapolitan	**e: iii** relative maj						
starts m#	1			19	22	25					
Allegro											
Sonata section	**Intro**	**Exposition**							**Development**		**Retransition**
Rondo section	**Intro**	**A**					**B**				
theme	intro	c	d	c^1	a^3 from Andantino	trans	e	e^1	*Fortspinnung*	e^2	transition, incl. "c" at 159
starts m#	40	60	71	80	88	106	117	125	133	143	151
key	**C**	**→ G**	**→ C**	**→ G**	**e d C**	**mod**	**G**		**e C D^b**	**G**	**D E^b**
starts m#	40	66	78	84	88 94 103	106	117		133 136 139	143	151 159
Sonata section		**Reprise**									
Rondo section		**A**					**B**				
theme		c^2	d^1				e	e^3	sequence, *Fortspinnung*		
starts m#		164	173				183	191	197		
key		**C**					**(C)**		**modulation**		
starts m#		164							197		
Sonata section		**Coda**									
Rondo section		**A**		**Coda**							
theme		c^3	passagework								
starts m#		207	216	232							
key		**C**									
starts m#		207									

CHART 11.1 Fauré, *Fantaisie*: Analysis.

examinations on July 28, 1898. Gaston Blanquart won first prize. In August the composer wrote to his publisher, Julien Hamelle, offering the *Fantaisie*, the Seventh Nocturne, and the *Sicilienne* for seven hundred francs.[11]

Seven years later, at the age of sixty, Fauré once again succeeded Théodore Dubois, this time as director of the Paris Conservatory, a position he held for fifteen years. As he grew older, he was plagued with migraine headaches and devastating hearing loss. Still, he continued to compose, creating his Second Cello Sonata, the Second Piano Quintet, a piano trio, string quartet, and the Nocturne no. 13 for solo piano. To the end, he devoted himself to his art and to meeting with young musicians, upon many of whom he exerted a profound influence.

Notes

1. Harold C. Schonberg, *The Lives of the Great Composers*, 3rd ed. (New York: Norton, 1997), 409.
2. Graham Johnson, *Gabriel Fauré: The Songs and Their Poets* (London: Ashgate, 2009), 143.
3. Jean-Michel Nectoux, *Gabriel Fauré: A Musical Life*, trans. Roger Nichols (Cambridge: Cambridge University Press, 1991), 26.
4. Nectoux, *Gabriel Fauré*, 146.
5. *Grove Music Online*, s.v. "Fauré, Gabriel," by Jean-Michel Nectoux, accessed August 2, 2014, http://www.oxfordmusiconline.com.ezproxy.bradley.edu/.
6. Nectoux, *Gabriel Fauré*, 482.
7. Philippe Fauré-Fremiet, ed., *Lettres intimes* (Paris: La Colombe, later Grasset, 1951), quoted in Nectoux, *Gabriel Fauré*, 150.
8. Rolf Haglund, recording booklet for *Joueuse de Flûte*, Áshildur Haraldsdóttir, flute, with Love Derwinger, piano (Lerum, Sweden: Intim Musik, 2006).
9. James M. Keller, *Chamber Music: A Listener's Guide* (New York: Oxford University Press, 2011), 196.
10. Adrian Corleonis, http://www.answers.com/topic/fantaisie-for-flute-piano-or-orchestra-in-e-minor-op-79#ixzz1XyYaxv9L, accessed October 1, 2011.
11. Jean-Michel Nectoux, ed. *Gabriel Fauré: His Life through His Letters* (London: Marion Boyars, 1984), 235.

12 Cécile Chaminade—Concertino, op. 107

CÉCILE CHAMINADE (1857–1944) enjoyed a youth of privilege. Growing up in Paris and Le Vésinet, an affluent suburb, she became acquainted with the leading French composers of her day through biweekly soirées hosted by her parents. The Chaminades were highly regarded amateur musicians and counted Georges Bizet, Emmanuel Chabrier, and Benjamin Godard among their friends. It was Bizet who discovered and encouraged young Cécile's musical talent. He suggested that she attend the Paris Conservatory, but Cécile's father rejected that idea on the grounds that it was not appropriate for a young woman of her class.[1] He did, however, allow her to study privately with professors from the school.

Chaminade studied piano as well as harmony, counterpoint, and fugue. In 1877, at the age of twenty, she made her professional debut, performing a piano recital at the Salle Pleyel in Paris. The following year she presented a recital of her own compositions at the home of her piano teacher, the conservatory's Félix LeCouppey. "Widely reviewed and well received the program would serve as a model for the typical Chaminade recital some twenty years later: repertoire consisting entirely of her works, a mixture of piano solos and songs, and the composer at the keyboard."[2]

During the 1880s, Chaminade composed a large array of pieces, including the four-movement *Suite d'Orchestre*, op. 20; the comic opera *La Sévillane*; a dramatic symphony with vocal soloists and a large chorus titled *Les Amazones*; a ballet, *Callirhoë*;

and a *Concertstück* for piano and orchestra. By the end of the decade, however, her focus turned almost exclusively to small-scale solo piano pieces and *mélodies* for solo voice with piano accompaniment. Certainly these genres served her well as she embarked on concert tours that brought her great fame; the immediate publication of these salon pieces enhanced their popularity and her earnings. There were frequent trips to England, where she became a favorite of Queen Victoria, and concert tours of Austria, Germany, Belgium, Poland, Hungary, Romania, Bulgaria, Greece, and Turkey.[3] Finally, after many invitations, she agreed to visit the United States in the fall of 1907. She performed the *Concertstück* as soloist with the recently founded Philadelphia Orchestra and cultivated a huge following with recitals in twelve cities. She presented recital programs in New York's Carnegie Hall, Orchestra Hall in Chicago, and major venues in Milwaukee, Minneapolis, and St. Louis. More than one hundred women's amateur musical societies, called "Chaminade clubs," sprang up at this time, and their popularity continued through the 1940s and 1950s.

In 1902, during Paul Taffanel's tenure as flute professor, Théodore Dubois, director of the Paris Conservatory, commissioned Chaminade to write a piece for the annual flute concours. Since 1832, the concours had been dominated by works composed by Taffanel's two predecessors, Tulou and Altès, but Taffanel inaugurated the practice of commissioning pieces from a variety of contemporary composers, including Andersen, Fauré, Enescu, and Gaubert. This change led to the creation of many of the best-known works in the repertoire.

Chaminade worked on the project with vigor.[4] She knew that she had to write a piece that contained "all the difficulties of the instrument"[5] within the confines of a short, one-movement work. One logical option was to compose a concertino, a free-form piece with multiple sections varying in tempo and character. (See Chart 12.1)

The composition opens in D major with an expansive, soaring melody, one of the hallmarks of Chaminade's style and a good example of her avowal that "I am essentially of the Romantic School, as all my work shows."[6] A version of the first half of this melody, now in A major, leads by way of a deceptive cadence to B♭ major and a presentation of the first two measures of the melody in that key. Passagework serves as transition to a *fortissimo* outpouring of the same theme back in D major.

The "B" section, in B♭ major, sets a different tone, signaled by the syncopated solo line and, in the accompaniment, a change of texture from block chords to tremolos and rapid arpeggios. The brighter tempo, increased chromaticism, and stringendo contribute to the agitation. Then, beginning in m. 45, Chaminade develops the section's opening motive, one presentation tumbling over the next.

The transition to "C" features a flirtation with minor keys, their diminished-seventh chords resolving to C minor, G minor, and D minor in mm. 68–70 before an authentic cadence establishes A minor at the start of "C" itself (m. 73). This

section	**Intro**	**A**				**B**												
starts m#	1	3				33												
theme		a	a^1	a^2	a^1	m	n	n	n/o	o	o	*Fortspinnung*						
starts m#		3	11	19	27	33	36	37	38/39	41	43	45						
key	**D**		**A**	**B^b**	**D**	**B^b**						**F**						
section						**B^1**								**C**				
starts m#						57								73				
theme						m	n	n	n^1	codetta		trans		x	y	x	y^1	trans
starts m#						57	60	61	62	64		68		73	79	84	90	96
key						**B^b**							**a**					**e C**
section	**cadenza**	**A^1**				**Coda**												
starts m#	111	112				136												
theme		a	a^3 *	a^2	a^1													
starts m#		112	120	124	132													
key	**various**	**D**	**A**	**B^b**	**D**													
			* cf mm 15–18															

CHART 12.1 Chaminade, Concertino: Analysis.

delightfully playful section is enlivened not only by its dazzling technical virtuosity but also by its varied articulation, rapid leaps, and jabbing accents. The deceptive cadence into m. 79 would seem to herald a more lyrical passage, but the playfulness resumes in the next measure. Measures 84–89 are virtually identical to mm. 73–78, only the melodic figuration being changed. The "y^1" that follows is also essentially identical to "y," except that its French-sixth-to-dominant chord progression is extended from one measure (83) to two (94–95). A long, harmonically complex transition leads to a cadenza built on just three chords: F♯ major, including an embellished fragment of the piece's opening melody; then, F♯ minor, which begins with a presentation of the fragment in that key; and finally a dominant pedal of D that prepares the way for the return of the "A" section in the tonic key. The coda, presto, brings the piece to the kind of brilliant conclusion that is perfect for competition repertoire.

Chaminade also wrote the sight-reading piece for the 1902 concours. The signed autograph of each competition piece was to be submitted to the conservatory's library. Unfortunately, the manuscript of both the concertino and the corresponding sight-reading piece are missing or have been misfiled.[7] Chaminade once revealed that she thought through new compositions in her head, then, when they were completely worked out, notated them. The remarkably clean manuscripts of many of her compositions substantiate this claim,[8] but because of the missing manuscript and the lack of any comment by her, it is not possible to ascertain details about the creation of the concertino.

It was the composer herself who later orchestrated the work for the London debut of flutist Marguerite de Forest Anderson,[9] an American who studied in Boston and New York and with Albert Fransella in London before launching a successful solo career.

In 1913 Chaminade was awarded France's highest decoration, the Legion of Honor. As the twentieth century progressed, however, most of her four hundred compositions were forgotten, as salon music gave way to the more progressive compositions of Debussy and Ravel. Only the concertino has retained its popularity, often serving as a coming-of-age piece for talented young flutists.

Notes

1. * Cécile Tardif, "Cécile Chaminade and the Concertino, op. 107," *Flutist Quarterly* 15 (Spring 1990): 19.

2. Marcia J. Citron, *Cécile Chaminade: A Bio-Bibliography* (Westport, CT: Greenwood Press, 1988), 4.

3. Citron, 12.

4. Cécile Tardif, *Portrait de Cécile Chaminade* (Montreal: Louise Courteau, 1993), 138.

5. Letter to Dr. Chapotot, February 28, 1934, quoted in Tardif, *Portrait*, 139.

6. "Mme. Chaminade, Greatest Woman Composer, Who Is Now Visiting America, Tells of Her Dreams," *Washington Post*, Nov. 1, 1908, quoted in Citron, 21.

7. Tardif, *Flutist Quarterly*, 22.

8. Citron, 20.

9. Mary Jean Simpson, "Marguerite de Forest Anderson," *Flutist Quarterly* 15 (Spring 1990): 13.

13 George Enescu—*Cantabile et Presto*

BORN IN THE northeastern corner of Romania, in the historic province of Moldavia, George Enescu (1881–1955) was a remarkably gifted child who became his country's greatest musician. He began violin lessons at the age of four and piano lessons at five; at seven, he entered the Vienna Conservatory. Only the second student ever to be accepted under the age of ten (Fritz Kreisler was the first in 1882),[1] Enescu studied harmony, counterpoint, music history, chamber music, violin, piano, and organ and also became a first-rate cellist by the time of his graduation at twelve.[2]

After an additional year of composition studies with Robert Fuchs, Enescu moved to Paris, guided by the desire to study composition with Jules Massenet. Massenet accepted Enescu (later known in Paris as Georges Enesco) into his class at the conservatory, and the young composer found his new teacher to be "the most approachable, talkative and enthusiastic person I've ever known . . . highly intelligent, a born musician and a great teacher."[3] Enescu and the other students appreciated Massenet's broad-minded approach, which contrasted with that of many of the other conservatory professors.

When Massenet resigned the following year, Enescu studied with his successor, Gabriel Fauré. Fauré was a very different teacher, but one whom Enescu also adored and with whom he would later play chamber music.[4] Classmates included Florent Schmitt, Jean Roger-Ducasse, Alfredo Casella, Charles Koechlin, and Maurice Ravel.

It was a formidable group, and many remained lifelong friends. Simultaneously, Enescu studied counterpoint and fugue with André Gédalge, who later wrote that of all his pupils, Enescu was "the only one to have real ideas and inspiration."[5]

One of the astonishing aspects of Enescu's genius was his prodigious musical memory. According to biographer Noel Malcolm, he could sit at the piano and begin at any point in Wagner's *Ring* cycle, and he could play 150 of Bach's cantatas, bringing out every nuance of each composition.[6] In the 1940s, Alexandru Rădulescu, a violinist in his quartet, asked "if it were true, as d'Indy had once said, that if the works of Beethoven were destroyed, Enescu would be able to reconstruct them all from memory. 'Oh no,' said Enescu, 'only the Symphonies, Quartets and Trios, the *Missa Solemnis* and *Fidelio*.'"[7]

In 1899, after winning the *premier prix* in violin, Enescu left the Paris Conservatory and launched his musical career as both a composer and one of the greatest violin virtuosi of his generation. Throughout his life, he divided his energies between these two pursuits and his time between Paris and his homeland.

During the early years of the twentieth century, Enescu spent most of his time in the French capital, where in 1904 Fauré persuaded him to serve as a member of the performance jury at the conservatory. For the next six years, Enescu evaluated pianists and violinists almost every year.[8] He also composed four competition pieces: in 1904 (at age twenty-two), the *Cantabile et Presto*, his only work for flute and piano, as well as a work for the harp concours (*Allegro de concert*); then two years later, the *Concertstück* for viola and *Légende* for trumpet.

Enescu's early compositions reflect diverse musical influences: echoes of Schumann and Brahms in the First Cello Sonata (1898), folk music in his Romanian Rhapsodies (1901), and a debt to Fauré in the Violin Sonata no. 2 (1899) and *Cantabile et Presto* (1904). At the same time, he spoke of his rapid development and believed that he was "becoming himself" as a composer during these years.[9] Pascal Bentoiu proposes that the varied styles in which Enescu composed "demonstrate a superlatively rich personality which—before accomplishing the grandiose synthesis—had to express its manifold facets in each direction."[10]

In formulating *Cantabile et Presto*, Enescu chose the same structure that his teacher Fauré had used for his flute concours piece (the *Fantaisie* of 1898): an expressive Andante followed by an exuberant finale. Each composer's work begins with a short, simple introduction out of which emerges a lyrical gem. The Cantabile opens in E♭ major with a tonic pedal point that continues through m. 5. As the "B" section begins (m. 9), the harmonic rhythm accelerates, with the pianist's sixteenth notes outlining a different chord on each beat. The lower notes of the arpeggios provide a bass line (mm. 9–18) while the upper notes offer a "sweet, melting" (and syncopated) countermelody (mm. 9–12 and 14 [last beat]–18). The intensification of chromaticism in

m. 13 and the tonicization of A♭ minor in m. 16 add drive to the section before it returns to the opening key, diatonic harmony, and soft dynamic level for its conclusion.

After a short fermata, the introduction and "A" section return. This time the accompaniment's sixteenth-note motion extends to the fourth beat of each measure under a lovely melodic variation in the flute. Piano arpeggiations in the "B^1" section (mm. 26–31) increase in speed to sextuplets, and the chromatic harmony invigorates excursions to C♭ major and E♭ minor before returning to the tonic key in m. 30. It is in m. 27 that the "B^1" section departs from its original outline, here descending from G to G♭ in the melody, supported by the somewhat unusual progression of a German augmented-sixth chord in third inversion (respelled: E𝄫–F–A𝄫–C♭; spelled: D–F–G–B), resolving directly to C♭ major (the tonic triad) in first inversion.

Noel Malcolm suggests that Enescu's remarkable musical memory guided him toward the creation of a complicated web of thematic connections within a piece.[11]

EXAMPLE 13.1 Enescu, *Cantabile et Presto*, "Cantabile," mm. 16–18 and mm. 31–33.

The changes that occur between the first and second presentations of the "B" material offer one example. Another may be seen in mm. 17 and 31. In its first appearance, the pianist's right-hand motive ("p" in Example 13.1) leads to a rest and the conclusion of the "B" section in m. 18. In its second iteration, the same motive propels the line onward into the "C" section and the movement's climax in m. 33. This section concludes with a short cadenza, after which Enescu returns to the melodic pattern of m. 8 as the basis for a codetta that prolongs tonic harmony in the home key.

Enescu launches the Presto with an emphatic E♭ major chord. As the harmonic progression unfolds, however, it becomes clear that the key is G minor. The composer reinforces the arrival of the tonic chord in m. 59 with a ten-measure tonic/dominant drone.

The movement is in rondo form, and its principal recurring section (labeled "D" on Chart 13.1) introduces one of the movement's distinctive features: contrasting melodic directions between the flute and the right hand of the piano. Rapid descending octaves in the piano (motive "t") precede the presentation of "D" and recur five more times in the course of the movement, each time effecting a transition to a new section (or, at m. 73, a repetition of the previous one).

Five measures into the next section, "E," Enescu offers ingenious, temporarily "atonal" chromaticism: a descending chromatic scale in parallel minor sixths harmonized by the piano's left hand, creating a series of half-diminished seventh chords alternating with augmented triads. Underlying this passage are both of the whole-tone scales, one supporting the seventh chords on the fourth and second eighths of each measure, the other supporting the triads on the first and third eighths. The nearly continuous sixteenth-note motion is interrupted by a march of quarter-note chords over a descending bass line leading to a sixteen-measure prolongation of dominant harmony. The rhythmically playful passage beginning at m. 113 presents a series of hemiolas: three eighth notes in the piano versus two groups of three sixteenth notes in the flute. As an additional rhythmic treat, four of these hemiolas fit into three measures. Here again, contrasting melodic contours enhance the delight of this diaphanous scherzo.

The appearance of the lyrical and impassioned "F" introduces the movement's only prolonged contrasting key, that of the parallel major, G. Woven into this section in mm. 151–154 is the sinuous passagework that Enescu used at the start of "E." Again, subtle motivic relationships achieve unifying connections.

Noteworthy in the coda are the uniformly *p* and *ppp* dynamics and, at mm. 202–205, the two plagal Neapolitan-tonic cadences, the first arrived at deceptively after an eight-measure dominant pedal. The contrast in the contour of melodic lines is exaggerated in the eight measures leading into the coda and in the coda itself. Only in the final seven measures do the two instruments move in the same direction for a resounding conclusion.

section	**Introduction**				**D†**				**D**				**E**						
# of mm	13				16				18				29						
starts m#	48				61				77				95						
recurring elements*	Δ	Δ	t	Δ	u	u	v	t	u	u	v^1	t^1	**w**	Δ	Δ	Δ	Δ	Δ	Δ
# of mm	4	4	4	1	4	4	4	4	4	4	4	6	4	4	4	6	5	5	1
starts m#	48	52	56	60	61	65	69	73	77	81	85	89	95	99	103	107	113	118	123
key	**g**										**mod**	**c**				**g**			
starts m#	1										89	93				107			

* Roman letters indicate recurring elements, Δ's non-recurring elements (often passagework).

section									**D**				**F**						
# of mm									15				26						
starts m#									124				139						
recurring elements									u	u	v	t^2	x	y	w^1/u^2	y^1	t^2		
# of mm									4	4	4	3	7	5	4	7	3		
starts m#									124	128	132	136	139	146	151	155	162		
key									**g**				**G**						
starts m#									124				139						

CHART 13.1 Enescu, *Cantabile et Presto*: Analysis of the "Presto."

section			**D**	**F**
# of mm			13	16
starts m#			165	178
recurring elements			u u^1 v^2 t^2	x^1 Δ
# of mm			4 4 2 3	8 8
starts m#			165 169 173 175	178 186
key			**G**	**E^b** **g**
starts m#			165	178 182
section			**(D) Coda**	
# of mm			18	
starts m#			194	
recurring elements			u^2 Δ $Δ^1$ Δ	
# of mm			4 4 4 6	
starts m#			194 198 202 206	
key			**g**	
starts m#			194	

† See text for discussions of Sections "A," "B," and "C" in the preceding Cantabile.

CHART 13.1 Continued

Cantabile et Presto lives on as one of the conservatory's great commissions, and both Philippe Gaubert and Marcel Moyse returned to it during their tenures at the institution: Gaubert selected it for the concours in 1921, Moyse in 1940. In the years after composing it, Enescu enjoyed a flourishing reputation as a violinist while suffering some delay and disappointment as he tried to launch his career as an orchestral composer.

With the outbreak of World War I, he returned to Romania, which, though initially neutral, became an ally of England, France, and Russia in August 1916 and then, within a few months, was overrun by Germany, Austria-Hungary, and Bulgaria. Romania suffered over three-quarters of a million military and civilian dead. Cut off from cosmopolitan musical influences during these years, Enescu, in his mid-thirties, gave almost daily concerts in hospitals and refugee camps, performed benefits for the Red Cross and other organizations, and devoted himself to developing the musical life of his native land. Of his wartime concertizing, he later said:

> I have often noticed how great an uplifting of the spirit could be seen in the faces of the wounded after the first few notes. This transformation of the soul is the supreme raison-d'être of music. If it did not have this wonderful effect of calming and purifying the human spirit, music would just be a meaningless sequence of sounds.[12]

During these years, he founded the Enescu Prize for Romanian composers, formed a symphony orchestra consisting largely of refugees, and created the country's first national opera company. And he fell in love. Marie Cantacuzino, unhappily married to the eldest son of a Romanian prince, was a beautiful and fascinating woman with whom Enescu carried on a lengthy affair. The young composer promised marriage upon the death of the princess's husband, a commitment he realized in 1939.

After the war, he continued touring internationally as a violinist, including a visit to the United States, where he also performed as conductor and met the young man who would become his most acclaimed student: Yehudi Menuhin. Throughout the twenties he also devoted enormous energy to his favorite work, the opera *Œdipe*, which he had begun sketching in 1910, completed in 1931, and finally saw premiered in Paris in 1936.

Tragedy filled Enescu's later life: when the Communist Party took control of Romania after World War II, he left his homeland for the last time. His wife had become mentally unstable and squandered his assets, and poor health consumed him until his death in 1955. While Romania would later honor him by staging celebrations of his music, imprinting his image on one of its most commonly used banknotes, and changing the name of his hometown from Liveni to George Enescu, the humble, kindly, loyal genius would die an impoverished, burdened man in a tiny Parisian apartment at the age of seventy-four.

Notes

1. Noel Malcolm, *George Enescu: His Life and Music* (London: Toccata, 1990), 35.
2. Malcolm, 42.
3. George Enescu, *Contrepoint dans le miroir*, ed. Bernard Gavoty (Paris: Éditrice Nagard, 1982), quoted in Malcolm, 49.
4. Malcolm, 54.
5. Marc Pincherle, *The World of the Virtuoso* (London: Gollancz, 1964), 115.
6. Malcolm, 13.
7. C. Răsvan, Interview with Alexandru Rădulescu, *Muzica* 25 (June 1975), 12–13, quoted in Malcolm, 213.
8. Malcolm, 92–93.
9. Enescu, 36, quoted in Malcolm, 82.
10. Pascal Bentoiu, *Masterworks of George Enescu: A Detailed Analysis*, trans. Lory Wallfisch (Lanham, MD: Scarecrow Press, 2010), 516.
11. Malcolm, 13–14.
12. Adrian Ranta, "Sub vraja lui George Enescu," *Lupta* 15 (October 18, 1936): 5, quoted in Malcolm, 118.

14 Philippe Gaubert—*Nocturne et Allegro scherzando*

SERENDIPITY LED PHILIPPE GAUBERT (1879–1941), the son of a cobbler and a housekeeper, to his place as one of France's most prominent musicians. Gaubert's mother worked for Paul Taffanel and sometimes took her young son with her when she cleaned the apartment of the eminent flutist and conductor. Taffanel adored the boy and offered to teach him to play the flute. Having already had some basic musical instruction from his father,[1] Gaubert soon began flute, harmony, and solfège studies with Taffanel. This was the beginning of a close, lifelong relationship, Taffanel guiding his student toward a career much like his own, as flutist, composer, and conductor.

Gaubert entered the Paris Conservatory in 1893, the same year that Taffanel was appointed professor of flute. Like his teacher, Gaubert, who was just fifteen, won the *premier prix* at the end of his first year of study; he performed Ferdinand Langer's Concerto in G Minor. In 1897 he became a member of the two most important orchestras in Paris[2] (both conducted by Taffanel): those of the Société des concerts du Conservatoire (which Gaubert usually referred to as "the Concert Society"), a virtuoso orchestra of professors and the finest students at the conservatory, and of the Théâtre national de l'Opéra, as the Paris Opera was then known, called by Gaubert simply "l'Opéra." He also continued composition studies at the conservatory, winning first prize in fugue in 1903. Two years later, Gaubert placed third in the prestigious Prix de Rome composition competition, the year of the travesty in which Maurice Ravel entered for the fifth time and was eliminated in the qualifying round.

In November 1904, Gaubert launched the third prong of his musical career, when the position of assistant conductor of the Concert Society became available.

> They decided to fill it by means of a competition. . . . My revered mentor, Paul Taffanel, told me: "Go for it!" "But, Master, I replied, I have never conducted, never dared to." . . . "Come see me" [he said]. He gave me two lessons, and one fine day there I was in front of the celebrated orchestra. The audition lasted a good hour-and-a-half. . . . I can still see [pianist] Ricardo Viñes playing the Saint-Saëns [Second] Concerto, bass [Armand] Narcon singing the [fourth movement of Beethoven's] Ninth, and I still remember an awful attack of nerves in the 2/8 trio [*sic*; actually 2/4] of the Schumann [Second Symphony] Scherzo . . . and the coda of this same scherzo! What a time I had with it! . . . A nearly unanimous vote rewarded my efforts and my audacity, and I was chosen Assistant Conductor of the Concert Society. I was twenty-five years old! Taffanel was beaming with joy![3]

Gaubert's career was progressing beautifully when in 1906, at the age of twenty-seven, he was asked to compose a piece for the conservatory's concours. The resulting composition, *Nocturne et Allegro scherzando* (the first of three he would write for the flute competition), became his best-known work.[4] Dedicated to Taffanel, it demonstrates the colorful harmonic language, elegant melodic lines, and brilliant passagework that characterize much of his oeuvre.[5]

Gaubert unifies the Nocturne with a three-note *Kernmotiv* (core or basic motive) announced immediately. This motive will sometimes descend the interval of a third, sometimes a second, its inversion will be used, and in two iterations its rhythm will vary a bit, but the twenty-three occurrences are always clearly recognizable.

The movement is cast in conventional ternary form, but there are intriguing aspects with regard to its harmonic language. (Enharmonic equivalency is established in m. 16, where in the flute, A♭ is tied to G♯.) The five-measure piano introduction is built on a whole-tone scale based on G♯. It is not until the start of the "a" theme that a key—D♭ major—is established, whereupon the first five measures are understood to have been a kind of extended dominant harmony.

In m. 15, there is an interesting modulation to E major: D♭ major, interpreted as C♯ major, is the parallel major of C♯ minor, the sixth degree of the scale of E major. Recurrences in "B" of the *Kernmotiv*, in both the flute and the right hand of the piano, link this section to the surrounding "A" sections.

Interestingly, Gaubert returns to "A" and D♭ major via an enharmonic Neapolitan chord (E♭♭–G♭–B♭♭) in second inversion (A–D–F♯), enhanced by a minor seventh (D♭♭/C). With the resolution of this chord, the melody of "A" returns, this time an octave higher, with the only significant changes, expressed as a^2 (mm. 29ff.) instead of a^1 (mm. 10ff.), occurring when Gaubert adds a half-measure (m. 32) and then a melodic embellishment in the penultimate measure of the phrase (m. 33). A four-measure codetta ends the section in D♭ major.

The Allegro scherzando begins in the same key but moves abruptly to F minor as the introduction gives way to the principal theme of this ternary-form movement. Gaubert inserts virtuoso passagework, almost always in four-measure phrases, and usually in pairs of these, between reiterations of the jaunty melody ("d," mm. 53–60). In m. 89, the piano emerges from its role as accompanist to engage in dialogue with the flute in a modulation from E♭ major via A♭ minor and its relative, C♭ (B) major, to A♭ major. Here Gaubert presents a contrasting lyrical section supported by syncopated chords.

Following a return to F minor and the Allegro's principal theme, "d," a transition built on the same whole-tone scale as the first five measures of the Nocturne, but this time starting on C (the dominant of F), prepares a final modulation to F major and a restatement of the Nocturne's principal theme adapted to the Allegro's 2/4 meter. This adaptation involves, successively, two different levels of (notated) augmentation: a broad one, in which four measures of the Allegro equal one of the Nocturne (mm. 167–174 and 179–184), and a speedier one, where two of the Allegro equal one of the Nocturne (mm. 175–178). Having already offered the movement's principal material in two extended presentations (mm. 51–104 and 129–166), Gaubert moves directly to a brief coda that blazes with brilliant passagework and ends with a plagal cadence.

Louis Ganne composed the sight-reading piece for the 1906 competition. The thirteen-member jury awarded seventeen-year-old Marcel Moyse, who was completing his first year of conservatory study, and René Bergeon the *premier prix*.

Gaubert enlisted in the army and saw action at Verdun during World War I. After a tour of the United States and Canada in 1919, he returned to Paris, where within a year he was awarded the three positions that put him at the center of French musical life between the wars. First, by unanimous vote, he was appointed principal conductor of the Société des concerts. Then he was named Adolphe Hennebains's successor ("after an interregnum maintained by Lafleurance")[6] as professor of flute at the conservatory. And, a few months later, he was offered the position of principal conductor of the Opéra. Gaubert juggled these three demanding positions until

1932, though he "put his flute in the closet" in 1920 and was entrusting Marcel Moyse with most of the teaching of the flute class by the end of the decade.

Paul Taffanel left extensive notes for a flute method book when he died in 1908. Fifteen years later, the very busy Gaubert finished compiling and editing this material, which Leduc published in 1923. In the end, even considering Gaubert's many contributions as flutist, composer, and conductor, it is this Taffanel-Gaubert method that is his most enduring legacy, one that forever ties him to the mentor who took a little boy, taught him to play the flute, provided his early training in harmony, and gave him the two conducting lessons that launched the most successful aspect of his career.

Notes

1. Claude Dorgeuille, *The French Flute School (1860–1950)*, trans. Edward Blakeman (London: Tony Bingham, 1986), 26.

2. *Grove Music Online*, s.v. "Gaubert, Philippe," by Edward Blakeman, accessed August 2, 2014, http://www.oxfordmusiconline.com.ezproxy.bradley.edu/.

3. Philippe Gaubert, "Comment je suis devenu chef d'orchestre," *Le Monde Musical* 49, no. 13 (Dec. 31, 1938), 281, quoted in Penelope Peterson Fischer, "Philippe Gaubert (1879–1941): His Life and Contributions as Flutist, Editor, Teacher, Conductor and Composer" (DMA diss., University of Maryland, 1982), 19–20, trans. William Wilsen.

4. The other two pieces were the *Fantaisie* (used in 1920, 1932, 1941) and the Ballade (1928).

5. Blakeman, *Grove Music Online*.

6. Dorgeuille, 33.

15 Georges Hüe—*Fantaisie*

BORN IN VERSAILLES, Georges Hüe (1858–1948; pronunciation: OO-eh, with OO pronounced like the "ue" in the French word *vue* [view]) celebrated his twelfth birthday about two months before the outbreak of the Franco-Prussian War. While staying in Cabourg (140 miles west of Paris, on the English Channel), the young boy, whose mother had taught him to play the piano, composed a mazurka. One day, as he was playing the work yet again, his grandmother suddenly declared, "This child is truly gifted. He carries something special in him. I must introduce him to [Charles] Gounod." Gounod encouraged Hüe, believing that he could have a glorious musical career if he devoted himself to it.[1]

Hüe was referred to Gounod's friend Émile Paladilhe, who pronounced the mazurka "worthless" but moderated his harsh appraisal in the face of the boy's shocked reaction: "Let's get to work. We'll see." As Hüe began to study harmony and counterpoint, Paladilhe quickly recognized his ability.[2]

Though Hüe's father, an architect, had hoped his son would enter the École des beaux-arts (School of Fine Arts) and take up his own profession, Georges instead enrolled at the Paris Conservatory in 1875. There he studied composition with Napoléon Henri Reber and organ with César Franck. In 1879 he won the prestigious Prix de Rome with his cantata *Médée* and enjoyed two years in Italy, traveling and composing. Two years later he won acclaim for the comic opera *Les pantins* ("The Jumping Jacks").[3]

The young composer attended the fourth performance of *Parsifal* in 1882 and, like so many others at the time, fell under Wagner's spell. He later became an honorary citizen of Bayreuth but confessed that, as his career developed, Wagner's influence began to weigh heavily on him. He eventually freed himself from its stranglehold.[4]

In 1883, Hüe was awarded second prize (Vincent d'Indy won first) in a composition contest sponsored by the city of Paris.[5] In subsequent years he wrote operas, songs, symphonic and choral works, and after a trip to the Far East, the ballet *Siang-Sin* (1924), which garnered a hundred performances in its first twenty years.[6]

In 1913, during Adolphe Hennebains's tenure as professor of flute, the Paris Conservatory commissioned Hüe to write a piece for its annual concours. The *Fantaisie* was originally written for flute and piano, as required for the competition, but its popularity led Hüe to orchestrate it ten years later.

The work, in bar form (A-A-B: a, b; a, b; c, c), opens boldly in G Phrygian; the consistent presence of A♭ and F♮ distinguishes this mode from the key of G minor. Hüe intensifies the second phrase with a crescendo molto enhanced by a dramatic vii^9 chord. A modulation in m. 9 leads to D Dorian in m. 11 for the start of the third phrase: varied repetitions of m. 2 precede a brief cadenza over a B♭ pedal. With the arrival of the next section ("b") in A major (mm. 19ff.), it would seem that the B♭ may have been functioning as a Neapolitan.

As expected of a concours piece, Hüe introduces technical challenges and quick changes of mood, moving in mm. 19-21 from the brilliance of the opening to *bien chanté*. A modulation in m. 31 ushers in the distant key of E♭ major and a linking passage (mm. 35ff.) that includes a modulation (mm. 38–39) to D minor, where in m. 40 Hüe employs both German and French augmented-sixth chords, resolving them to the dominant in the following measure. The return of the mm. 21–24 theme at m. 41 leads to a deceptive cadence into the reprise of "A" at m. 44.

While this return draws on the material of the opening, Hüe stresses it with tremolos in the left hand of the piano and by beginning in the flute on the fourth degree of D Dorian (the same pitch as the first degree of G Phrygian in m. 2). At m. 52 he forgoes the quiet lyricism and harmonic stability that prevailed at the start of the first "b" section. Instead, the flute continues with melodic content from the "a" section as the piano begins a new version of "b." This four-measure phrase leads inexorably to a *fortissimo* outpouring of the "b" theme followed by a transition (mm. 60ff.) to *très vif*, "B."

A *fantaisie*, by definition, invites the composer to indulge in flights of fancy, and in the romantic era such pieces often suggested idyllic scenes. Hüe borrows this concept and evokes *Midsummer Night's Dream* fairies and sprites with playful, staccato eighth notes in 3/8 meter. The flute's chromaticism tempers the playfulness while spicing up an otherwise static fifty-two-measure dominant pedal accompaniment. Links connect appearances of "c" material, first heard in m. 118, then again in m. 140 in the right hand of the piano, and a third time beginning in m. 206. Each iteration begins in B♭ minor. In m. 230, the key abruptly changes to B♭ major (the preceding twelve measures having been in B major) for a reappearance of the emotive theme first heard in m. 164. The hemiola with which it begins suggests an expansive outcry above the fluid accompaniment. One phrase drives on to the next until m. 274, when the thrust relents and gives way to a sense of anticipation in advance of the coda (m. 290). Here the meter changes from 3/8 to 2/4. Ten measures on the dominant of the relative major of B♭ minor (V^9/III) lead to a V^7 chord that resolves to B♭ major for the piece's triumphant ending.

Georges Hüe, who lived to the age of ninety, composed during the late romantic era and continued through the rapidly changing first half of the twentieth century. Influenced by the harmonic language of the impressionists, he established a temporary niche, but as he grew older, he displayed no interest in newer trends. His large-scale compositions are now rarely heard, and the charming *Fantaisie* has become his best-known and most often performed composition.

Notes

1. Paul Landormy, *La musique française: Après Debussy* (Paris: Gallimard, 1943), 192, trans. William Wilsen.

2. Landormy, 192.

3. *Grove Music Online*, s.v. "Hüe, Georges," by Richard Langham Smith, accessed August 2, 2014, http://www.oxfordmusiconline.com.ezproxy.bradley.edu/.

4. Landormy, 193.

5. Landormy, 193.

6. Landormy, 194.

Heralds of a New Era

16 Claude Debussy—*Syrinx*

"PARISIAN TO HIS VERY FINGERTIPS" was Nadezhda von Meck's description of Claude Debussy (1862–1918) in the summer of 1882. Two years earlier, Madame von Meck, the famous patron and confidante of Tchaikovsky, had engaged the eighteen-year-old Debussy to give piano lessons to her children and play duets with her during the family's summer vacation. She continued to employ him during his summer breaks from studies at the Paris Conservatory in 1881 and 1882, as she and the children enjoyed visits to Interlaken, Rome, Naples, and Vienna in addition to various Russian cities.[1] A few years later her observation about his attachment to Paris was confirmed: in 1884 Debussy won the conservatory's Prix de Rome with the "reward" of a protracted residency in that city funded by the French government. In love with (the married) Marie-Blanche Vasnier, Debussy deferred his departure for Italy until the last minute and, once there, "took a prompt dislike to everything."[2] He wrote letters detailing his desire to return to Paris and later described his stay as "forced labor." He fulfilled the minimum residency[3] and, after just over two years of "forced exile" (January 1885 to March 1887), fled back to Paris. He couldn't bear to be away from the charms of his beloved city any longer.

In the years that followed, he continued his association with Ernest Guiraud, his former composition teacher, who listened and offered encouragement as the young composer formulated his artistic ideals. Debussy was invited to the elite Tuesday evening salon of Stéphane Mallarmé, where he got to know leading symbolist poets and impressionist painters, along with composers Ernest Chausson and Vincent d'Indy. In 1894, at the age of thirty-two, he completed his first major orchestral work, the revolutionary *Prélude à l'après-midi d'un faune*, which was inspired by Mallarmé's famous poem of the same name. Five years later came the *Nocturnes*, and then, after years of on-and-off work dating back to 1893, the groundbreaking opera *Pelléas et Mélisande* premiered in 1902. In between, there were creatively barren years, matrimonial rejections, and the much-needed financial support of generous friends.

Both personal scandal—abandoning his wife, Lilly Texier, for a new, married lover—and the continued creation of highly original works (*Fêtes galantes, Masques, L'isle joyeuse, La mer*) characterized the early years of the new century. Plans for a Tristan opera, proposed to Debussy by symbolist poet and playwright Gabriel Mourey, foundered because Joseph Bédier, author of the novel on which the libretto was to be based, had already granted rights for a stage adaptation to his cousin.

His thoughts never far from further theatrical projects and his financial situation never far from disaster, Debussy agreed, in 1910, to a less promising proposal than Tristan when Gabriele d'Annunzio asked him to compose incidental music for *Le martyre de Saint Sébastien*. Three years later, Mourey approached the composer again, this time asking him to write music for his three-act dramatic poem based on the ancient myth of Psyché and Cupid. Skeptical, Debussy responded, "Have you thought what genius would be needed to rejuvenate this tired old myth, already so exploited that it seems that the feathers of the wings of love are all withered away?"[4] Finally, however, he agreed to the project. The third act includes a secondary plot that tells of the death of the supposedly immortal god, Pan.[5] Debussy created *La flûte de Pan*, later retitled *Syrinx*, to be performed during this act.

Embarking upon and finishing a composition were often agonizing for Debussy: "It is not without a certain amount of terror that I see the moment approaching when I shall positively have to write something," he had admitted to d'Annunzio in January 1911.[6] The music for *Psyché* was to be completed for a performance on December 1, 1913, but on November 24 Debussy had to admit to Mourey that the three-minute piece was not yet finished. Somehow, he managed to get it done during the course of the week, however, and it was performed as scheduled. Debussy did not attend because of a trip to Russia that commenced the same day.[7]

La flûte de Pan is a remarkable little piece that has fascinated theorists and stimulated them to unearth its mysteries. Debussy knew that analysts would try to explain his compositions: no piece in the flute repertoire has been subjected to so many published analyses as this one, by as diverse a crowd as William Austin, Carol Baron, Robert Cogan and Possi Escot, Julia Larson, Jean-Jacques Nattiez, Robert Orledge, and Ernestine Whitman. However, earlier in the year during which he composed *La flûte de Pan*, Debussy warned: "The beauty of a work of art will always remain mysterious. That is to say, one will never be able to discover exactly 'how it was done.' Let us preserve at all costs, this magic which is peculiar to music."[8]

Debussy died only five years after completing *La flûte de Pan* and would have been surprised by the title under which it was eventually published in 1927, *Syrinx*. Neither would he know how scholars have labored to solve mysteries surrounding it and that, in fact, some questions still remain.

Mourey described the music as "the last melody that Pan plays before his death," a characterization that led many to believe that the piece was to be played at the end of *Psyché*. In 1991, however, a manuscript copy was found in Brussels and a facsimile edition of the piece was published. "The manuscript indicates that the music belongs to Act 3, scene 1, in the course of dialogue between an oread (mountain nymph) and a naiad [water nymph]. The oread is trying to allay the naiad's fear of Pan and suddenly indicates that an invisible Pan is about to play again: 'Mais voici que Pan de sa flûte recommence à jouer . . .' ['But look, Pan begins to play his flute again']. This is the cue for the first eight measures of *Syrinx*."[9]

The attitude of the naiad immediately changes and the two maidens become enraptured by Pan's performance. After m. 8, there is a fermata—omitted from the later Jobert edition—and the words: "Tais-toi, contiens ta joie, écoute" ("Be silent, restrain your joy, listen"), after which Pan performs the rest of the piece. When Debussy delivered the manuscript, he specified that the piece was to be played offstage: Pan was hidden inside his cave.

The questions that linger relate to the manuscript used by French flutist Louis Fleury, who was engaged to perform *La flûte de Pan* for the premiere of *Psyché* in 1913, and by Jean Jobert, when he published the work in 1927. Who penned the manuscript from which Fleury played? Was his copy the Brussels manuscript that was rediscovered in 1991? And what did Jobert use as the primary source when he first printed the work?

Fleury is known to have held on to his music after the performances of *Psyché* and to have played *La flûte de Pan* during the remaining years of his life. After his death in 1926, it seems that his widow gave the manuscript to Jobert to publish. The name of the piece was changed to *Syrinx* at that time, presumably to avoid confusion with the song of the same title in Debussy's *Chansons de Bilitis*, which Jobert had also published.

Researchers do not know what happened to Debussy's original manuscript or if, as suggested by Michael Stegemann, Fleury's copy was itself the original, penned either from Debussy's sketches or written down in collaboration with Debussy as he hastily tried to complete the work.[10] Stegemann believes that the creases in the paper of the Brussels manuscript suggest that "it had been folded up small enough to be packed into Fleury's flute case for safe-keeping."[11]

The three breath marks (mm. 2, 4, and 14) in the Brussels manuscript contrast with eighteen in Jobert's edition. This important incongruity probably occurred when Jobert, perhaps hearing that Moyse had played the piece for Debussy, asked the flutist to look over the work prior to its publication. In addition to adding the breaths he needed when he played the work (Debussy was adamant that a breath not occur in m. 25), Moyse may have contributed some other "emandations." Because Moyse refused to have his name listed as editor, the markings were erroneously attributed to Debussy.[12]

Psyché had two more performances during the week of its premiere while Debussy continued with his trip to Russia, the first of five he would undertake over the next eight months "in a final bid for something like solvency."[13] These were difficult times, as evidenced by letters sent to his wife, and were soon exacerbated by the start of World War I. On June 30, 1915, he wrote to his publisher Jacques Durand, "I have suffered much from the long drought forced upon my brain by the war."[14]

Only a week later, this weight was lifted when Debussy, along with his wife and daughter, Chouchou, left Paris for a three-month summer sojourn in Pourville, a coastal resort near Dieppe, in northwestern France, about seventy miles west of the World War I battle lines. In a beautiful villa overlooking the sea, which had always inspired him, Debussy enjoyed an enormously happy and productive time. At the start of his stay, he sent Durand a proposal for six sonatas; by the end, he had already completed the Cello Sonata and his masterful Sonata for Flute, Viola, and Harp. (The Violin Sonata of 1916/17 was the only other major work he would complete during his lifetime.) Debussy was reluctant to leave Pourville that September, and indeed, his departure coincided with a decline in health, as he battled the cancer that would take his life in 1918. But in the flute-viola-harp sonata composed during that final surge of inspiration in Pourville, he created one of the finest works in the flutist's chamber music repertoire.

Notes

1. Roger Nichols, *The Life of Debussy* (Cambridge: Cambridge University Press, 1998), 13.

2. Marcel Dietschy, *A Portrait of Claude Debussy* (Oxford: Clarendon Press, 1990), 40.

3. Dietschy, 46.

4. Nicholas Rauch sale catalogue, Geneva, November 24, 1958, 25, no. 93, quoted in Robert Orledge, *Debussy and the Theatre* (Cambridge: Cambridge University Press, 1982), 253.

5. Anders Ljungar-Chapelon, "Preface," *Debussy Syrinx La Flûte de Pan für Flöte solo*, ed. Michael Stegemann and Anders Ljungar-Chapelon (Vienna: Wiener Urtext Edition, Schott / Universal Edition, 1996), 3.

6. Guy Tosi, ed. *Debussy et d'Annunzio: Correspondence inédite* (Paris: Denoël, 1948), 63–64, quoted in Orledge, 1.

7. Nichols, 148.

8. François Lesure, ed. *Monsieur Croche et autres écrits: Édition complete de son oeuvre critique* (Paris: Gallimard, 1971), 224, quoted in Orledge, 254.

9. David Grayson, "Bilitis and Tanagra: Afternoons with Nude Women," in *Debussy and His World*, ed. Jane F. Fulcher (Princeton, NJ: Princeton University Press, 2001), 132.

10. Michael Stegemann, "Notes on the Sources," trans. Peter Owens, *Debussy Syrinx La Flûte de Pan für Flöte solo*, 16.

11. Stegemann, 16.

12. Trevor Wye, *Marcel Moyse: An Extraordinary Man* (Cedar Falls, IA: Winzer Press, 1993), 68–69.

13. Nichols, 148.

14. Dietschy, 178.

17 Albert Roussel—*Joueurs de flûte*, op. 27

ALBERT ROUSSEL (1869–1937) was born midway between Debussy (1862) and Ravel (1875) in Tourcoing, on France's northern border, midway between Dunkirk and Brussels. He turned to music only at the age of twenty-five, after launching a career as an officer in the French navy. As a child, he had learned the fundamentals of music from his mother and had then studied with the local cathedral organist, but he seems not to have considered a career in music until much later. Instead, he "devoured Jules Verne's maritime adventures, delighted in his family's seaside vacations [at Heyst, Belgium], and decorated his room to look like that of a ship's captain."[1] At fifteen he left for Paris to study at the Collège Stanislas and prepare for the entrance exams for the École navale (France's naval academy).

Passing the first part of the *baccalauréat* with flying colors, Roussel was accepted as a midshipman at the École in 1887 and reported for duty on the training ship *Borda*. Graduated and commissioned in 1889, he embarked on a series of assignments to the frigate *Iphigénie*, the battleship *Dévastation*, the sailing ship *Melpomène*, the cruiser *Victorieuse*, and the gunboat *Styx*. While assigned to the cruiser, he was finally able to enjoy some leisure time and the chance to compose and perform chamber music with two friends.

The first public performance of one of Roussel's compositions, Andante for String Trio and Organ, came Christmas Day 1892. He was twenty-three. The following year his *Marche nuptiale* was performed, and a short time later, one of his shipmates, Ensign Adolphe Calvet, offered to send the piece to French conductor and violinist Édouard Colonne for evaluation. Calvet returned the manuscript to Roussel weeks later, reporting Colonne's recommendation that Roussel resign from the navy and devote himself to music. Only years later did the budding composer learn that Calvet had, in fact, offered only his own opinion and had never sent the music to the esteemed conductor.[2]

When his assignment on the gunboat ended, Roussel requested a leave of absence. Visiting family in the northern French town of Roubaix, he met with Jules Koszul, director of the Roubaix Conservatory (and Dutilleux's grandfather), to discuss his desire to pursue a musical career. Offered encouragement and musical instruction by Koszul, Roussel resigned his commission in 1894 and moved to Paris. There, upon Koszul's recommendation, he was accepted as a student of Eugène Gigout. For four years, Gigout provided instruction in piano, organ, harmony, and counterpoint. Roussel must have enjoyed a shot in the arm when, in 1897, the two madrigals he submitted (under different pseudonyms) to the Société des compositeurs de musique each won first prize.[3]

A year later, at age thirty, Roussel entered the Schola Cantorum, where he began nine years of study with Vincent d'Indy, who had co-founded the school five years earlier. Beginning in 1902, d'Indy entrusted him with the Schola's counterpoint class, a position Roussel held until 1914. During this period, his students included Satie and Varèse. Ten years later Martinů would come to him for private study.

Roussel married in 1908 and the following year embarked on a three-month voyage to India and Cambodia. There he became fascinated with the medieval Hindu legend of Queen Padmavati, who sacrificed her life for love, and decided to set her story as an opera. His work on the composition, however, was interrupted by the outbreak of World War I. Roussel applied for active duty; the army recommissioned him as a transport officer and sent him to the Battle of the Somme and to Verdun. The ill health he had experienced all his life forced him to retire in January 1918.[4]

Several years later, Roussel and his wife purchased property on the Normandy coast. In this quiet, idyllic place, Roussel enjoyed long walks by the sea, completed his Second Symphony, and created many of his best-known works. It was here during the 1920s that his mature style evolved and that he created *Deux poèmes de Ronsard*, op. 26 (for voice and flute), and *Joueurs de flûte*, op. 27.

One of six chamber works in which the flute plays a major role, *Flute Players* was composed in August and September of 1924,[5] when the composer was fifty-five. He dedicated the piece to French composer and conductor J. Guy Ropartz, then added a separate dedication for each movement to a leading French flutist of the day. The titles of the movements refer to religious figures (Pan, Krishna) and fictitious ones (Tityrus, Péjaudie).

Pan, the best-known of Roussel's four flutists (at least to westerners), was the Greek god of nature, hunting, and shepherds, who looked like a satyr (a goat-man), consorted with nymphs, and was associated with not only music but sexuality. Roussel's tribute is cast in three parts, with much of the harmony determined by voice leading—not surprising given that he was a pupil and professor at the Schola Cantorum, where the study of older music was emphasized.

"Pan" begins and ends in G. Looking in detail at the first section of the piece (Très lent and Moins lent, with cadences at mm. 6, 11, and 18), one finds, after the initial measure in G Mixolydian, three voice-led, chromatic-atonal measures in which the vertical structures are determined by the piano's descent from the fifth g/d^1 to the fifth c/g, a "progression" ornamented (or ignored) by the flute as it pursues its melos. Arrival on c/g in m. 4 is reinforced by mm. 5–6, in which the flute gives up its wandering and participates in a V^{11} chord in C minor.

Measures 7–11 modulate from C to A♭ and return to C (m. 10). This passage cadences on an A minor eleventh chord followed by two sixteenths that anticipate the B♭ tonality that prevails for the first two beats of the next segment, mm. 12–18. The salient harmonic features of this segment include the three f^3's in the flute (mm. 12–14); the G♯ diminished-seventh chords bracketing mm. 12–13 and 13–14 (supported fully by the piano in m. 12, less so in m. 13); the A♭ tonality of m. 14; chromatic, voice-led atonality in the piano, mm. 15–16, accompanied by another flute emphasis of f, culminating, in mm. 17–18, in a G^7 chord that soon turns into the G♯ diminished-seventh that the flute outlined so insistently at the ends of mm. 12 and 13.

The Modérément animé can be seen to consist of five measures in C minor followed by eight in F. In this scheme, the chords of mm. 19–20 are ♭II^9, vii^9, V^{11}, V^9. The first and fourth of these chords are heard again in m. 21, while 22–23 are the same as 19–20. The tonality shifts to F with a V^9 chord in mm. 24–25. The harmonic goal of mm. 26–30 remains F major, attained in m. 31, but voice leading determines the sonorities as the range of the passage decreases from just short of four octaves in m. 26 to two octaves in m. 31. The conflict in the flute between B♭ and B♮ in mm. 26–27 is resolved in favor of B♭ in m. 28; from here on the flute remains solidly in F major. Meanwhile the left-hand piano moves chromatically up a tritone (B♮ to F) for two measures of vii^{o7} harmony before an arpeggiated F major in m. 31. The middle voice (right-hand piano), in contrary motion to the flute, follows its own (incomplete) path to F from five measures on D♭/C♯ through D to E♭ on the second beat of m. 31. At this point, the listener must change trains (right-hand piano to flute) and complete the journey with the flute's intonation of F on the third beat.

A modest but abrupt shift in tonality from F major to its relative minor inaugurates the final Lent, in which the flute is again entrusted with the primary melodic material and its ornamentation. The piano's right hand operates for six measures within a narrow range to express versions of an accompaniment motive that are unified by their rhythmic and melodic contours. Harmonically, this segment begins with three measures of the German-sixth chord of D minor. Roussel reinterprets the following measure of dominant harmony (A^7) as a German-sixth chord that resolves to its tonic, C♯ minor (mm. 36–37). Measures 38–43 offer another example of voice-led sonorities, the bass descending stepwise on the downbeats from D to the tableau's ultimate goal, G, while the right hand ascends in parallel thirds and sixths.

Measures 43–44 and 45–46 reprise mm. 32–33. Tonally, this last segment (m. 43 to the end) is in G, with a three-measure excursion to the Neapolitan in mm. 47–49, after which the bass resumes its descent from G in m. 50 through F, E♭, D♭, C, B, B♭, and A to its final G. Meanwhile, the piano's right hand descends for four measures (43–46), assumes flute-like characteristics for three, and drops out as the flute begins a three-measure reprise of the piece's first three measures.

The piper Tityrus ("Tityre" being its vocative case) is one of the two characters in Virgil's first *Eclogue*. Absorbed in his own good fortune, he enjoys wealth and ease as he offers a musical tribute to his beloved. The other character, Meliboeus, like many others around Mantua (Virgil's birthplace), has been dispossessed and is heading into exile, his property given to veterans of the winning army in a recent civil war. (Tityrus's land was restored to him after he went to Rome to plead his case.) Meliboeus addresses Tityrus in the poem's first stanza:

> *Tityre, tu patulae recubans sub tegmine fagi . . .*
>
> You, Tityrus, lying there beneath the shade of a spreading beech tree making woodland music on a slender pipe! We are leaving our country and our sweet fields; we are being exiled while you, Tityrus, at your ease in the shade, teach the woods to resound with the name of beautiful Amaryllis.

In Roussel's treatment, "Tityre," by virtue of its tempo, articulation, texture, and form (A-B-A^1), assumes the character of a scherzo, an expression often used for the second movement of a four-movement sonata. And it shares its tonality (E) and its atypical duple meter with another famous quasi scherzo, the overture to *A Midsummer Night's Dream* (which features a real scherzo as one of its other movements).

"Tityre" begins in E Phrygian and ends with a very nice plagal cadence in E Aeolian. In between one hears closely related keys: G major from m. 8, B minor at

m. 17, G major again at 23, a modulating passage from 37–40, E minor at 41, and as mentioned, E Aeolian from 43 to the end.

Although there is nothing humorous about Tityrus nor the events depicted in the first *Eclogue*, Wendell Dobbs suggests that the staccato, disjunct melodic lines and upward rushes of thirty-second notes seem "to depict Tityrus' stroke of luck and his casual, superficial attitude towards Meliboeus' plight." He associates the flute's lyrical melody in the "B" section (mm. 21–32) with Tityrus's recounting of his good fortune and the music's evaporating "to nothing at the end" with the encounter's drawing to a close.[6]

The two "A" sections are built around a three-measure *Kernmotiv* (core or basic motive), "a," which, in the piano, serves as an introduction. The flute then offers it three times, followed in mm. 7 and 11 by a one-measure link, "w." After the third iteration of "a," a one-measure motive, "x," is heard six times, its first two statements accompanied by a lyric, legato moment in the flute that foreshadows its melody in "B."

The "A" section's *Kernmotiv* continues in the piano in section "B," but the obbligato flute line is so different from what has gone before that one clearly senses new terrain. Six iterations of a one-measure motive first heard in the flute in m. 37 lead to a reprise of mm. 1–2 (the first two-thirds of "a"), followed in mm. 45–46 and 47–48 by sequential treatment of the first one-half of "a" (one and a half measures) as presented earlier by the flute at m. 8 and by the piano at m. 25. Finally (mm. 49–52), Roussel drives the piece home with four one-measure sequential iterations of the first one-third of "a."

Roussel dedicated "Krishna," the third of his tableaux, to Louis Fleury, who premiered the piece with pianist Janine Weill in a concert of La revue musicale held at the Théâtre du Vieux-Colombier in Paris on January 17, 1925. For this piece the composer drew on his voyages in the navy and a later trip to India with his wife.

Krishna is a Hindu god, the eighth incarnation (avatar) of Vishnu, protector of mankind. In the Bhagavad Gita, Krishna declares: "For the preservation of the righteous, the destruction of the wicked, and the establishment of dharma [virtue], I come into being from age to age."[7] The young Krishna is often portrayed playing the flute, with which he enchants the milkmaids (wives and daughters of the cowherds) to leave their homes and dance with him in the moonlight.

Roussel composed the piece using a Western adaptation of the raga *shree* (A, B♭, C♯, D♯, E, F, G♯, A), a traditional north Indian scale often used for religious gatherings at sunset. The raga, of course, determines the sonorities and pitch centers. "Krishna" is in ternary form, with pitch centers focused on A, C, and A, respectively. The middle section (mm. 20–44) transposes *shree* to C, D♭, E, F♯, G, A♭, B, C. The only deviations from strict use of the raga (except for enharmonic equivalents of the raga's D♭ and A♭) are the F♮s that occur in mm. 20–22 (neighboring tones in the piano's left hand) and in m. 44, where they contribute to the mostly chromatic contrary motion between the two hands of the piano. The exotic scale, 7/8 meter, supple melodic lines, and the piano's hypnotic one-measure ostinatos clearly evoke the youthful enchanter.

The use of an Indian raga does not preclude Western ears (and probably Western composers) from hearing (and creating) Western tonality. For example, the first five measures in the piano might be perceived as A major with, in each measure, a tonic triad followed by an altered German-sixth chord (with augmented fifth as well as sixth above the F).

In m. 6, a new tonal center emerges, C♯, extending to m. 9, where the two opening measures recur, perhaps back in A major but more likely continuing in C♯ (reinterpreting the alternating chords as VI/c♯ and I^9/C♯, a tonality that, as D♭ minor, prevails through m. 27). Notable are the repetitious dominants occurring from 20 through 26, first in the flute, then the bass.

Measure 27 is a transitional one, its bass "descending" from the preceding A♭ to the persistent $f♯^1$ that supports the first three measures of the second part of "B" (mm. 28–44). C is the tonal center here, with a brief excursion into E (major and minor) in mm. 31–34 before C reasserts itself and rules until the opening key, A, is reestablished at the moment of reprise (m. 45).

Measures 47–53 present the "a-b" of mm. 3–9 as "a-b^1," but instead of the modulation of "b" to C♯, the tonal center remains A as the flute turns the last measure of "b^1" into a five-measure evanescing sequence. The tableau's initial key of A is confirmed by the final cadence (mm. 56–57), VI^{+5} of A minor resolving, Picardy-wise, to A major, the kind of subdominant-tonic cadence Roussel adopted for the ending of the other three numbers of *Joueurs*.

Monsieur de la Péjaudie was the protagonist in the 1920 novel *La pécheresse* ("The Sinful Woman") by French symbolist author Henri de Régnier. Roussel appreciated Régnier's work and had already set three of the author's texts. The tableau's title character is a flutist whose fine playing assists him in his escapades with women, though he is eventually sent to the gallows for his sins. Roussel dedicated the movement to Philippe Gaubert, who also reportedly had an eye for the ladies.

Of the four tableaux, the slender "Péjaudie" is the most unified. Except for the first four measures of its coda, it is entirely in F major, its tonality emphasized by long dominant pedals (six measures starting at m. 13, eight starting at m. 24) and by strongly directional bass lines descending stepwise to the dominant ($B♭_1$ to C_1, mm. 24–27) or to the tonic (f^1 to F_1, mm. 30–41, with breaks in this long line only between the c^1 of m. 31 and the e of m. 32 and between the three final notes: E_1–$B♭_1$–F_1).

Another unifying factor is that twenty-four of its forty-one measures feature the distinctive rhythm and texture of the piano's first measure. Yet so acute is Roussel's muse that, though unified, the piece is anything but monotonous.

theme	a	b	a^1	$b^{1\ extended}$	c	$c^{extended}$	coda		
starts m#	5	9	13	17	24	28	34	38	39
key	**F**						**e**	**f**	**F**

CHART 17.1 Roussel, *Joueurs de Flûte*, Op. 27: Analysis of "Monsieur de la Péjaudie."

After an introduction of four measures, in which the upper notes of the piano rise from c^1 to b^1 (preparing the entrance of the flute on c^3), the themes unfold as shown in Chart 17.1.

The phrase rhythm of "b^1" deserves mention: its first measure is harmonically and melodically equivalent to the first two of "b" (mm. 9 and 10); its second, in the flute's elaboration of D♭ and the piano's characteristic rhythm, equivalent to m. 11. The third and fourth measures (19 and 20) can be seen as an extension of the single m. 12, after which the flute extends "b^1" to a cadence on the dominant in m. 24 (an elision, in that the flute's cadence coincides with the beginning of "c" in the piano). The upper notes in the piano's right hand in mm. 21–24 are a variant of the ascending scale in mm. 1–4 but this time offer a deception in that the cadential tonic expected to close the phrase on the downbeat of m. 24, f^1, is ousted by a dominant beginning a new phrase and a new section.

F major is obscured by augmented-sixth chords in mm. 31–33. By beats, these seven chords may be interpreted in F as: (1) V^9 of F major, (2) German-sixth of B♭ minor (iv of F minor), (3) ditto, (4) simultaneous French-sixth and German-sixth of D minor (vi of F major), (5) German-sixth of D minor, (6) A minor (iii of F major), (7) G minor (ii of F major). Continuing into the coda, the chords, now in E minor, by measure, are (1) C augmented (iii^{+5}/iv), (2) F♯ (V/V and V^{11}/V), (3) F♯ (V^{13}/V), (4) (last eighth note of m. 36) G♯ diminished-seventh (vii^{o7}/iv), (5) E major ($I^{\#3}$). The next chord (on the third beat of m. 37) functions as both V^9/iv in the preceding E minor and V^9/iii in F major. However, the following chord, a B♭ minor seventh, functions not in F major but as iv^7 of F minor, which then resolves in a plagal cadence to I of F major in m. 39.

The solidness and independence of Roussel's music are reflective of the way he lived his life. While he had been born the only child of a well-to-do, loving family (industrialists who produced textiles), Roussel endured hardships early on, including the deaths of his father the year after his birth, his father's parents by the time he was seven, and his mother when he was eight. Three years later, his mother's father—with whom he had lived since the death of his mother—also died, at which time he went to live with his mother's sister and her husband until, at fifteen, he left for schooling in Paris. His marriage at thirty-nine, the idyllic home he and his wife shared by the sea, and the positive reception of his compositions made the postwar years happy and productive, which helped counter the earlier tragedies. Frail health had plagued him throughout his life, however, and on August 13, 1937, he suffered a heart attack that led to his death ten days later. Recognized as one of the finest French composers of his generation, he died in the same year as one of the others, Maurice Ravel.

Notes

1. Phillip Huscher, "Roussel: Suite no. 2 from *Bacchus and Ariadne*, op. 43," Chicago Symphony Orchestra program book, May 19–24, 2011, 10.

2. Robert Follet, *Albert Roussel: A Bio-Bibliography* (Westport, CT: Greenwood Press, 1988), 4.

3. Huscher, 11.

4. Follet, 6.

5. Follet, 20.

6. Wendell Dobbs, "Roussel: The Flute and Extramusical Reference," *Flutist Quarterly* 22 (Winter 1996/7): 55.

7. *Columbia Encyclopedia*, 5th ed., s.v. "avatara."

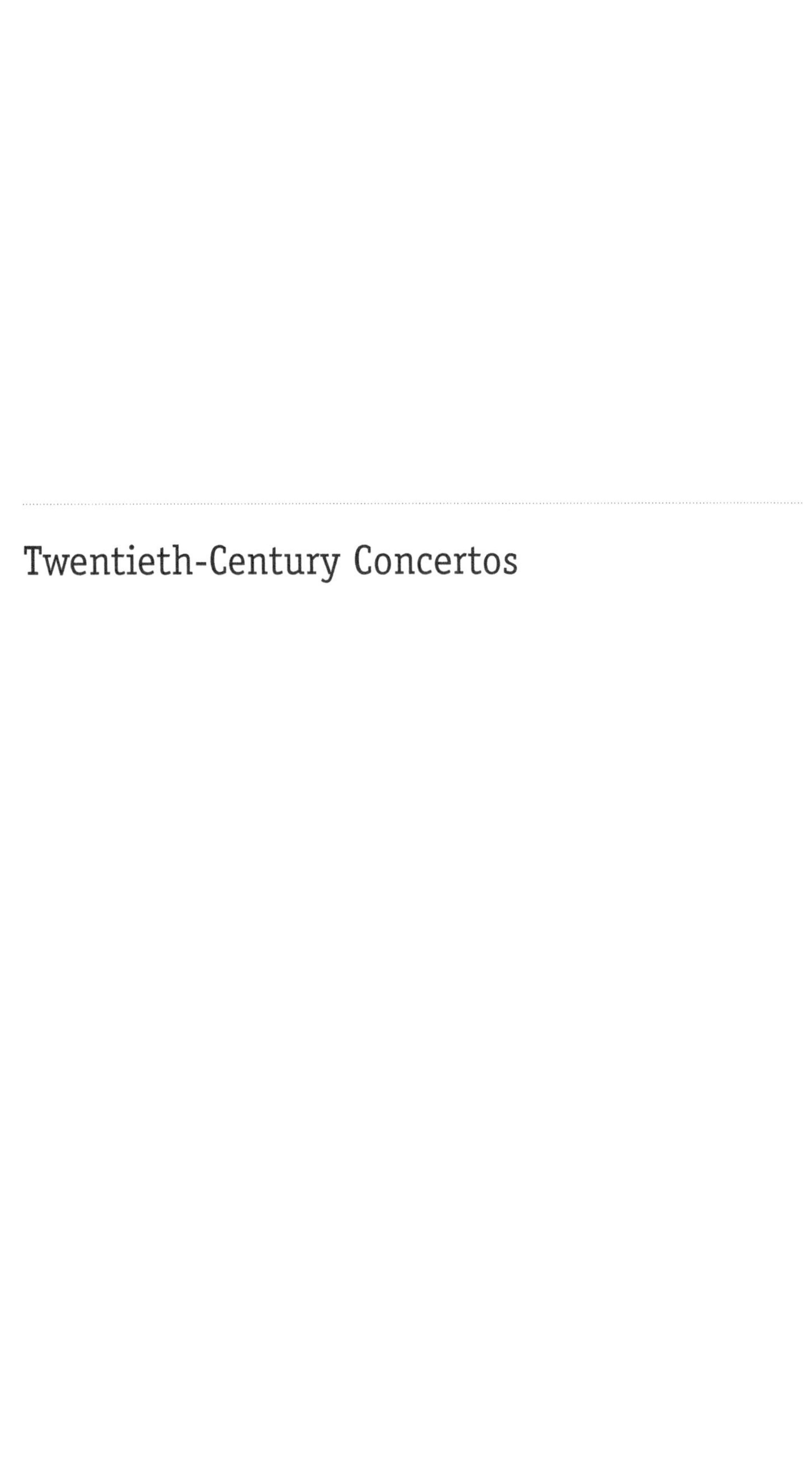

Twentieth-Century Concertos

18 Carl Nielsen—Concerto for Flute and Orchestra

IN HIS ESSAY "Mozart and Our Time," Carl Nielsen (1865–1931) writes, "When one reflects on the great artists of the past one seems to be conscious of two main types. One, grave and gloomy, his brows contracted and hands clenched, strides heavily and determinedly forward. The other comes swinging along with light springy steps, free and easy and with a friendly smile, as if walking in the sun."[1] Nielsen cites Beethoven as belonging to the first group, Mozart to the second. "The man and the works resemble one another and it is possible to form an approximate idea of the nature of his mind from his facial expression. Turn to Beethoven, Tolstoy, and Ibsen. In the faces of these and similar men, with their deep lines, stern features, and introspective eyes, we read plainly of bitter struggle with themselves and their material; and their works resound with the clash of will-power and energy."[2] While Nielsen does not bring himself or his music into the discourse, listeners of the concerto might speculate as to the group to which he belongs.

The foremost Danish composer of the twentieth century, Carl Nielsen achieved international recognition with his six symphonies (1894–1925) and three solo concertos: for violin (1911), flute (1926), and clarinet (1928). He spent most of his life in Copenhagen, first studying violin and music theory at the Copenhagen Conservatory of Music (now known as the Royal Danish Academy of Music), then performing as violinist in the Royal Orchestra, a prestigious ensemble he later served as assistant music director. He was awarded an annual state pension beginning in 1901, his thirty-sixth year, and with this, plus conducting, composition, teaching, and a subsequent annual retainer from publisher Wilhelm Hansen, he managed to piece together a comfortable living for his family and himself.

In 1921, after hearing four members of the Copenhagen Woodwind Quintet rehearse Mozart's Sinfonia Concertante, Nielsen was inspired to compose a work for them. Stimulated by the way Mozart captured the distinctive characteristics of each instrument,[3] Nielsen sought to extend this concept by incorporating into his woodwind quintet (and the nascent wind concertos) a fundamental aspect of his own compositional method. He once stated that whereas in his early years, he composed at the piano and then transcribed for orchestra, he later wrote, in full score, music conceived for specific instruments. By the time of the woodwind quintet and the flute concerto (1921–1926), he was trying to "creep into the instruments," believing that they "have a soul."[4] Not only did each instrument have a soul, but he also tried to write for the personality of each of the players for whom the quintet was being composed. This personal approach is one of the most notable aspects of both the woodwind quintet and the flute concerto. In the latter work, he pared down the performing forces (pairs of oboes, clarinets, bassoons, and horns, plus bass trombone, timpani, and strings) to achieve textural clarity.

As he was completing the quintet in 1922, Nielsen developed a new plan: he decided to compose a series of five solo concertos, one for each member of the Copenhagen group. Four years later, after his Sixth Symphony, Nielsen began a flute concerto, the first of his planned series. "In every man or woman there is something we would wish to know,"[5] he wrote. Believing that he could convey the essence of his subjects through music, capturing what couldn't be communicated in any other way,[6] he planned to create a musical portrait of the instrument and of the individual in the Copenhagen Woodwind Quintet who played that instrument. "The flute cannot belie its true nature, it comes from Arcadia and prefers the pastoral moods. Thus the composer is obliged to conform to its mild nature unless he would risk being branded as a barbarian."[7] Although he stated in his prose writings that music could "proclaim nothing definite,"[8] writers and listeners who know the origin of the concerto suggest that it paints a witty and revealing portrait of the newest member of the quintet, Holger Gilbert-Jespersen.

Nielsen was living in Florence during the summer of 1926 as he worked on the concerto. On the backs of postcards, he sent snippets of the work to Gilbert-Jespersen, who was to give the first performance of the work that October[9] on an all-Nielsen program by the Paris Conservatory Orchestra. Unfortunately, Nielsen became ill and fell behind schedule. Gilbert-Jespersen later remembered that as he was on his way to Paris for the premiere, Nielsen was still correcting the work and changing things around. "My head was starting to spin as I was thinking about the fact that I wouldn't get to see this poor piece."[10] Not only that, but Gilbert-Jespersen had to play a silver flute because he had developed an allergic reaction to his wooden one.[11] In spite of the flute, his nervousness, and last-minute changes to the concerto, the Paris premiere was a success, a sold-out performance attended by Ravel, Honegger, and Roussel and remembered by the composer as one of the greatest experiences of his life.[12] Shortly after the premiere, Nielsen replaced the ending, which he had written in haste, with the brilliant and, especially in terms of tonality, more satisfying conclusion that flutists play today.

The concerto features virtuosic writing not only for the flutist but also for the principal woodwinds of the orchestra, often in counterpoint. Orla Rosenhoff, the teacher who most profoundly influenced Nielsen during his student years, focused his attention on the art of counterpoint. It's interesting to hear the flute engage in virtuoso conversations with the oboe, clarinet, bassoon, and horn when one realizes that the composition was inspired by a group of five musicians who knew each other well. Other quirky, sometimes raucous dialogues engage the timpani and bass trombone.

The vigorous opening of the concerto immediately establishes a key conflict, treble D Dorian over a sustained grand unison E♭. From this moment on, tonal conflict is a primary force in the concerto. (See Chart 18.1) Just at the time when many composers were exploring atonality and searching for new ways to organize pitch, Nielsen was demonstrating his unique sense of tonality.

After the ferociously energetic introduction, the first theme, "a," begins cheerfully in E♭ minor. The voluptuous second theme, "b," in F major, is introduced by oboes, bassoons, and violins, then taken up by the soloist, clarinet, and bassoon in a lovely moment of chamber music. Nielsen then turns this theme into a riot (mm. 70–80), tutti, treble versus bass, from which the concerto's two protagonists disengage themselves like champions for their respective sides. The solo flute and bass trombone carry on in an angry duet while the other instruments slip into the role of bystanders, only to erupt and interrupt the brawlers (mm. 96–97) with an assertion of "a," fugato, which leads to the concerto's most important theme, "c," in E Lydian, presented boldly by the orchestra and then tenderly by the flute (mm. 110ff., E major) in the concerto's most sublime moment. (See Example 18.1)

The key of E major is not closely related to any of the other keys in the first movement except for a briefly referenced G♯ minor. However, in Nielsen's process of "emergent tonality," E major is the tonal goal of the concerto. In this system, Nielsen embarks on a journey in which he lays "greater weight on the dynamic progress of a work rather than on the reprise of a theme or the closing cadence as a goal for the musical evolution."[13] This highly individual approach to tonality, in which the final

section	**Intro**	**"Exposition"**			**"Development"**								**"Reprise"**			**Coda**
theme		a	b	trio/cad	b	a	c & a	c	a (& c)	mini-cad	a	cad	c & b	c (& a)	(a)	b
starts m#	1	12	34	59	70	97	101	110	122	133	134	146	158	163	167	179
starts in	**D dorian over E^b**	**e^b**	**F**	**C**	**C**	**E**	**E lydian**	**E**	**g#**	**—**	**f**	**—**	**G^b**	**a^b**	**F#**	**G^b**

CHART 18.1 Nielsen, Concerto for Flute and Orchestra: Analysis of the first movement.

EXAMPLE 18.1 Nielsen, Concerto for Flute and Orchestra, Mvt. 1, mm. 107–114.

EXAMPLE 18.1 Continued

harmonic goal is not the key of the opening, differs markedly from the organizing principle of sonata form. While thematic aspects of the flute concerto's first movement suggest sonata form, that form's tonal essence does not figure in Nielsen's conception. Here, the concerto's final tonality, far removed from those of the opening and the first theme, is foreshadowed in the development section before the movement closes in G♭ major.

After the first movement's tranquil close, one is startled by the furious beginning of the second, *fortissimo*. This chromatic, tonally ambiguous opening gradually calms in preparation for the movement's principal theme, "d," which begins lightheartedly in G major as the search for the final key continues. Sparse texture highlights dialogue between the flute and other instruments, beginning with violins, then bassoon. After three presentations of the second theme, "e," and a calming transitional passage, there begins at m. 62, adagio ma non troppo, a gorgeous elegy for flute, legato, in eighth notes soaring above violins in quarter notes. So must Orpheus have grieved for Eurydice.

Nielsen considered this movement "rondo-like,"[14] and indeed, recurrences of "d" shape the movement. (See Chart 18.2) After three appearances in G major, it is this theme that, in m. 195 above a pedal E, heralds the work's arrival at its tonal destination. Other hallmarks of Nielsen's style are evident: vivid contrasts, driving rhythmic energy, adroit counterpoint, and a unique sense of harmonic progress. Nielsen's

section	**Intro**	**A**		**B**		
theme	x	d *	e	f		
starts m#	1	12	39	62		
starts in (on)	**→G**	**G**	**g# aeolian**	**f**		
section		**A**		**transition**		
theme		d	e	x	f	
starts m#		93	115	130	138	
starts in (on)		**G**	**g**	**C**	**G**	
section		**A**		**C**		
theme		d		g	d	g, d, c
starts m#		145		180	195	200
starts in (on)		**G**		**b**	**E pedal**	**E**
section	**cadenza**	**A**		**Coda**		
theme		d^1		e^1		
starts m#	211	231		239		
starts in (on)	**A pedal**	**E**		**E**		
* Themes "a," "b," and "c" occurred in the first movement.						

CHART 18.2 Nielsen, Concerto for Flute and Orchestra: Analysis of the second movement.

often comical portrayal of the bass trombone epitomizes his idiosyncratic approach to writing not only for an instrument but perhaps also for a player. The composer had played trombone in a military band during his youth, and it has been suggested that perhaps this instrument represents Nielsen himself.[15]

Because of Nielsen's illness during the summer of 1926 as he worked on the concerto, he had to compose an ending for the Paris premiere quickly. Robert Simpson explains that this "cheerful ending in D major" had "no significance beyond its gaiety. After the first performance, however, he saw that he had not fulfilled a process that had already almost completed itself"[16] and created a new ending in E major. In the later version, with changes beginning at m. 169, the bass trombone reintroduces theme "c," the E major melody from the first movement. It's ironic that the instrument generally presented as a buffoon is the very one that reintroduces the work's tonal goal, E major, and its most exquisite theme (at m. 200). At the end of its foray into sublimity, however, the oaf reasserts its oafishness with two sneering, descending glissandi (mm. 208–211), exacerbating the already incongruous interaction between the elegant flute and the obstreperous trombone.

The orchestra confirms E major with metrically altered presentations of "d," the rondo theme (mm. 231ff.), and "e" (mm. 239ff.). In the last six measures, the refined flute (Gilbert-Jespersen?) once again struggles for primacy with the orchestra and the boisterous trombone (Nielsen?), who contributes four more raspberries. Happily the flute enjoys the last word with a high E, sustained *forte* as the rest of the orchestra fades away.

Nielsen's wit in including a single brass soloist, the bass trombone, to serve as foil in the concerto, suggests that while perhaps he saw himself as an artist like Beethoven who "strides heavily and determinedly forward" in "bitter struggle" with his material, in this late work, written when he was sixty-one, he was able to add a bit of the "light springy steps" of his favorite composer, Mozart. Nielsen's is a brilliant concerto—sparkling, dramatic, virtuosic, highly individual—and a worthy successor to those written by his musical hero. What a gift it would have been if he had lived to complete the series of concertos he planned.

Notes

1. Nielsen, Carl. *Living Music*, trans. Reginald Spink (London: Hutchinson, 1953), 13.

2. Nielsen, 14.

3. The Carl Nielsen Society. ". . . a whole pile of works," http://www.carlnielsen.dk/pages/biography.php, accessed June 18, 2010.

4. Jack Lawson, *Carl Nielsen* (London: Phaidon, 1997), 196.

5. Carl Nielsen, *My Childhood*, trans. Reginald Spink (London: Hutchinson, 1953), 7.

6. Phillip Huscher, "Carl Nielsen: Flute Concerto," Chicago Symphony Orchestra program book, December 18–20, 2008, 64–65.

7. Carl Nielsen, quoted in Lawson, 196.

8. *Living Music*, 33.

9. Amy Catherine Nelson, "The Flute Concerto by Carl Nielsen and the Contributions of Holger Gilbert-Jespersen" (DMA diss., University of Colorado at Boulder, 2003), 100.

10. Nelson, 101.

11. Nelson, 101.

12. Lawson, 197.

13. Kirsten Flensborg Petersen, "Carl Nielsen's Flute Concerto: Form and Revision of the Ending," *Carl Nielsen Studies* 2 (Copenhagen: Royal Library, 2005), 215.

14. Petersen, 201.

15. Lawson, 26, quoted in Nelson, 8.

16. Robert Simpson, "Carl Nielsen and Tonality," *Det Virtuelle Musikbibliotek*, http://dvm.nu/hierarchy/periodical/dmt/1965/04, accessed November 4, 2008.

19 Jacques Ibert—Concerto for Flute and Orchestra

JACQUES IBERT (1890–1962) was a contemporary and classmate of Darius Milhaud (1892–1974) and Arthur Honegger (1892–1955), musicians who became members of Les Six, the group that was to dominate French music between the world wars. Ibert, however, followed an independent but no less successful path. He entered the Paris Conservatory in 1910, at the relatively advanced age of twenty, interested in both drama and music. Gradually he moved into classes in harmony (taught by Émile Pessard), counterpoint (André Gédalge), and composition (Paul Vidal).

Just as Ibert was to begin the orchestration curriculum, the outbreak of World War I interrupted his musical studies. He was initially rejected by the military because of poor health, but his fervent desire to serve his country led him to submit numerous letters to organizations involved in the war effort. He was accepted by the Red Cross and served as a medic and ambulance driver on the front lines and then as a surgical nurse, frequently as an anesthetist, in over eight hundred operations during the sixteen-month period between November 1914 and February 1916.[1] In the fall of 1916, he contracted paratyphoid and had to accept a medical discharge. Again, his desire to serve led him to seek an alternative. He applied for and won a position as a communications intelligence officer with the navy. In 1918 he was awarded the Croix de Guerre for his naval service.

It seems astonishing that in 1919, after four years when he could barely find time to compose, Ibert won the conservatory's coveted Prix de Rome with *Le poète et la fée*, a "cantata" for three voices and orchestra. (While some reports suggest that he won this award having had no instruction in orchestration, his biographer Alexandra Laederich relates that Professor Gédalge organized a private class for the best of his counterpoint students in which he advised them with regard to orchestration. It was in these sessions that Ibert met Honegger and Milhaud,[2] who would become lifelong friends.)

Just as Les Six debuted in Paris, Ibert left for Rome: as the prix winner he was awarded a three- to four-year residential scholarship at the Villa Medici, during which time he composed prolifically and traveled. The Prix de Rome was Ibert's big break, and he rose to the occasion admirably, composing works that would receive critical acclaim. He returned to Paris in May 1923 and presented the required concert of works composed in Rome in December of the following year, then spent the next fourteen years completing a steady stream of commissions and enjoying a career as one of the most successful composers in France. It was toward the end of this period that he penned his most enduring work, the Concerto for Flute and Orchestra.

In 1932, Marcel Moyse was appointed flute professor at the Paris Conservatory, succeeding his teacher, Philippe Gaubert. Moyse had been assisting with the class for many years, but his official appointment came only when Gaubert was promoted to music director of the Opéra during the middle of the 1931/32 season.[3] Almost immediately, Moyse asked the forty-two-year-old Ibert to compose a work.

Ibert was fascinated by the timbres of wind instruments and was particularly adept at writing for them, so he must have been enthusiastic as he embarked on his first woodwind concerto. He approached his work pragmatically, stating:

> I impose a strict discipline on myself, going to work at my desk every day. It's an essential training, as it is for sportsmen. Inspiration often arrives when you're working, and she's a lady you must never keep waiting. The material components of an orchestra help me a great deal, just as a sculptor is served by the stone he carves. I try to keep in mind a visual picture, such as the instrumentalist's posture or the positions of leading ballet dancers. By some audio-visual process I then hear the music playing.[4]

One wonders if his family influenced his ideas regarding a "visual picture": his wife was a sculptor, and her father a painter.

In its broadest outline, Ibert's flute concerto is classical in construction: three movements, arranged fast-slow-fast. But from the opening polytonal chord of the first movement, the listener is drawn into the highly original sound world of Ibert's music. The ascending treble line in mm. 3 and 4 is supported by the dominant of F minor leading to a resolution on the downbeat of m. 5. However, beginning in m. 8, Ibert suggests A♭ major and G♭ major on the way to A minor (m. 11). This is but one example of the composer's nebulous tonality; a clear sense of key, when present, is often fleeting. Darting through the opening section, the solo flute presents a jaunty, staccato passage of cascading sixteenth notes, a principal theme unlike that of any other flute concerto.

As can be seen on Chart 19.1, the first movement is constructed in the form of an arch, the contrasting "B" section beginning in m. 55 after the once vigorous sixteenth notes have dissipated. The long-breathed, legato theme, over an accompaniment in the lower strings, begins in D♭ major with an ascending, then descending, bass line and a demonstration of Ibert's ability to evoke a strong contrast of mood.

The subsequent transition passage and "C" section include three tonalities that are expressed through their dominants: mm. 87–93 and 97–105, extended dominants of C minor; mm. 106–110, V of A♭ major; and mm. 112–119, V in F minor. This tonal instability, this lack of resolution, combined with the busy yet transparent texture of solo orchestral winds interacting in short spurts with the solo flute, creates a frenetic tapestry. It is often the counterpoint that determines the harmonic progression, as in mm. 97–99 and 116–119. The rich texture, in which each voice scurries about with its idea, continues until the return of "B" at the pickup to m. 158, where the solo clarinet gives out the sostenuto melody as the flute embroiders with elaborate counterpoint. A strongly expressed, syncopated theme (mm. 194ff.) leads to the return of "A" and a spirited conclusion that sets up the next movement, a serene respite between the hectic pace of the concerto's opening movement and its rambunctious finale.

Cast in a simple ternary design, the middle movement opens with a two-measure introduction in D♭ major, the initial tonic chord appearing in its weak second inversion in muted strings. The flute enters in the same mood but in the key of G, a tritone away from the key of its accompaniment. A two-measure motive, presented sequentially in mm. 18–19, 20–21, and 22–23, leads to the climax of the opening section.

The appearance of wind instruments and strong dotted rhythms introduces the middle section, which will feature solo flute countermelodies sometimes interwoven with, sometimes floating above, the voices of the orchestra. As in the first section, a short sequential phrase propels the movement to its high point. This time (mm. 59–67) it is a four-beat motive, animando, at m. 64, that presses forward against the 3/4 meter and leads to the impassioned climax of the movement. Tension is released through the return of rhythmic stability, a five-measure calando, and a cadence in F minor with a Picardy third. Ibert modulates back to the opening key of D♭, where elegant arabesques in the flute become, at m. 82, the accompaniment for the return

section	Intro	A													B							
starts m#	1	5			15						33	44			55	71				83		91
theme		a			a+						b	c			d	e				f		transition
# of mm	4	3	3	4	3	3	3	3	3	3	4 4 3	3 4 4			16	4	4	2	2	4	4	3 3
motive*†	Δ	m	n - n	o	m	n - n	n+	n+	n+	n+						p	p^1	q	q^1	r	s	n - n Δ
key§	**f**			**a**		**D^b**			**mod**		**G^b f**				**D^b**	**F**		**A**		**C**	**V^{ped}**	**mod**
starts m#	3			11		19			27		33 37				55	71		79		83	87	94
section		**C**																				
starts m#		97	100				112				126			136								
theme		intro	g				g^1				g^2			(trans)								
# of mm		3	2	2	2	3 3	2	2	4	2 4	2	2	3 3	6								
motive*†		Δ	v (=μ+1)	v	w	x	v	v	w+	x^1	v	v	y	Δ								
key§		**c**				**A^b f**				**D^b**	**b^b**		**D^b**	**V^{ped}**								
starts m#		97				106 111				120	126		133									
section		**transition**													**B**							
starts m#		142													158	174				186		194
theme															d	e				f^1		transition
# of mm		2	2	1	3	2	2	4							16	4	4	2	2	4	4	3 3 4 4
motive*†		μ+1	μ+1	μ	μ+2	1+μ	1+μ	Δ (μ at 157)								p	p^1	q	q^1	r	t	Δ
key§		**modulation**				**D^b**									**G^b(F#)**	**B^b**		**C**		**D**	**f**	**chrom. vii**
starts m#		142				150									158	174		182		186	190	200 206

CHART 19.1 Ibert, Concerto for Flute and Orchestra: Analysis of the first movement.

section		A											Coda									
starts m#		208			218						236	247	256									
theme		a & d			a+						b	c^1										
# of mm		3	3	4	3	3	3	3	3	3	4 4 3	3 4 2	2	2	4	2						
motive*†		m	n - n	o	m	n - n	n+	n+	n+	n+			v	v	v+	Δ						
key§		**f (continued)**		**b♭**			**D♭**		**mod**		**G♭ f**											
starts m#		208		214			224		230		236 240											

*** μ = rhythm & contour of first 8 notes of motive "m."** † Δ = non-thematic, incl passagework. **§** chromatic and modulatory passages of fewer than 4 mm may not be noted.

CHART 19.1 Continued

of the movement's principal theme in G, now presented by a soaring solo violin. At m. 97 the solo flute and strings exchange roles, the flute now taking over the principal theme, second violins and violas the arabesques. The movement ends with a reprise of the flute's sequential motive from mm. 59ff. of the "B" section, still in conflict with the meter, as a solo viola plays the "accompaniment melody" from mm. 1–4 over a D♭ chord, now in root position. As the flute rises to its final high D♭, all dissonance drops away: harmonic resolution brings this hauntingly beautiful reverie to a close.

The brilliant finale is a technical tour de force that was immediately selected for the Paris Conservatory's 1934 concours. Brightly colored and witty, it begins with boldly stated chords in cross-rhythm followed by a 9/8 measure of triplets. This refrain, appearing in different keys, becomes the movement's signature. In between, "Ibert asks everything of his soloist, from daredevil leaps and racing scales to tongue-twister melodies and rhapsodic ornamented tunes, and then writes a mini–mad scene of a cadenza for good measure."[5]

The movement is cast in large-scale ternary form, with the tarantella-like "A" sections embracing a cantabile Moderato assai introduced by the solo flute. (See Chart 19.2) The fleeting tonal centers of the outer sections are largely in the major mode, and Ibert intensifies their scherzando mood by means of fast-paced exchanges between the solo flute and members of the orchestra. In contrast, the "B" section, beginning in B♭ minor, features melody-and-accompaniment texture with duple eighth notes supplying the rhythmic background. The flutist's triplets pull against these duplets. Chromaticism within largely minor keys adds a poignant touch.

Ibert was a composer of great breadth. During his long career he created operas and ballets, film scores, incidental music, cadenzas for Mozart's Clarinet Concerto, and orchestral and chamber works. What's more, he was able to evoke many moods, from the tender and evocative to the festive and humorous;[6] the flute concerto is a particularly good example.

Marcel Moyse premiered the concerto on February 25, 1934, at a concert of the orchestra of the Société des concerts du Conservatoire, conducted by Gaubert. Milhaud, Honegger, Poulenc, Martinů, Stravinsky, and Roussel all attended the performance, which introduced them to what would become one of the flute repertoire's most enduring concertos. Several years later, Ibert conducted a performance of the work in Prague, again with Moyse as soloist. A reception was held afterward at the French Embassy, at which "the ambassador's wife asked Moyse if he would 'play something' for the guests. Sensing the flutist's discomfort, Ibert announced he would compose something new for the occasion."[7] He set to work and, within an hour, completed *Pièce pour flûte seule*, which Moyse premiered immediately.

section	A															
starts m#	1	8	15	25	33	41	49	57	65	73	81	89	97	103		
theme	a	a	trans	**b**	**b^1**	**a^1**	**c**	**c**	**d (= tr)**	**b**	**b^1**	**a^1**	**a^2**	transition		
# of mm	7	7	10	8	8	8	8	8	8	8	8	8	6	14		
motive*	μ	μ		π+		μ	π^1+ π^1+	π^1+ π^1+		π+		μ	μ π^2	μ^1 μ^1 Σ Σ Σ^1		
# of mm	4 3	4 3	4 2 2 2	4 4	4 4	4 4	4 4	4 4	4 4	4 4	4 4	4 4	4 2	3 3 1 2 2 3		
key	**F**	**A C**		**F**	**A^b**	**a^b A^b**		**f**	**E A**	**F**	**A^b F**	**f**	**F**	**D^b modulation**		
	* μ = mm. 1-4. π = mm. 29-30. Σ = mm. 111-112.															
section	**B**															
starts m#	117	126	135	144	153	162	174	180	189	198						
theme	intro	e	f	e^1	f^1	g	trans	e	f	e^2						
# of mm	9	9	9	9	9	12	6	9	9	9						
phrasing (# of mm)	6 + 3					4 + 4 + 4										
key	**(mod) b^b**		**e^b**	**b^b mod**		**D^b b^b**		**a**	**d**	**a**						
section				**A^1**											**Coda**	
starts m#				207	215	223	231	239	247	255	263	271	275	276	280	284
theme				**b**	**b^1**	**a^1**	**c**	**c**	**d (= tr)**	**b**	**b^1**	**a^3**	cadenza	transition		
# of mm				8	8	8	8	8	8	8	8	4	1	4	10	
motive *				π+		μ	π^1+ π^1+	π^1+ π^1+		π+		4			μ	π^3
# of mm				4 4	4 4	4 4	4 4	4 4	4 4	4 4	4 4	μ			4	2 4
key				**G^b**	**A**	**a**	**A**	**f#**	**F B^b**	**G^b**	**A F**	**f**	—	**F**		
	* μ = mm. 1-4. π = mm. 29-30.															

CHART 19.2 Ibert, Concerto for Flute and Orchestra: Analysis of the third movement.

In 1937, Jacques Ibert was granted the prestigious position of director of the French Academy at the Villa Medici, at which time he moved back to the city and the palatial villa where he had enjoyed his Prix de Rome years. Excepting the very difficult period of war when the Vichy government banned his music and Mussolini seized the villa, he lived happily in Rome until his retirement in 1960.

Notes

1. Gérard Michel, *Jacques Ibert* (Paris: Seghers, 1967), 25.
2. *Grove Music Online*, s.v. "Ibert, Jacques (François Antoine Marie)," by Alexandra Laederich, accessed August 2, 2014, http://www.oxfordmusiconline.com.ezproxy.bradley.edu/.
3. Ann McCutchan, *Marcel Moyse: Voice of the Flute* (Portland, OR: Amadeus, 1994), 119.
4. Hugh Macdonald, "Jacques Ibert: Concerto for Flute and Orchestra." Boston Symphony Orchestra program book, Nov. 19–21, 2009, 47, 49.
5. Phillip Huscher, "Jacques Ibert: Flute Concerto, op. 37." Chicago Symphony Orchestra program book, Sept. 23–Oct. 8, 2011, 36A.
6. Laederich, *Grove Music Online*.
7. McCutchan, 147.

Midcentury Solo and Chamber Masterpieces

20 Paul Hindemith—Sonata for Flute and Piano

PAUL HINDEMITH (1895–1963) composed his Sonata for Flute and Piano at a pivotal time, both in his life and in the history of his country. The year was 1936, and he was living in Berlin.

Since 1927, this extraordinarily versatile musician had been teaching at the Hochschule für Musik, facilely dashing off one composition after another and performing as a world-class violist (and a capable violinist, clarinetist, and pianist). Things began to change in 1929, when Alfred Rosenberg founded the Kampfbund für deutsche Kultur[1] (Militant League for German Culture), and especially in 1933, when Adolf Hitler, as leader of the largest party in the Reichstag (Parliament), was appointed chancellor of Germany. Like so many of his countrymen, Hindemith underestimated the significance of the ascendancy to power of the National Socialist German Workers' Party, as evidenced by his advice to fellow composer Berthold Goldschmidt to "stay put—'They are idiots, they won't last.'"[2] Hindemith was married to the daughter of the Jewish director of the Frankfurt Opera (though she and her mother were Christians), naively expressed anti-Nazi views, continued to perform with Jewish colleagues, and had, early in his career, written astonishingly avant-garde works. Rosenberg's operation watched him like a hawk.[3]

In 1932, Hindemith turned his attention to composing the music for his eighth opera, *Mathis der Maler* and, before completing that, to an orchestral version that would fulfill his commission from music director Wilhelm Furtwängler for the Berlin Philharmonic. The *Mathis der Maler* Symphony was premiered to great acclaim in March 1934. Believing that Germany wouldn't remain "hypnotized" for much longer, Hindemith was caught off guard when the Kulturgemeinde (literally "Culture Community," better understood as "Culture Authority"), the organization that succeeded the Kampfbund and served as the "cultural guardian" for the Nazi Party, refused permission for a second performance of the orchestral work and boycotted future performances of his music.[4]

Their decision provoked Furtwängler to write a passionate defense of the composer; it was published on the front page of the *Deutsche Allgemeine Zeitung* that November. Furtwängler was dismissed from the Berlin Philharmonic on December 4, then after a meeting with Propaganda Minister Joseph Goebbels on February 28, reinstated.

The attacks on Hindemith and the boycotting of his music continued, and in January 1935 he agreed to a six-month leave of absence from the Hochschule. He completed *Mathis der Maler*, the opera he considered his masterpiece, then began a series of instrumental sonatas the following year. Between 1918 and 1924, he had written sonatas for violin, viola, cello, and viola d'amore, but the flute sonata, written in 1936, the prime of his career, would be the first of his wind compositions in this genre.

Hindemith received a cablegram in September 1936 from Oliver Strunk, chief of the Music Division of the Library of Congress, inviting the composer to be the featured artist at the Eighth Washington Festival of Contemporary Music, to be held in April 1937. Hindemith accepted the invitation, appreciating the importance of this, his first appearance in America.

The second concert of the festival would showcase his music exclusively. Strunk proposed a program of chamber music written between 1921 and 1928, asking for the composer's impressions. Hindemith finally replied ten weeks later, suggesting a program that included the solo viola sonata (which Strunk had included) but rejecting the other pieces in favor of more recent works. He suggested that the program open with his flute sonata, adding, "The flute sonata has not yet been performed for I have just written it."[5] The piece, which Hindemith completed on December 16, 1936,[6] had in fact been scheduled for a premiere in Berlin by Gustav Scheck, professor at the Hochschule, and Walter Gieseking . . . until the Nazi Party forbade it.

Just before embarking on his trip, realizing that he was not going to reconcile with the government, Hindemith resigned from the Hochschule. He then set sail from Hamburg, arriving in the United States on April 2, at which time he jotted a quick note to his wife back home in Germany. His communication ended: "Keep your fingers crossed for me."[7] He spent a week in New York overseeing rehearsals, writing the final chapter of *Unterweisung im Tonsatz*, Teil I (*Craft of Musical Composition*, Part I: *Theory*), and taking in the sights of the city, then took a train to Washington on the evening of April 9.

The Washington Festival engaged impressive players for Hindemith's concert, including Georges Barrère and Jesús Maria Sanromá to premiere the flute sonata. The composer reported a "first-class performance" with a large audience who received it warmly.[8]

The sonata is in three movements, the first in sonata form. Though Goebbels had accused the composer of writing degenerate atonal music, in truth Hindemith considered it impossible to escape the influence of tonality, "a natural force like gravity."[9]

The piece opens in B♭ major, though the opening theme's consequent phrase turns to B♭ Aeolian. A transition (mm. 12–18) modulates to A major for a presentation of the disjunct second theme, heard unequivocally as sol–sol–do–sol–do–sol–do–la–mi (in movable do), though that interpretation is not always supported by the accompanying chords. Variations of the final phrase of this theme, µ (final beat of m. 22–beginning of m. 24), assume importance as the movement progresses, serving as both a calm closing theme (mm. 35ff.) and a forceful exclamation point at the end of the exposition (mm. 41–43).

The development begins in m. 44, the piano, *ppp*, creating anticipation for the flute's reentry. Six times in this section, one hears the opening sol–do–re–sol of theme 1 (Σ), each time except the last (in the piano) in a new key and louder than its predecessor. The compression and proximity of statements 3 through 6 also contribute to the growing intensity of the section. (Actually, the first four notes of Σ appear eleven times if one includes the elided statements in mm. 61, 63 (twice), and 64 and notes 2 through 5 in the piano's right hand, m. 68.) The sequential presentations of Σ lead unobtrusively into the reprise: a *fortissimo* statement of the complete theme 1, now back in the home key of B♭ major (then Aeolian). This time the piano's right hand echoes the flute's announcement of the theme. An example of Hindemith's adroit counterpoint occurs in m. 75, where the piano repeats the first four notes of Σ (theme 1's antecedent phrase) as the accompaniment to that same theme's consequent phrase, Δ.

A large-scale descending bass line, beginning on beat 2 of m. 86 and moving every two and a half, then three and a half, then three beats, accompanies the second statement of the second theme. A sequence of three presentations of the six-note motive first heard as part of theme 2 (flute, m. 20) begins at the end of m. 90 and effects a modulation that leads to the closing theme. Stated three times, this "closing" ends inconclusively, in mid-modulation, on a sustained B♭ in a chord comprising five of the six notes of a whole-tone scale and sounding like a French augmented-sixth chord in D. What follows?

The coda begins in D Aeolian and relies largely on the consequent phrase of theme 1. But Hindemith appends compressed versions of theme 1's opening motive, Σ, and theme 2's closing motive, μ. He repeats the whole structure (mm. 111–118) but expands its last two measures, μ, to close the movement. With its Lydian E♮, it first appears softly, tentatively in flute and piano. Then as if to confirm the "rightness" of this essay, the flute states it again, now *forte* and faster, its final "tonic" confirmed by a resolute B♭ major chord in the piano.

The second movement, formally clear (A-B-A-B) but tonally ambiguous, draws on Hindemith's propensity for freely chromatic melody operating within a framework of clear tonality. In mm. 1–7, for example, the flute has all twelve pitches except A♯, which, with D♯, is also avoided in the piano. The absence of A♯ and D♯, leading tones of B and E, respectively, weakens the aural case for these pitches as tonal centers, though E Mixolydian seems to be an acceptable compromise.

Throughout this movement, Hindemith uses sequential passages to build intensity. Already from m. 2, the Δ motive (four notes beginning on the second half of the second beat) leads the opening phrase from *piano* to *forte*. When the "A" section returns in m. 33 a third higher, the same structure leads inexorably to the climax: c^4 *ff* above the movement's most rhythmically agitated accompaniment. The long transition from "B" to the return of "A" includes two modulating sequences (mm. 24–29 and 29–32), both built on the Δ motive but each ending with a fragment of the motive first presented in m. 14. The close-order imitation and crescendos of the second sequence pour into the passionate return of "A."

The final movement, in rondo form, returns to B♭ for its tonal center but includes modulations to remote tonal reaches, the "B" section, for example, beginning in C♯, moving to G♯ in m. 50, then back to C♯ and finally to C major. (See Chart 20.1) The flute and piano take turns presenting the movement's melodies. Often, after each has had its say, the two engage in conversation. However, there is one extended canon (mm. 150–167) in which the texture becomes polyphonic, both players performing theme "d" simultaneously.

Pianist and composer John Colman studied with Hindemith in Berlin and related that in 1936 the out-of-favor Hindemith was assigned a basement room for his teaching at the Hochschule. From a small window he observed a Nazi marching band practicing. "He told the class that the last movement of the sonata, a sarcastic march, came from this experience."[10] Although emphasis on the downbeats of mm. 262–264 and 266–268 lends authenticity to Hindemith's *Marsch*, the insertion of an extra measure and a half at m. 247 (actually a repetition of the preceding measure and a half) and of an extra measure at 268 destroys the metrical symmetry

Scherzo (rondo)																				
section	**A**							**B**										**transition**		
theme	**a**	**b**	**trans**		**a**		**b^1**	**c**	**c^1**		**c^2**									
# of mm	8	8+	1*+	7+	1*+	7	7	10+	1*+	15+	1*+	11						16		
starts m#	1	9	17		25		33	40	50		66							78		
motive																		μ	μ	μ
# of BEATS																		11	11	11
starts m#																		78	83	88
tonal center	**B^b**							**C#**	**G#**		**C#**	**mod**						**C**		
starts m#	1							40	50		66	72						77		
			*elision		*elision				*elision		*elision									
section	**A^1**							**C**												
theme IMITATED													**d^2 piano**							
# of mm													14+							
starts m#													152							
theme	**a**				**a**		**b^2**	**d**		**d^1**		**d^2 flute**			**d†**			**trans**		
# of mm	8+				1*+	7	10+	1*+	12+	1*+	16	16+			1*+	15		13		
starts m#	94				102		110	120		133		150			166			182		
tonal center	**B**				**B^b**			**E^b**				**C^b**		**mod**	**E^b**		**E**	**E^b**		
starts m#	94				102			120				150		154	166		170	182		
					*elision			*elision		*elision					*elision					
															† Last iteration of d (16 mm) = 12 mm of d, a 2-m insertion, & a new 2-m ending					

CHART 20.1 Hindemith, Sonata for Flute and Piano: Analysis of the third movement.

section	**A²**																	**transition**		
theme	**a**	**b**			**a**		**b³**													
# of mm	8	9			8		6											16		
starts m#	195	203			212		220											226		
motive																		μ	μ	μ
# of BEATS																		11	11	11
starts m#																		226	231	236
tonal center	**D♭**	**A♭**			**D♭**		**C**											**(C)**		
starts m#	193	203			212		220													
March (rounded binary)																				
section	**E**		**E**		**F**					**F¹**										
theme	**e**		**e**		**f**		**e¹**			**f¹**		**e²**								
# of mm	10		10		9+		1*+	7		9+		1*+	11							
starts m#	242		252		262		271			279		288								
phrase	u	v	u	v	w	x	u¹		y	w	z	u¹		y^extended						
# of mm	4	6	4	6	4	5+	1*+	3	4	4	5+	1*+	3	8						
starts m#	242	246	252	256	262	266	271		275	279	283	288		292						
tonal center	**B♭**				**F**	**B**	**B♭**			**F**	**mod**	**B♭**								
starts m#	242				262		271			279	283	288								
							*elision					*elision								

CHART 20.1 Continued

expected in a march. Likewise, the bubbly, cheerful flute part (including triplets) and the asymmetrical four-bar antecedent and six-bar consequent phrases (mm. 242–251 and 252–261, 262–271, 279–288) all contribute to Hindemith's mockery of a four-square march. The crowning glory, however, is the waltz accompaniment to the flute's steady eighth notes (mm. 283–285) during the final modulation back to the home key of B♭.

The Nazis had a "tortured relationship with modernity,"[11] and their views of Hindemith, the preeminent modern German composer, had always been inconsistent: at times they believed he might conform; at other times they vilified him. He had gotten into trouble before for writing *Variante eines Militärmarsches*, a parody of a Bavarian military march, as the finale of his *Kammermusik* no. 5 ("Viola Concerto"). Now, in December 1936 the great musical craftsman subtly composed a parody that the government would never discover.

No one could single-handedly take on the Third Reich, and in the end, Hindemith and his wife left Germany, vowing never to live in the country again. They moved to Switzerland in 1938 and on to the United States in 1940, where he spent thirteen years as a professor at Yale University. He continued his series of instrumental sonatas, composing works for oboe, English horn, clarinet, bassoon, horn, alto horn, trumpet, and trombone, ending the series in 1955 with a work for tuba and piano.

Hindemith had planned to appear in Germany only minimally after the war, but in 1949, encouraged by an invitation from the US government to tour the American zones of occupation as conductor and lecturer, he reengaged with his homeland.[12] Then in 1953, he resigned his position at Yale and moved to Zurich. Ever the well-rounded musician, he spent his final years conducting, recording, fulfilling commissions, teaching, performing as violist, and lecturing throughout western Europe and the United States. He died in Frankfurt in 1963.

Notes

1. Michael H. Kater, *Composers of the Nazi Era* (New York: Oxford University Press, 2000), 34.
2. Guy Rickards, *Hindemith, Hartmann, and Henze* (London: Phaidon, 1995), 80.
3. Kater, 37.
4. Ian Kemp, *Hindemith* (London: Oxford University Press, 1970), 28.
5. Luther Noss, *Paul Hindemith in the United States* (Urbana: University of Illinois Press, 1989), 14–15.
6. Stephen Luttmann, *Paul Hindemith: A Research and Information Guide*, 2nd ed. (New York: Routledge, 2009), 406.
7. Letter, Paul Hindemith to Gertrude Hindemith, April 16, 1937, cited in Noss, 16.
8. Paul Hindemith, Journal, April 10, 1937, quoted in Noss, 20.

9. Kemp, 36.

10. Katherine Hoover, http://johnranck.net/studio/clinic/practice_corner/hindemith.html, accessed August 14, 2012.

11. "Paul Hindemith," *Music and the Holocaust*, http://holocaustmusic.ort.org/politics-and-propaganda/third-reich/hindemith-paul/, accessed August 17, 2012.

12. Geoffrey Skelton, *Paul Hindemith: The Man behind the Music* (London: Gollancz, 1975), 237.

21 Edgard Varèse—*Density 21.5*

FROM THE START, Edgard Varèse (1883–1965) lived an unconventional life, and as the years passed and he embarked upon a career, he became a most unconventional composer. Born in Paris to a violent, overbearing father and his eighteen-year-old wife, the infant Edgard, only weeks after birth, was sent to the small Burgundian village of Le Villars to live with the family of his great-uncle.[1] He "seems to have spent part of each winter, at least, with his parents in Paris,"[2] rejoining them permanently in the late 1880s and subsequently moving with them to Turin, Italy. Varèse was only fourteen when his young mother died; on her deathbed, she called his father "an assassin"[3] and made the boy promise to protect his siblings from the man's vicious temper. When some six years later, he witnessed his father mistreating his second wife, Varèse beat him up and left for good. The two would never see each other again.

Henri Varèse had opposed his son's interest in music, but now Edgard, determined to become a professional musician, moved to Paris and entered the Schola Cantorum. There he studied counterpoint with Albert Roussel, a strong influence as he formed his fundamental musical beliefs, and conducting with Vincent d'Indy.

He completed a one-year preliminary course, then turned to the conservatory to continue his studies. Fellow student Nadia Boulanger recalled:

> Varèse . . . used to bring in every week a little sketch of a few measures and the teacher, I've forgotten who it was (maybe Widor), would say, "Well, now, Mr. Varèse, this is very interesting, go on and finish it." And the next week there would be another little sketch and the following week another different one; there was never anything finished.[4]

Such would be the case throughout Varèse's professional career: he left only a dozen completed works, less than two hours of music.

Varèse spent just four months at the conservatory, after which he founded and conducted a choir for the Université populaire du Faubourg Saint-Antoine.[5] At the end of 1907 he abruptly relocated to Berlin, one of the many seemingly capricious moves that would season his life. During his years there, he became well acquainted with the eminent Italian pianist and composer Ferruccio Busoni (1866–1924), who was also living in the German capital. Varèse was enthralled by the revolutionary ideas the older man put forth. In *Entwurf einer neuen Ästhetik der Tonkunst* (*Sketch of a New Aesthetic of Music*), Busoni called for a musical language that would "break down the barriers erected by 'the law-givers.'"[6] He asserted the need for new scales, microtones, and electronic instruments, believing that "Music is born free and destined to regain its freedom."[7] Varèse later remarked:

> I owe an enormous debt of gratitude to this extraordinary man. . . . [H]e crystallized my half-formed ideas, stimulated my imagination, and determined, I believe, the future development of my music. Treating me as he did, as a colleague and a friend, he was as fructifying to me as the sun and rain and fertilizer to soil.[8]

After five and a half years, Varèse returned to Paris. Then in December 1915, just as he turned thirty-two, he moved to the United States. He had at the time only a rudimentary knowledge of English, a couple of scores, and ninety dollars in his pocket.[9] Biographer Malcolm MacDonald suggests that he "appeared to welcome the opportunity for a totally fresh start in the USA, with a blank sheet that allowed his new works to appear as if from nowhere."[10] Indeed, he left behind the Debussy-inspired titles and works and, after a couple of years in the States, entered his most productive period, composing *Amériques, Offrandes, Hyperprism, Octandre, Integrales*, and *Arcana* between 1918 and 1928. This decade also included exertions to encourage the performance of contemporary music through his founding in 1921 (along with Carlos Salzedo, a fellow French musician living in the USA) of the International Composers' Guild and, after its demise, the Pan American Association of Composers (1928–1934).

Throughout his career, Varèse strove to produce music that was unlike anything that had ever been heard. He "saw the willingness of composers to adopt approaches devised by others as tantamount to confession of a failure of imagination [and believed] that *inventing a system oneself* was hardly any better" (emphasis in source).[11] Each of his compositions is scored for a different instrumentation; each is unique.

Varèse spoke often of the need for new instruments:

> "We need new instruments very badly," he said in 1916 in an interview for the *New York Telegraph*. ". . . In my work I have always felt the need of new mediums of expression. . . . What I am looking for is new mechanical mediums which will lend themselves to every expression of thought and keep up with thought."[12]

Scholars have suggested that Varèse's frustration with the encumbering limits of traditional instruments and his inability to interest others in research and funding for new instruments led to deep discouragement and resulted in his being able to complete only one work between 1935 and 1954: the thirty-one-measure original version of *Density 21.5*.

In January 1936, as Varèse, age fifty-three, was struggling with two large-scale works (*The One-All-Alone* and *Espace*), Georges Barrère asked him to compose a work for the inauguration of his new, specially constructed Haynes platinum flute. Varèse agreed, composing a solo flute piece and then using the density of platinum as its title. Barrère premiered the work on February 16, 1936, at Carnegie Hall as part of a benefit concert for New York's Lycée français.

Felix Meyer, in "Flute Piece with a Past: *Density 21.5* Revisited," reproduces an autograph copy of the work in its original version of 1936. While acknowledging that the matter cannot be ascertained with certainty, Meyer argues that this thirty-one-measure piece was probably the version performed by Barrère.[13] It must also have been this version that Varèse described as "pretty" in a letter to his wife after hearing the flutist play it in the second of two sessions prior to the premiere.[14]

After completing *Density*, Varèse wrote to his wife, "started *Espace*—It is underway and augurs well—The discipline imposed by the little flute piece is bearing fruit."[15] Immersed in *Espace*, he did not pursue publication of *Density*, but neither did he forget the work. In a letter to Carlos Salzedo dated July 19, 1937, Varèse wrote, "Has B[arrère] bottled up *Density*? He should do it side by side with *Syrinx*."[16] Certainly the two works that inaugurated twentieth-century solo flute music have often been linked, even in their contrast: "Debussy's soulful masterpiece is a blank, despairing outcry, its trend always downward, in weeping, sighing phrases. Varèse's line seeks from the first to rise (if only by a semitone), to walk, to fly."[17]

Varèse substantially reworked the piece a decade after its composition, and in the summer of 1946 it was published in the *New Music Quarterly*. For this fifty-six-measure 1946 version, Varèse rewrote the middle section and included the now famous key clicks for the first time.[18] Further revisions led to a 1951 edition, this one written out by Varèse's protégé Chou Wen-chung "with several alterations by the composer." This edition, from which Ricordi published the work, is the version known today.[19]

Although *Density* was written at a time when Varèse was frustrated by the limitations of traditional instruments, forcing him to compose within confines he wished to reject, his piece for solo flute demonstrates the originality of a composer who refused to retrace the steps of others. From the opening constricted three-note gesture (falling half-step, rising whole step) that expands to outline the tritone C♯–G and goes on to exploit the full range of the flute, Varèse built a composition that explored the extreme registers of the instrument in a way that had never been considered. But as Jonathan Bernard explains, Varèse's piece ascends only to b^3, not the instrument's accepted highest note, c^4:

> Like other Varèse endings, the purpose of this final ascent is not to close off by emphasizing the limits of the medium, not to reach a climax by neatly summing up, but to suggest the limitless possibilities of musical space [i.e., above b^3]. Varèse's phrase "open rather than bounded" is nowhere more appropriate. Like other musical compositions, *Density 21.5* must end somewhere, but the "journey into space" may go on, in however figurative a sense.[20]

In *Density 21.5*, Varèse pushed the flutist to expand the instrument's dynamic capacity, put forward a rhythmic complexity never before demanded of a solo flutist, and, with the key clicks of 1946, introduced the first avant-garde technique, a technique that forged the way for composers to begin to conceive of new realms of possibilities. The only work Varèse ever composed for a solo instrument, *Density* has been the subject of numerous analyses, including those by Carol Baron, Jonathan Bernard, Julia Larson Mattern, Jean-Jacques Nattiez, George Perle, and Marc Wilkinson, each of whom attempts to understand and explain the mastery of its construction.

Though speculation abounds, the rationale behind important events in Varèse's life remains unconfirmed, as do a surprising number of details: Why, for example, did he leave the conservatory after only four months of study? Why did he abruptly move to Berlin in 1907, having only days earlier married French actress Suzanne Bing? The two divorced in 1913, after which Varèse returned to Paris, leaving his scores—some twenty works[21]—and other belongings in storage. It was nine years before he returned to Berlin (1922), later reporting that everything had burned in a fire. Why did he leave the scores for so long and why, if he left almost all of them behind, was it announced just after his arrival in New York in 1915 that he was "setting out on a tour 'with an orchestra that he will conduct himself and which will play in the main his own compositions'"?[22] Louise Varèse, Edgard's second wife, later offered: "Varèse always gave reasons for his sudden changes, but not the reason, unconscious of it as he was, that gave [those sudden changes their] final impetus: his demon of unrest."[23]

Notes

1. Malcolm MacDonald, "'Only One Thing of Value': Varèse the Burgundian," in *Edgard Varèse: Composer, Sound Sculptor, Visionary*, ed. Felix Meyer and Heidy Zimmermann (Woodbridge, UK: Boydell, 2006), 16.
2. MacDonald, *Edgard Varèse*, 20.
3. Alan Rich, *American Pioneers: Ives to Cage and Beyond* (London: Phaidon, 1995), 77.
4. Elliott Carter, "'Elle est la musique en personne': A Reminiscence of Nadia Boulanger" (c. 1985, rev. 1995), in *Elliott Carter: Collected Essays and Lectures, 1937–1995*, ed. Jonathan Bernard (Rochester: University of Rochester Press, 1997), 282.
5. Dieter A. Nanz, "A Student in Paris: Varèse from 1904 to 1907," in *Edgard Varèse: Composer, Sound Sculptor, Visionary*, 30.
6. Antony Beaumont, "Busoni, Ferruccio," *New Grove Dictionary of Music and Musicians*, 2nd ed., vol. 4, ed. Stanley Sadie (London: Macmillan, 2001), 671.
7. Beaumont, 671.
8. Malcolm MacDonald, *Varèse: Astronomer in Sound* (London: Kahn and Averill, 2003), 69.
9. Rich, 83.
10. MacDonald, *Varèse*, 7.
11. Jonathan W. Bernard, *The Music of Edgard Varèse* (New Haven, CT: Yale University Press, 1987), xvii.
12. MacDonald, *Varèse*, 149.
13. Felix Meyer, "Flute Piece with a Past: *Density 21.5* Revisited," in *Edgard Varèse: Composer, Sound Sculptor, Visionary*, 248.
14. Meyer, 249.
15. Edgard Varèse, letter to Louise Varèse, February 9, 1936, Edgard Varèse Collection, Paul Sacher Foundation, quoted in Meyer, 250.
16. Meyer, 250.
17. MacDonald, *Varèse*, 292.
18. Meyer, 253.
19. Meyer, 254.
20. Bernard, 232.
21. MacDonald, *Edgard Varèse*, 20.

22. Heidy Zimmermann, "The Lost Early Works: Facts and Suppositions," in *Edgard Varèse: Composer, Sound Sculptor, Visionary*, 51.

23. Louise Varèse, *Varèse: A Looking-Glass Diary* (New York: Norton, 1972), 47, quoted in David Schiff, "A Red but No Communist: Varèse in the 1930s and 40s," in *Edgard Varèse: Composer, Sound Sculptor, Visionary*, 239.

22 Frank Martin—*Ballade* for Flute and Piano

FRANK MARTIN (1890–1974) matured musically at an interesting and rapidly changing time. A contemporary of Ibert, Martinů, Prokofiev, and Hindemith, he was influenced by the great avant-garde composers of his day—Debussy, Ravel, and Schoenberg—though his training began under the conservative tutelage of Swiss composer Joseph Lauber.

Martin entered the world as the tenth and youngest child of a Calvinist minister in Geneva, Switzerland. "[A]ll of the children played musical instruments, but . . . there were no professional musicians and no interest in having one."[1] The young boy demonstrated unusual talent, especially for composition, and was profoundly affected when he heard a performance of Bach's *St. Matthew Passion* in 1902. At eighty-one, he described the experience as "the greatest influence of my life."[2] Martin knew that he wanted to become a composer but acquiesced to his parents' wishes, enrolling at the University of Geneva to study mathematics and physics. At the same time, he pursued piano and composition lessons privately with Lauber.

Martin's first break came in 1911 when the Association of Swiss Musicians premiered his *Trois poèmes païens* for baritone and orchestra at its annual festival. During the following years, his style developed slowly, perhaps in part because Switzerland was outside the mainstream of contemporary European music. He would later state that his avoidance of fashionable trends contributed an element of timelessness to his music.[3]

After serving as a sergeant in Swiss Army communications during World War I, Martin met Ernest Ansermet, founder and music director of Geneva's Orchestre de la Suisse Romande. A highly regarded conductor recognized especially for fine performances of challenging contemporary music, Ansermet conducted the premiere of Martin's cantata *Les Dithyrambes* and became a lifelong friend and Martin's most important musical advocate.

Martin moved to Zurich in 1918, then on to Rome and Paris in the early 1920s. For the composer these were difficult but crucial years, as he immersed himself in contemporary European music. With a wife and child, he struggled to make ends meet in Paris. In 1925 he returned to Geneva, where his marriage ended.

Back in his native city, Martin founded a chamber music ensemble with which he performed as pianist and harpsichordist. Initially a trio that played only the works of J. S. Bach, the group soon expanded its membership and repertoire and took on the name Société de musique de chambre de Genève. Martin also enrolled at the Dalcroze Institute. After two years of study, he became a certified instructor of eurhythmics, staying on at the institute as a part-time teacher for the next decade.

The final element of Martin's formation came during the early 1930s, when he devoted his attention to the twelve-tone system of Arnold Schoenberg. While Martin would ultimately reject aspects of the system because he was not willing to break away from tonality completely, he was "drawn to the concept by the new freedoms it afforded, especially the idea of setting aside the limitations of the traditional cadence and the diatonic scale."[4]

Martin accepted a position teaching chamber music at the Geneva Conservatory but left the post in 1933 to become artistic director and professor of composition, harmony, and improvisation at a new private school in Geneva, the Technicum moderne de musique. The short-lived institution closed in 1940, after which Martin returned to his chamber music position at the conservatory for an additional five years. One of his great joys at the Technicum was getting to know the young flutist Maria Boeke, the last student to earn a diploma from the school.[5] Martin's second wife, Irène Gardian, had died of septicemia in 1939, leaving the composer with three young daughters under the age of eight (and an older child from his first marriage). He married Maria the following year, and she would prove a loving supporter. After his death, she worked tirelessly to establish and maintain a society in his honor.

By the late 1930s, when Martin composed his *Ballade* for Flute and Piano, he was clearly hitting his stride. The work was commissioned by the first International Music Competition in Geneva to serve as the piece required of each flutist in the 1939 competition. It was the second of six pieces that Martin titled "Ballade." Four of them—for saxophone, flute, piano, and trombone, respectively—were composed between 1938 and 1940 as Martin was "perfecting his new-found style."[6] The ballades for cello and viola followed in 1949 and 1972.

Each ballade is a single-movement work full of dramatic tension. Changes (highlighted by double bars) in tempo, meter, expression, and texture invite consideration of the one for flute and piano in eight sections:

1. 1–43: Allegro ben moderato
2. 44–94: Vivace
3. 95–153: Dolce cantabile
4. 154–193: Cadenza
5. 194–199: Lento
6. 200–282: Con moto, animando and crescendo, Presto
7. 283–323: Molto vivace
8. 324–358: Meno mosso, animando and crescendo, Presto

It will be shown that when one adds considerations of thematic content and tonality to the parameters above, it is possible to synthesize the eight sections of the *Ballade* into a ternary form plus coda: A, sections 1–3; B, section 4; A^1, sections 5–7; coda, section 8.

Eight thematic elements and their variants play an important role in the *Ballade*.[7] (See Chart 22.1)

Martin, in *Interviews about Music*, described the process of development as central to his art:

> Since I was little, I have always preferred, in the piano sonatas I played, the development to the exposition because in the development there is this more or less dramatic element. . . . I have a hard time constructing something that is simply "*posé*" [presented]—that which is static is not in my nature. I am always *en route*, in a development or progression.[8]

In "Reflections on the Work of Art," he admits to a "distressing childishness" as he tries to begin a new work.

> You find yourself in the presence of something very vague, very indeterminate, which has to be realized by means of notes and rhythms, i.e., by extraordinarily precise technical processes. . . . Even in the best case, this is a very bad time to get through. . . . On scraps of paper you scribble little tunes that seem absurd to you, successions of chords without rhyme or reason, work out little technical exercises according to this or that strict canon. . . . And then, one fine day, it happens that you have discovered a musical element that can serve as a beginning.[9]

thematic elements	1st appearance starts at m.*	in Fl (flute) or Rt (piano right hand)	number of beats or mm.	SUBSEQUENT APPEARANCES start at m. # in Fl (flute) or Rt/Left/Bo (piano right/left/both hands)													
				at m.*	in	at m.*	in	at m.*	in	at m.*	in	at m.*	in	at m.*	in	at m.*	in
a	1	Fl	6 beats	11	Fl	22	Fl	32	Fl	34	Rt	36	Rt	245	Fl	329	Fl
a^1	229.5	Fl	5.5 mm														
b	17	Fl	3 mm														
b^1	30	Fl	2 mm														
b^2	38	Fl	2 mm														
b^3	259.7	Fl	8th+3 mm														
c	44	Rt	4 mm	54	Rt	75	Rt	81	Rt	194	Fl	283	Rt	293	Rt		
c^1	51	Rt	1 m	61.3	Bo	149.3	Rt	290	Rt	300.3	Rt						
c^2	337	Fl	2 beats														
d	61	Fl	16th+2.5 mm	300.7	Fl												
d^1	147	Fl	3 mm														
e	66	Fl	2 mm	305	Fl												
e^1	71.3	Fl	5 beats														
e^2	89	Fl	6 mm														
f	80.3	Fl	5 beats														
f^1	83.3	Fl	2 beats	107	Fl	116	Fl	134	Fl	137	Fl						
f^2	84	Rt	2 mm														
f^3	86.7	Rt	2 beats	87.3	Fl												
f^4	199.7	Fl	qtr+4 mm	242.5	Bo	324	Bo										
f^5	206.7	Fl	qtr+3 mm	211.5	Bo	250.7	Bo	255.5	Bo								
g	95.5	Fl	qtr+3 mm	122.5	Fl	123.5	Left										
h	143	Fl	1 m	155	Fl	156	Fl	159	Fl								
h^1	157	Fl	1 m	160	Fl	161+	Fl										

* "**.3**," "**.5**," and "**.7**" indicate elements starting **1/3**, **1/2**, or **2/3** of the way into a given measure.

CHART 22.1 Martin, *Ballade* for Flute and Piano: Identification of the piece's eight fundamental elements and their variants.

As Jean-Clair Vançon points out, Martin's entire effort at this stage of composition is devoted to the quest for the prime, the germinating, element. "From the prime idea, the work sort of develops on its own, like an organism that grows, without the composer's being able to intervene except as an arborist does who 'steers' his apple tree and gives it the desired shape."[10] The development (or *Fortspinnung*, "spinning out") of thematic elements, as shown on Chart 22.2, is central to Martin's creative process.

It is interesting that no new elements are presented after "A." Even the thematic material of the cadenza, "B," is briefly foreshadowed toward the end of "A." Element "g" never returns after "A," nor does element "h" after its fulsome elaboration in the cadenza.

The cadenza stands alone as one of the work's four principal divisions, not only because it is the only section wholly devoted to one element but because of its texture, range, and free rhythm. The monophonic texture, relatively limited range (the flute exceeds the octave-plus-diminished-octave range of the cadenza in every section except for the six-measure no. 5), and absence of beat render it unique.

Thus, thematic considerations support dividing the work into eight sections and combining these into four divisions constituting a ternary form with coda. In the ballades of Chopin and Brahms, thematic recurrence *and* tonality determine the A-B-A form. Similarly, tonal considerations support the form revealed by thematic analysis in Martin's composition. (See Charts 22.3 and 22.4)

The *Ballade* is in E. Not only does the work start and end in that key, but E is the most important way station on the voyage from beginning to end. The first of the eight sections closes in E (mm. 30–43). The heart of the work, section 4, and the first two-thirds of section 5 (mm. 154–197) are in E. The prevalent centers of the sixth section are E and B, including an ending in E (mm. 273–282), and the last third of the seventh section and all of the coda (mm. 310–358) are emphatically in E. Interestingly—perhaps to create contrast and tension and later a sense of return—Martin avoids the tonality of E in sections 2 and 3 and in the first two-thirds of sections 6 (until m. 256) and 7 (until m. 310), where E returns for good in a "plagal" progression following ten measures of A.

A is the second most prevalent tonality in the work, playing the primary role in section 2 as the tonality of the central passage (mm. 61–74) and second fiddle in section 7, where it functions as the piece's penultimate tonality, preceding the final return to E. F♯, C♯/D♭, and B are the next most prevalent tonalities. F♯ is the final tonality of section 2 and the main one of section 3. An eighteen-measure pedal beginning in m. 89 extends well into the next section, where it "resolves" to B. Tonal centers in descending fourths lead to section 3's second tonality, C♯/D♭ (m. 122). C♯ prevails for four measures but gradually yields to another pedal on F♯ (mm. 134–144). Five measures of "dirty triads" usher in the final measures on the section's second

No new material is introduced after "A"; "g" appears only in "A"; "h" first appears at the end of "A," monopolizes cadenza, then disappears.																								
	A: 153 mm, 1–153																							
	Section 1: 1–43									**Section 2:** 44–94														
a	a	a		a		a	a	a																
starts in m#	1	11		22		32	34	36																
b			b		b^1				b^2															
			17		30				38															
c										c	c^1	c	c^1				c		c					
										44	51	54	61				75		81					
d														d										
														61										
e															e	e^1								e^2
															66	71								89
f																		f		f^1	f^2	f^3	f^3	
																		80		83	84	86	87	

	A (continued)										**B (cadenza):** 40 mm, 154–193								**A^1:** 130 mm, 194–323					
	Section 3: 95–153										**Section 4: 154–193**								**Section 5:** 194–199					
c										c^1									c					
										149									194					
d									d^1															
									147															
f		f^1	f^1			f^1	f^1																	
		107	116			134	137																	

g	g			g	g																			
	95			122	123																			
h								h			h	h	h^1	h	h^1	h *fortgesponnen**								
								143			154	156	157	159	160	161								
	* An element that is *fortgesponnen* is spun out, continued, extended, developed, as opposed to symmetrically repeated or varied.																							
	A¹ (continued)																		**Coda:** 35 mm, 324–358					
	Section 6: 200–282												**Section 7:** 283–323						**Section 8:** 324–358					
a				a^1		a														a				
				229		245														329				
b									b^3 chromatic bravura															
									259															
c													c	c^1	c	c^1					c^2 bravura passagework			
													283	290	293	300					337			
d																	d							
																	300							
e																		e						
																		305						
f	f^4	f^5	f^5		f^4		f^5	f^5											f^4					
	200	206	211		242		250	255											324					

CHART 22.2 Martin, *Ballade* for Flute and Piano: Deployment of the eight thematic elements in the piece's eight sections and four major divisions (A B A' Coda).

Division	Section #: measure #s	Total mm	Tonal center	Operating in measures	Tonal center's total mm within Section	Tonal center's prevalence within Section
A	1: 1–43	43	**E**	1-6, 30-43	20	47%
			G	11-14, 22-27	10	23%
	2: 44–94	51	**A**	50-51, 61-74	16	31%
			Bb	44-47, 75-78, 85-88	12	24%
	3: 95–153	59	**F#[1]**	95-106, 130-144	27	46%
			C#[1]/D♭	122-129, 149-153	13	22%
B	4: 154–193	40	**E[2]**	154-193	40	100%
A′	5: 194–199	6	**E**	194-197[3]	4	67%
	6: 200–282	83	**E**	256-263, 273-282	18	22%
			B	210-211, 223-231, 243-249	18	22%
			C/B#	206-209, 235-237, 254-255, 267-272	15	18%
			C#/D♭	200-205, 250-253	10	12%
	7: 283–323	41[4]	**E**	310-323	14	34%
			A	289-290, 300-309	12	29%
Coda	8: 324–358	35	**E**	324-358	35	100%

[1] Mm. 126-133 could be in either C# or F#; half (126-129) have been allocated to C#, the rest (130-133) to F#.

[2] 22 of 24 of the repeated or sustained notes or the highest notes of repeated or sequential patterns belong to the scale of E major/minor; mm. 154-178 outline a descending scale from e^3 to e^2 and on down to c^2.

[3] These 4 mm. are a reprise of mm. 44-47, transposed up a tritone.

[4] Mm. 283-312 are a reprise of mm. 44-73; the fast repeated f#'s in mm. 71-72 & modulation in m. 73 are replaced in mm. 310–312 by slower and more emphatic F#s.

CHART 22.3 Martin, *Ballade* for Flute and Piano: Primary tonal centers in the piece.

tonal center, this time as D♭ instead of C♯. B joins the aforementioned E, C/B♯, and C♯/D♭, four of the work's five most important tonal centers, to play a leading role in section 6.

Competitions have engendered many compositions, and Martin's complex, carefully crafted work ranks among the very best. So highly regarded was this piece that Ernest Ansermet arranged it for flute and orchestra shortly after it was performed in the competition. Two years later, Martin himself created a version for flute, string orchestra, and piano.

After contributing so much to Swiss musical life through his commissioned compositions, performances, and teaching, Martin and his wife left Geneva, moving to her native Amsterdam in 1946. Martin believed that he was too well known in Switzerland and there were "too many demands on his time to properly devote himself to the discipline and hard work of composing."[11] Indeed, composition had never come easily to him, producing anxiety as he began each new work. His widow

Tonality by sections										Tonal centers in order of prevalence		
	Number of measures in Section											
	Division	**A**		**B**	**A′**			**Coda**				
Tonal Center	**Sect 1**	**2**	**3**	**4**	**5**	**6**	**7**	**Coda**	Total mm	Total mm	Tonal Center	% of 358 mm
E	20			40	4	18	14	35	131	131	**E**	36%
F		8	6				4		18	38	**A**	11%
F#		6	27			3			36	36	**F#**	10%
G	10	3	3			1	3		20	27	**C# (D^b)**	7%
G#	2				2	3			7	25	**B**	7%
A	5	16				5	12		38	20	**G**	6%
B^b		12				2	6		20	20	**B^b**	6%
B		2	3			18	2		25	18	**F**	5%
C (B#)			3			15			18	18	**C (B#)**	5%
C# (D^b)	4		13			10			27	8	**D#**	2%
D	2								2	8	**none**	2%
D#						8			8	7	**G#**	2%
none		4	4						8	2	**D**	1%
mm per section	43	51	59	40	6	83	41	35	358	358	<totals>	100%
primary tonal centers per section	**E, G**	**A, B^b**	**F#, C#/ D^b**	**E**	**E**	**B, C/B#, C#/D^b, E**	**E, A**	**E**				

CHART 22.4 Martin, *Ballade* for Flute and Piano: Tonality in the piece as a whole.

recalled, "An idea or a commission for a new work had to 'mature.' That could take a long time and often it was as if he had the flu. But the flu disappeared the day the composition process started, so I called it 'compositis.'"[12]

In 1956 the family, now including two young children, purchased a home in the small town of Naarden, ten miles east of Amsterdam. "For my husband, it was like paradise,"[13] Maria Martin recalled. For one more year, he traveled regularly to Cologne, having taught since 1950 at the Hochschule für Musik, where he counted Karlheinz Stockhausen among his students. And then, at the age of sixty-seven, he retired from teaching and devoted the rest of his life to fulfilling as many commissions as he could. Given his renown as Switzerland's foremost composer and besieged with requests, he continued in this endeavor until the final days of his life.

Notes

1. Charles W. King, *Frank Martin: A Bio-Bibliography* (Westport, CT: Greenwood Press, 1990), 4.

2. Dorle J. Soria, "Artist Life: Frank Martin, Master of All Trades," *High Fidelity / Musical America* 22 (March 1972): MA-12.

3. Elmer Schönberger, "Een jong componist van tachtig jaar." *Preludium* 30 (Dec. 1970): 77–78, cited in King, 125.

4. King, 6.

5. Lukas Näf, "Musinfo—the Database of Swiss Music: Martin Frank Biography," http://www.musinfo.ch/index.php?content=maske_personen&pers_id=258&setLanguage=en, accessed June 27, 2012.

6. Lori P. Shortall, "Thematic, Harmonic, and Formal Aspects of Frank Martin's *Ballade* for Flute and Piano" (master's thesis, University of Western Ontario, 1996), 9.

7. Shortall, 43ff.

8. Frank Martin and Jean-Claude Piguet, *Entretiens sur la musique* (Neuchâtel: La Baconnière, 1967), 34–35, cited in Jean-Clair Vançon, "La Ballade pour flute et piano de Frank Martin: Le style et l'écriture," *Traversières* 69 (2001): 12, trans. William Wilsen.

9. Frank Martin, "Réflexions sur l'oeuvre d'art" (1950), in *Un compositeur médite sur son art, écrits et pensées recueillis par sa femme* (Neuchâtel: La Baconnière, 1977), 51, cited in Jean-Clair Vançon, 12.

10. Frank Martin, "L'expérience créatrice" (1950), in *Un compositeur médite sur son art*, 46, cited in Jean-Clair Vançon, 12–13.

11. King, 7.

12. Maria Martin, http://www.frankmartin.org/index.php/en/frank-martin-house, accessed June 28, 2012.

13. Maria Martin, http://www.frankmartin.org/index.php/en/frank-martin-house, accessed June 28, 2012.

23 Sergei Prokofiev—Sonata for Flute and Piano

FOR MANY COMPOSERS in the first half of the twentieth century, the upheavals of world wars caused such disruption to their lives that they composed little, whether because of military service or because of emotional distress. Sergei Prokofiev (1891–1953) was a notable exception.

An unusually precocious child, he was a facile pianist by the age of six. At thirteen, he arrived for his audition at the St. Petersburg Conservatory with manuscripts of four operas, a symphony, two sonatas, and many piano pieces in hand. Gaining admission, he studied composition with Reinhold Glière and Nikolai Rimsky-Korsakov and piano with Anna Esipova, graduating with honors in 1914. During his final year at the conservatory, he had set his sights on winning the prestigious Rubinstein Prize and went about the student piano competition in an unorthodox way.

> . . . instead of a classical concerto, I chose one of my own. While I might not be able to compete successfully in performance of a classical concerto, there was a chance that my own might impress the examiners by the novelty of technique; they simply would not be able to judge whether I was playing it well or not! . . . My most serious competitor was Golubovskaya . . . a very subtle and intelligent pianist. We were extremely gallant and courteous to each other: on the eve of the examination we inquired after the condition of each other's fingers,

> and in the long hours of suspense while the judges were deciding our fate, we played chess. After a long and stormy session the prize was awarded to me . . .
>
> [Glazunov, director of the conservatory] lost his temper and flatly refused to announce the results of the voting, which, he declared, encouraged a "harmful trend." Since, however, the "harm" had already been done, there was nothing for it but to read the announcement, which he did in a flat, toneless mumble.[1]

With that, the "cocky young man of undeniable talent"[2] launched his career.

In the midst of the Russian Revolution only a few years later, Prokofiev headed to the USA; then in 1922, he settled in Paris. He returned permanently to the Soviet Union in 1936, where he spent the last seventeen years of his life "stimulated as well as stifled by the cultural policies dictated by Stalin."[3]

When Russian-American composer Vernon Duke asked Prokofiev "how he could live and work in the atmosphere of Soviet totalitarianism," the composer replied, "I care nothing for politics—I'm a composer first and last. Any government that lets me write my music in peace, publishes everything I compose before the ink is dry, and performs every note that comes from my pen is all right with me."[4] While the Second World War uprooted him from Moscow, he remained astonishingly prolific during these years, completing the first version of his opera *War and Peace*, the Fifth Symphony, the second string quartet, two piano sonatas, five film scores, the symphonic suite *The Year 1941*, the *Ballad of an Unknown Boy*, and the Sonata for Flute and Piano.

After Hitler broke his nonaggression pact and attacked the Soviet Union on June 22, 1941, the Soviet Committee on Artistic Affairs evacuated leading artists from Moscow, fearing that the city might fall to the Germans. On August 8, 1941, Prokofiev and other luminaries boarded a train for the thousand-mile, three-day trip south to Nalchik, in the foothills of the Caucasus Mountains. For three months, he lived and worked in this pleasant little town alongside his new love, Mira Mendelson, until, under threat of attack, the two and their colleagues were "loaded into railroad cars, overcrowded and uncomfortable,"[5] and taken to Tbilisi, capital of Georgia.

Six months later, the prominent film director Sergei Eisenstein, with whom Prokofiev had collaborated on *Alexander Nevsky*, invited the composer to Alma-Ata, the capital of Kazakhstan. Most of the Soviet film studios, "hard at work on morale-boosting projects,"[6] had relocated there in 1941. Eisenstein hoped that Prokofiev would join him to write the score for his film biography of Ivan the Terrible. Though Prokofiev had turned down an offer from Eisenstein before the war, now, in 1942, he accepted the filmmaker's entreaty, setting out with Mira in late May on the arduous monthlong journey. "Film work is interesting, profitable, and does not require strenuous creative energy. Alma-Ata is a pleasant city, and full of money,"[7] he later reported.

It was while in Alma-Ata that Prokofiev began serious work on the flute sonata. He had been attracted to the idea of writing for this "undeservedly neglected" instrument since his days in Paris, a center for great woodwind playing. Creating an abstract, apolitical work was "perhaps inappropriate at the moment, but pleasant,"[8] he told his friend Nikolai Miaskovsky.

Then in mid-June 1943, the Kirov Ballet invited Prokofiev to come north to its temporary home in Molotov (known today by its original name, Perm), an outpost so far east that it is closer to the capital of Siberia, Novosibirsk, than to Moscow. The Kirov hoped that he would complete *Cinderella*, the ballet he had begun two years earlier. So began the final leg of his wartime travels. During his four months in Molotov, Prokofiev finished the flute sonata and most of *Cinderella*. The former would have its premiere on December 7 in Moscow.

"The sunniest and most serene of his wartime compositions,"[9] the sonata demonstrates Prokofiev's ability to meld his melodic gift with classical form and a tonal framework to create a wholly fresh and original composition. Prokofiev believed that composing a work without tonality was "like building on sand," but like other twentieth-century composers, he was able to "broaden the traditional concept of loyalty to the tonic"[10]: chromatic inflection and change of tonality by simple juxtaposition (without modulation) contribute to the vitality of his music. For example, the work's first theme, chromatically inflected but clearly in the key of D major, detours into C major after only two measures, then returns to D four measures later. (This displacement is reminiscent of *Peter and the Wolf*, where after opening Peter's theme in C major, Prokofiev suddenly turns to E♭ major in the third measure.) A moment later, the transition turns to the distant keys of A♭ and B before arriving, as classical practice would prescribe, in A major for the introduction of the second theme.

Following the lyrical second theme, the development begins very differently: the flute announces a martial motive, staccato (labeled "x" on Chart 23.1 and distinguished by a group of sixteenth-note triplets). Two measures later, the piano takes up a motive (first heard in the flute in m. 9) that becomes ever more disjunct. Russian critics said Prokofiev's use of wide melodic leaps gave his music its "football" quality.[11] The "athleticism" of "y" stands in marked contrast to the repeated notes of "x." Prokofiev weaves both motives into the fabric of this section, using them to integrate and delight as he develops "a" and "b," the two principal themes of the exposition.

With regard to form, Prokofiev once stated, "I want nothing better, nothing more flexible or more complete than the sonata form, which contains everything necessary to my structural purpose."[12] Indeed, the first movement is a perfectly crafted example of this classical structure. But to the end, he infuses it with his personality: the

section	**Exposition**																
theme	**a**				**transition**						**b**			**b¹**			
# of mm	8				12						1	8		12			
starts m#	1				9						21	22		30			
phrase # of mm	4		4		2	2	2	2		4	1	4	4	2.5	2.5	3	4
starts m#	1		5		9	11	13	15		17	21	22	26	30	32.5	35	38
element					y*	y	y	v	(y)	v¹	intro						w
starts m#					9	11	13	15	(16)	17	21						
key	**D**	**(C)**		**D**			**A♭**	**B**			**A**		**E**	**A**		**e**	**A**
starts m#	1	3		7			13	15			21		26	30		35	38

* Element "y" = 14 sixteenth-notes + a longer note.

section	**Development**																
theme	**introduction**								**(a)**			**(b)**				**(a)**	
# of mm	10								6			4				5	
starts m#	42								52			58				62	
phrase # of mm	3		2		3			2	3.5	2.5		4				3	2
starts m#	42		45		47			50	52	55.5		58				62	65
element	x*	y*	x	y	x&y	x	y	x	x	x		y	v	x&y	v²	x	x
starts m#	42	44	45	46	47	48	49	50	52	55.5		58	59	60	61	62	65
key	**(A)**								**E**		**b**					**B**	**B♭**
starts m#	42								52		56					62	65

* Element "x" = triplet + a longer note.

section	Development (continued)															
theme	**(b)**							**(b)**						**trans**		
# of mm	7							11						4		
starts m#	67							74						85		
phrase # of mm	2		5					2	3		3		3			
starts m#	67		69					74	76		79		82			
element		$w^?$		x		$w^?$	$w^?$		x&y	x	x&y	x	flourish			
starts m#	67	68		70		72	73		76	77	79	80	82			
key	**(B^b)**				**d**		**B**		**G**					**mod**	**D**	
starts m#	67				71		73		76					85	87	

section	Reprise											Coda					
theme	**a**				**trans**			**b**			**b^2**				**(a)**		
# of mm	8				6			1	8		7		12				
starts m#	89				97			103	104		112		119				
phrase # of mm	4		4		2		4	1	4	4	3	4	4	3	3	2	
starts m#	89		93		97		99	103	104	108	112	115	119	123	126	129	
element					v	y	v^1	intro					w	(w)		(w)	
starts m#					97	98	99	103				115	119	123		129	
key	**D**	**(C)**		**D**						**A**	**a**	**D**		**b^b**		**D**	
starts m#	89	91		95						108	112	115		123		129	

CHART 23.1 Prokofiev, Sonata for Flute and Piano: Analysis of the first movement.

football quality of the flute's theme in the coda (mm. 119–122), the unexpected turn to B♭ minor (m. 123), the chromaticism underlying the flute's final wistful recollection of the first theme.

The essence of a classical scherzo lies in its compound beat at a fast tempo and its witty, sometimes surprising elements. At the start of the second movement, Prokofiev creates two conundrums: first, he does not immediately establish a key. Then when the flute enters in A minor, its rhythm and melodic contour suggest a meter of 2/4 in conflict with the already established 3/4 (only slightly vitiated by the piano's hemiola in mm. 4–5). As the section progresses, Prokofiev includes unpredictable modulations (See Chart 23.2) and harmonic deceptions to enhance the joke. The gossamer character is briefly interrupted by the entrance of a sturdier "b" theme (m. 83) and its varied restatement.

Following a return to "A," which this time moves from D minor to E major, one hears the pensive melody of the trio over a static accompaniment. Whether or not it was the composer's intention, the first measure of this section (especially its instrumentation and texture: flute over sustained fifths on the tonic in the piano) is reminiscent of the first measure of the "*Khorovod* [round dance] of the Princesses" from *The Firebird*: flute over sustained octave on the dominant in two horns. Perhaps a doffing of the hat to Stravinsky?

Prokofiev interrupts the trio's tranquility with several outbursts and then crafts a brilliant retransition: the piano's triplet quarter notes, beginning in m. 204, recall the opening of the movement and softly begin leading us back to the scherzo. It turns out that the trio has maintained the tempo of the scherzo and achieved "poco meno mosso" through a change from a compound to a simple beat (three to two prolations). Prokofiev has only to reinstate the compound beat (triple prolation) to achieve a seamless return to tempo 1. Though Prokofiev "always maintained that his interest lay not in rhythm . . . but in the invention of good themes,"[13] his rhythmic genius is evident here.

With its simple accompaniment, the exquisite theme of the third movement suggests the possibility of F Lydian until B♭s are introduced in the sixth measure. Just after, Prokofiev slips deceptively into the distant key of F♯ minor and touches on D minor before arriving more decisively in C major. (See Chart 23.3) A new quasi-canonic texture ushers in a second statement of the principal theme. The middle section introduces chromatic sixteenth-note triplets alternating between flute and piano, beguiling figuration that continues in the flute as the piano reintroduces the opening theme in octaves. This return is interesting in that not only does the triplet figuration perpetuate the mood of "B" (the middle section) but tonally the return achieves the tonic key of F only after seven measures in the Neapolitan (G♭ major) and six in the supertonic (G minor). The coda returns to the simplicity

Note: Δ = non-recurring thematic material

			Scherzo																													
theme	**intro**		**a**		**a^1**				**a**		**a^2**						**trans**					**b**		**b^1**								
starts m#	1		7		15				34		42						58					83		103								
# of mm	6		8		19				8		16						25					20		20								
phrase	Δ	Δ	h	i	h	j	k	l	h	i	h	m	j			k	l^1		p			n	n^1	n	n^2							
# of mm	3	3	4	4	4	4	4	7	4	4	4	4	4			4	2	9	6	4	4	8	12	8	12							
key	**n/a**		**a**		**C**	**A^b**		**d^b= c#**	**d**		**(F) (A)**						**d**			**D^b**		**A**	**G C**	**A^b**	**G^b**							
starts m#	1		7		15	19		27	34											75		83	93 99	103	113							
harmony								**7th degree of D minor**															**V$^{6/5}$/IV**									
									Scherzo (continued)																	**Trio** (proportions miniscule compared to Scherzo)						
theme									**a**		**a^3**						**trans**									**c**		**d**	**c**			
starts m#									123		131						149									162		182	190			
# of mm									8		18						13									20		8	22			
phrase									h	i	h	m	j^1	j^2	j^3		l^2	Δ	Δ							r	s*	t	r	s*		
# of mm									4	4	4	4	3	3	4		4	4	5							12	8	8	12	10		
key									**d**					**e**			**E**									**D/d**		**E**	**D/d**			
starts m#									123					142			149									162	174	182	190	202	209	
harmony														**vii°**			**vii^9**										**IV^9**			**IV^9**	**iv$^{6/5}$ - V**	
																										*The two "s" elements differ in # of mm, but, because of the metrical notation, they have exactly the same number of beats.						
			Scherzo																									**Coda**				
theme	tr		**a**		**a^1**				**a**		**a^2**						**tr**					**b**		**b^2**		**trans**		**coda**				
starts m#	212		228		236				255		263						279					304		324		340		348				
# of mm	16		8		19				8		16						25					20		16		8		23				
phrase	r^1	Δ	h	i	h	j	k	l	h	i	h	m	j	k			l^1		p			n	n^1	n	n^3	Δ	Δ	(b)	(a)	(b)	(a)	Δ
# of mm	8	8	4	4	4	4	4	7	4	4	4	4	4	4			2	9	6	4	4	8	12	8	8	4	4	1	5	3	4	10
key	**a^b**	**d**	**a**		**C**	**A^b**		**d^b/c#**	**d**		**(F) (A)**						**d**			**D^b**		**A**	**G C**	**A^b**	**G^b**	**(D^b)**	**(A^b)**	**a**				
starts m#	212	220	228		236	240		248	255											296		304	314 320	324	334	342	346	348	349	354		361 368 369
harmony	**ii^7**	**V**																											**IV$^{6/4+/3}$**	**i^{3+}**		**i vii$^{\circ 7}$/v i**

CHART 23.2 Prokofiev, Sonata for Flute and Piano: Analysis of the second movement.

Note: Δ = non-recurring thematic material											
section	**A**				**B**						
theme	**a**		**a**		**b**		**c**		**b^1**		**trans**
starts m#	1		18		35		43		53		61
# of mm	17		17		8		10		8		4
phrase	q	r	q	r	s	s^1	t	t^1	s	s^2	Δ
starts m#	1	10	18	27	35	39	43	47	53	57	61
# of mm	9	8	9	8	4	4	4	6	4	4	4
motive		μ		μ^1							
starts m#		14		31							
key	**F f#**	**d C**					**b**		**C**		**mod**
starts m#	1 8	10 14					43		53		61
section	**A**		**Coda**								
theme	**a**		**a^1**	**b^1**							
starts m#	65		82	90							
# of mm	17		8	5							
phrase	q	r	q^1	r^1							
starts m#	65	74	82	90							
# of mm	9	8	8	5							
motive		μ		μ^2							
starts m#		78		90							
key	**G♭ g**	**F**									
starts m#	65 72	78									

CHART 23.3 Prokofiev, Sonata for Flute and Piano: Analysis of the third movement.

of the opening and ends with a voice-led (rather than a harmonic) progression to the tonic.

The rousing "A" section of the finale again features one of Prokofiev's tonal detours: after opening in D major, he begins the second phrase in C major, then returns to D. (See Chart 23.4) The vigor of this opening section gives way to a comical insertion in m. 30: the pianist enters with a theme not unlike a Hanon exercise. To this, the flutist subsequently adds a syncopated, athletic (i.e., "football") theme filled in with grace-note flourishes.

Following a return to "A" and "B," the piano prepares the way for a central episode, the flutist entering with a tender melody that will gradually intensify toward a more dramatic outpouring, *fortissimo*. Prokofiev shines again as, at m. 113, he shapes a nine-measure modulating transition that gains momentum as it drives into a third treatment of "A."

Dmitri Shostakovich declared Prokofiev's sonata "a perfectly magnificent work," and it remains one of the finest pieces in the flute repertoire. Certainly it was a work

Note: Δ = non-recurring thematic material																									
section	**A**								**B**																
theme	**a**	**a^1**	**a**	**b**	**b^1**	**c**			**d**	**d**	**d^1**	**d^2**	**d^3**												
# of mm	5	6	5	4	4	5			5	5	5	4	5												
starts m#	1	6	12	17	21	25			30	35	40	45	49												
key	**D**	**(C)D**			**d**				**A**		**f#**	**b**	**A**												
starts m#	1	6 8			24				30		40	45	49												
section	**A**								**B**								**C**								
theme	**a**				**b^1**	**c^1**			**d**						**trans**		**int**	**e**	**f**	**e^1**	**f^1**	**e**	**f^2**	**trans**	
# of mm	5				4	4			5						11		4	4	6	4	6	4	2	9	
starts m#	54				59	63			67						72		83	87	91	97	101	107	111	113	
phrase															Δ	Δ								(a)	Δ
# of mm															4	7								4	5
starts m#															72	76									
key	**D**				**d**				**A**						**F**					**(f#)**	**F**	**A^b**		**A**	**mod**
starts m#	54				62				67						72					100	103	107		113	117

CHART 23.4 Prokofiev, Sonata for Flute and Piano: Analysis of the fourth movement.

section	**A**								**B**						
theme	**a**	**a**^{1}		**b**	**b**^{1}				**d**^{4}		**d**^{1}	**d**$^{2?}$	**d**$^{3?}$	**d**^{5}	
# of mm	5	6		4	4				4		5	4	3	4	
starts m#	122	127		133	137				141		145	150	154	157	
key	**D**	**(C)**	**D**						**b**^{b}		**d**	**g**	**D**	**mod**	
starts m#	122	127	129						141		145	150	154	157	
section	**A (Coda)**														
theme	**a**^{2}					**a**^{3}									
# of mm	9					5									
starts m#	161					170									
element	(a)	(a†)	(a^)	(a*)	Δ	(a*)	(a*)	Δ							
# of mm	2	1	3	2	1	2	2	1							
starts m#	161	163	164	167	169	170	172	174							
key	**D**														
starts m#	161														
	† canonic entrance after 6 beats								^ canonic entrance after 4 beats						* compare 2nd m of "a"

CHART 23.4 Continued

that Soviet authorities would find appealing, but one must not assume that its style resulted from restrictions imposed by the regime. As English musicologist Gerald Abraham proposed in 1943:

> Why should Prokofiev, who was continuing a brilliant career outside Russia, have voluntarily returned to a land where he knew certain limitations would be imposed on his work, unless he felt that these limitations would be unimportant? The truth is, I think, that he had already been tending in this direction for some time.[14]

Abraham's hypothesis is certainly in keeping with Prokofiev's sentiment cited above: "I care nothing for politics." Perhaps this was true in the 1930s and early 1940s, but everything changed in 1948, when the Central Committee of the Communist Party denounced Prokofiev, along with all the other leading Soviet composers. Charged with "formalism," a condemnation invoked when composers were believed to have written works incompatible with the Soviet ideal, Prokofiev would be forever changed: like the other composers cited in the resolution, he was frightened and demoralized. Commissions were abruptly canceled, and musicians were afraid to perform his works.

Shostakovich lived on and composed after Stalin's death, perhaps even secretly "having the last word" with his Symphony no. 10, in the final movement of which his monogram, D SCHostakovich (D–Es [i.e., E♭]–C–H [i.e., B]) obliterates the brutal scherzo theme associated with Stalin. Prokofiev would have a much different fate. He died on March 5, 1953, the same day as the Soviet leader who had ruined his final years. As a last cruel blow, Prokofiev's death was not announced for days so as not to diminish the dictator's glorification.

Notes

1. David Gutman, *Prokofiev* (London: Alderman, 1988), 46.

2. Harold C. Schonberg, *The Lives of the Great Composers*, 3rd ed. (New York: Norton, 1997), 525.

3. Gutman, 7.

4. Vernon Duke, *Passport to Paris* (Boston: Little, Brown, 1955), 344.

5. Harlow Robinson, *Sergei Prokofiev* (New York: Viking, 1987; Boston: Northeastern University Press, 2002), 399. Reprint ed. cited.

6. Gutman, 140.

7. Robinson, 406.

8. Robinson, 421.

9. Israel V. Nestyev, *Prokofiev* (Stanford, CA: Stanford University Press, 1960), 345.

10. Joseph Machlis, *Introduction to Contemporary Music* (New York: Norton, 1961), 36.
11. Machlis, 277.
12. Machlis, 279.
13. Gutman, 13–15.
14. Gerald Abraham, *Eight Soviet Composers* (London: Oxford University Press, 1943), 32.

24 Henri Dutilleux—Sonatine for Flute and Piano

ALTHOUGH HIS COMPOSITIONAL career spanned some seventy years, Henri Dutilleux (1916–2013) composed his most frequently performed work, the Sonatine for Flute and Piano, when he was just twenty-seven. He had completed his studies at the Paris Conservatory only five years earlier, winning the prestigious Prix de Rome in 1938. Because of the turmoil leading up to World War II, however, the four-year residency at the Villa Medici accorded each winner became a mere four months for the young composer: he moved to Rome in February 1939 and returned to Paris in June. Taken into the army as a stretcher bearer when war broke out in September, he served for nearly a year, then was demobilized in September 1940.[1] He went back to Paris, where he struggled for over a year to make ends meet during the turbulence of the German Occupation. In early 1942, the Vichy government and the Institut de France, which granted the Prix de Rome, ordered former prizewinners to take up residence at the Villa Il Paradiso in Nice, which was in the Vichy-administered zone, or lose their grants. After only a month, however, Dutilleux, alone and ill at ease, couldn't stand it any longer and illegally escaped north into the occupied zone and back to Paris.[2] "I realized I would have to earn my living, which I did by giving harmony lessons, accompanying singers [at the conservatory], and making arrangements of music for nightclubs."[3] It was during this unsettled period that Claude Delvincourt, director of the Paris Conservatory, commissioned the young composer to write a series of examination pieces for wind instruments—bassoon, flute, oboe, and trombone. Although the flute piece, written in 1943, became Dutilleux's most often performed and recorded work, he considered it, like almost all of his early efforts (i.e., compositions before the Piano Sonata of 1948), to be derivative and without merit.

Indeed, Dutilleux had grown up influenced by the impressionists, and it would take some time for him to develop his own voice as a composer. His family had long been interested in the arts: one great-grandfather was a painter, printer, and friend of Delacroix and Corot, another was a composer, organist, and friend of Gabriel Fauré. Dutilleux's parents were amateur musicians, and the composer described his home as one filled with music and paintings.[4] "If I've followed the path of music, that is because of the intelligence of those around me and especially of my parents, who first of all took advice from many sources and then encouraged me wholeheartedly."[5]

Raised in Douai, in northern France, Dutilleux studied harmony, counterpoint, and piano with Victor Gallois at the local conservatory while simultaneously receiving his general education (French, Latin, English, natural science, and math) at a lycée. He later recalled:

> It meant going from one school to the other, and this entailed some extraordinary acrobatics because one lesson followed hard on the heels of another with no let-up. We had a lesson in solfège at 6:30 a.m. No sooner were we out of that than we had to get to the lycée, then we left that to go to a piano lesson between 12:30 and 2:00 then back to the lycée![6]

In 1933, at the age of seventeen, Dutilleux moved to Paris to begin studies at the conservatory. His association with the school led to composition of the sonatine and to a long life in the French capital.

Though the work of a young composer, the sonatine is a complex, masterful piece. Written as a single movement, it divides into three sections: an Allegretto with a cadenza, an Andante, and an Animé followed by a second cadenza and coda. Dutilleux's inclusion of a key signature (one flat) in the first and third sections intimates his dedication to tonality. "My main reservation over this twelve-tone technique has always been that I could not really accept the basic principle of abolishing all hierarchies between the different degrees of the chromatic scale."[7]

The opening section prior to the cadenza is in ternary form: A-B-A. Right from the start, one hears Dutilleux's expert handling of complex harmonic, rhythmic, and melodic material. Harmonically, he enriches the tonal palette by combining minor and later major scales with the Phrygian mode. The opening phrase (mm.

1–4) combines D minor with D Phrygian, then in mm. 5–7 he moves to A minor/Phrygian. At the same time the 7/8 meter, with alternating 4 + 3 and 3 + 4 groupings, veils the pulse in a manner reminiscent of Debussy. Melodically, Dutilleux foreshadows the principal theme with two variations of it (mm. 1–4 and 5–9 in the piano) in a sort of reverse variation procedure, before the theme itself is introduced by the flute in m. 10 with D major/Phrygian harmony. Although the D major and Phrygian scales combined include eleven of the twelve chromatic pitches, there is here, nonetheless, an emphasis on D as tonic. Dutilleux uses such combinations to enrich harmonic possibilities while still preserving a strong sense of harmonic direction. Measure 14 inaugurates a five-measure transition to "B": two measures in C♯ minor/Phrygian followed by three measures, again redolent of Debussy, that modulate by means of a whole-tone scale (F–G–A–B–C♯–E♭) over a G♯ pedal, a pitch that has lingered from the previous C♯ minor/Phrygian constellation.

The more-spritely "B" introduces two new motives, one featuring 3 + 4 and the other 4 + 3 groupings of eighth notes (mm. 19–22 and 23–26, respectively). A modulating transition ushers in the return of "A." As in the opening, Dutilleux incorporates complex major/Phrygian harmonies as he first presents two variations of the theme (mm. 30–31 and 32–37). The latter variation is extended by five measures in 6/8 (including a sustained dominant harmony, mm. 40–42) that prolong anticipation of the reprise of the main theme in D major/Phrygian at m. 43 (cf. mm. 10ff.). The brief closing statement (mm. 52–56) begins with a three-measure sequence in the piano built on material from m. 2, after which the two instruments diverge melodically and evaporate into silence.

Thematically, the Allegretto is remarkably tightly constructed, all of its fifty-six measures deriving from one of five motives, as shown in Example 24.1: v (first appears in the piano, m. 1), w (piano, m. 2), x (flute, m. 16), y (piano right hand, m. 19), and z (flute, m. 23).[8]

The cadenza introduces a dotted figure (thirty-second note, dotted sixteenth, thirty-second, long note) that Dutilleux states three times at the top and four times at the bottom of each of the two phrases. This figure will return at the end of the next section, the Andante, to propel it to its cliffhanging conclusion.

The expressive Andante, the most harmonically complex section of the piece, begins with a gentle motive in the piano that is taken up by the flute and extended to become the section's main theme (mm. 66–71; then repeated a minor sixth higher, where the ominous syncopations pervasive in the piano part give way to a more animated melodic and rhythmic accompaniment). Underlying this first half of the movement, the bass line progresses through the pitches of a circle of fifths: E in m. 64 moving to A, D, G, C, F, B♭, and E♭ in mm. 70, 71, 72, 75, 76, 77, and 78.

EXAMPLE 24.1 Dutilleux, Sonatine for Flute and Piano: Motives "v," "w," "x," "y," and "z."

Motive "v," piano, m. 1

Motive "w," piano, m. 2

Motive "x," flute, m. 16

Motive "y," piano right hand, m. 19

Motive "z," flute, m. 23

With the flourish into m. 78, a new melody is introduced in D♭ major, soaring above the piano's quiet cross rhythms. In the second half of m. 80, Dutilleux subtly reintroduces the dotted motive from the cadenza, at first descending a major and a minor third, then ascending a diminished fourth, ending on D♭. He repeats and then uses different intervals as the motive leads into the pitch D at the beginning of m. 83. As the dynamic level increases and the melodic lines rise, Dutilleux in m. 85 sharpens the rhythmic profile of the motive, thereby returning it to the rhythm as first stated in the cadenza. Presenting the motive five times in a rhythmically languid version before offering it as originally stated is another example of the reverse variations discussed with regard to the opening of the sonatine. After m. 85, the motive undergoes further variation, the length of its final note changing and then the dotted rhythm being abandoned altogether in the two statements making up the climax, m. 87. Further intensifying the drive to the climax in the last six measures of this section, which are in F major, is a dominant pedal point on C. (It will not resolve until m. 111, well into the final section of the piece.)

Like the first section, the Animé reveals ternary design (introduction-E-F-E). Structural cohesiveness is enhanced by Dutilleux's incorporation of the "E" section's principal theme (mm. 101–104) into the accompaniment of the latter part of "F" (mm. 151ff.) while the flute gives out, dolce cantabile, the section's only lyrical melody. Contrasting with the tonal stability of "E" (in F major), the central "F" (mm. 129–172) bounds through a series of major and minor keys leading to a climax (mm. 168–170) before subsiding into the return of "E," again in F major. Dutilleux builds tension again by increasing chromaticism as the second "E" progresses. In m. 190, a long crescendo begins, which, along with modulation, frenzied trills, syncopated rhythms, and an indication that the playing is to "become excited," leads to the climax of the work (to be played "avec exaltation") and the feverish opening of the second cadenza.

The coda begins with a slithering chromatic line in the flute, an expansion to twelve measures of the eight-measure triplet passage in mm. 143ff., this time over a dominant pedal point. As has occurred effectively so many times before, this quiet, mysterious passage gradually gains tempo and momentum, leading to the brilliant conclusion in which the flute ascends to its highest C before the piano plunges to its lowest F, the root of the final, emphatic tonic chord.

In 1942, the year before he composed this successful and enduring work, Dutilleux met Geneviève Joy (1919–2009), a star piano student at the conservatory who later taught sight-reading and chamber music there. The two married on September 17, 1946, a year after Dutilleux became director of music production at Radio France. In this position, which he held until 1963, Dutilleux was responsible for providing music that would, in his words, "support dramatic and literary broadcasts . . . a form of radio art, or radio theatre, if you like."[9] He commissioned music and then arranged for it to be performed and recorded in the studio. He spoke well of the position and managed also to compose film scores ("good training in how to compose fast"),[10] symphonies, chamber music, solo concertos, and ballet music through these years, but he decided to leave the post in 1963 and devote himself fully to composition. (He did teach at the École normale de musique between 1961 and 1970 and, as a guest professor, at the conservatory for two years beginning in 1970.) Dutilleux went on to become one of the most distinctive and highly regarded composers of the twentieth century.

All of the composers whose pieces are represented in this book would no doubt be pleased to have contributed one of the best-known works in the flute repertoire—save one: Henri Dutilleux. He wished to be remembered only for his later compositions, which he regarded as good work, and stated unequivocally that he derived "no pleasure" from the success of the sonatine.[11]

Notes

1. Pierrette Mari, *Henri Dutilleux* (Paris: Hachette, 1973), 35.

2. Caroline Potter, *Henri Dutilleux: His Life and Works* (Aldershot, UK: Ashgate, 1997), 6.

3. Roger Nichols, trans. *Henri Dutilleux: Music—Mystery and Memory—Conversations with Claude Glayman* (Aldershot, UK: Ashgate, 2003), 19.

4. Nichols, 3.

5. Nichols, 6.

6. Nichols, 6.

7. Nichols, 21.

8. Versions of "v" occur, in addition to its first appearance, in mm. 3, 5, 8, 10, 12, 14, 15, 30, 31, 32, 34, 36, 43, 45, 47, 50, 51; of "w" in mm. 4, 6, 7, 9, 11, 13, 27, 28, 29, 33, 35, 37, 38, 39, 40, 41, 42, 44, 46, 48, 49, 52, 53, 54, 55, 56; of "x" in mm. 17, 18; of "y" in mm. 20, 21, 22; and of "z" in mm. 24, 25, 26.

9. Nichols, 33.

10. Nichols, 27.

11. Nichols, 83.

25 André Jolivet—*Chant de Linos*

BORN IN MONTMARTRE, the artistic center of Paris at the turn of the century, André Jolivet (1905–1974) expressed interest in the arts at an early age, but his parents—his father, a repressed painter earning a living as a bookkeeper for the municipal bus company, and his mother, an amateur pianist—were adamant that he pursue a practical career as a civil servant (which included the possibility of teaching) and explore music only as a hobby.[1] So in contrast to many others, he never attended a conservatory and never became a virtuoso instrumentalist. He did, however, participate in a wealth of musical endeavors during his childhood, beginning with solfège and piano lessons at the age of four. Most valuable was his involvement in a fine religious choral society sponsored by his neighborhood church, Notre-Dame de Clignancourt, where he learned the rudiments of harmony and counterpoint. His desire to perform in the society's orchestra led to cello lessons, and in an autobiographical sketch, he humorously described playing in an "orchestra" of three at a nearby theater, where he learned to improvise by highlighting the action of silent films with "appropriate noise."[2] From the age of twelve, he attended performances at the Comédie-Française every Thursday afternoon; soon his only ambition was to be part of this august institution.

At the age of twenty, Jolivet completed his fourth year of higher education at the École normale d'instituteurs, a boarding school in Auteuil dedicated to the training of primary school teachers (of six- to fourteen-year-olds). He served in the military for about a year and a half and then obtained a position at a primary school in St. Denis. Only then, in September 1927, at the age of twenty-two, did he begin composition studies. His first lessons were with Paul Le Flem, professor of counterpoint at the Schola Cantorum, director of the Chanteurs de Saint-Gervais, and music critic of *Comoedia*, positions that accorded well with his conservative leanings as a composer. Le Flem directed Jolivet's studies toward harmony and counterpoint, including Renaissance polyphony.

Jolivet had more contemporary musical interests, however, and his introduction to atonal music through attendance at a series of concerts honoring Schoenberg's visit to Paris in 1927 made a profound impression. Two years later he heard Varèse's *Amériques*, which "opened the doors of [Jolivet's] audacity."[3] Le Flem, realizing his student's propensity for "daring experiment," recommended that Jolivet study with Varèse,[4] who had returned to Paris after an extended stay in the United States. Jolivet later wrote, "I must say, that it was Varèse . . . for whom I have the deepest admiration, who set me on my way. He helped me to discover one of music's most significant aspects; music as a magical and ritual expression of human society."[5]

Jolivet persevered during the late 1920s and throughout the 1930s, teaching school, composing, and attending concerts of contemporary music. With the completion of *Mana* for solo piano (1935) and *Cinq incantations* for solo flute (1936, the same year as Varèse's *Density 21.5*), he propelled himself to prominence on the Parisian musical scene. Still, he was disappointed by the lack of opportunity for performance of his music.

In staunch opposition to neoclassicism, which was all the rage in Paris at this time, Jolivet sought to "rehumanize" French music, believing that it had become too dryly abstract and, in its eclecticism, "undistinguished and lacking in purpose," especially in the hands of Satie and Les Six.[6] This conviction and his desire to have his music performed led him to become in December 1935 a founding member of La Spirale, an association that produced concerts of contemporary French and foreign chamber music. Jolivet served as the fledgling society's treasurer, presiding over deficits from the third month on, until he finally closed the books on July 1, 1938.[7]

Meanwhile, in June 1936, while Spirale was still in full (if deficit-ridden) bloom, Jolivet and two of Spirale's other members, Olivier Messiaen and Jean-Yves Daniel-Lesur, along with Yves Baudrier, associated themselves as La Jeune France. The group's goal, to foster the composition and performance of new symphonic music, required an entirely different level of organization and financing from that of Spirale. Jeune France had good connections and sponsored several successful concerts but met its demise with the onset of World War II. Jolivet's attempts to revive the group after the war couldn't be realized as he wished.

On August 26, 1939, Sergeant André Jolivet was mobilized, but ill health, described later by the composer as a "physiological crisis, quite severe, due to the overload I had been imposing on myself for a decade," required a nearly three-month convalescence before he could report for duty on November 18.[8] He joined his unit, an anti-tank artillery battery, at Paris's Fort Charenton on December 5, but had to spend another couple of weeks in a military hospital before rejoining his comrades in January in Fontainebleau, where life in the open air finally put him back on his feet.[9] A letter to Serge Moreux, dated April 8, 1940, during the *Sitzkrieg*, in which he bitterly refers to himself as a "babysitter of horses" (artillery being horse powered), tells of his psychological state: "I'm absolutely empty—and emptied. Am I the same person who started writing a symphony last August? It's someone else . . . someone I don't know. . . . The only thing that interests me is the music I could have written—should have written—and shall not write."[10]

The armistice signed on June 22, 1940, finds Jolivet and his battery in the Dordogne, where they had retreated as part of the rear guard protecting the civilian exodus from Paris, 450 kilometers to the north. The composer is working on the *Mass for the Day of Peace*, which is partially premiered in Pressignac on Bastille Day, just before medals are distributed to the soldiers in the village square. Jolivet is awarded the bronze star and the Croix de Guerre in the presence of his wife and son, who have managed to join him in the south.[11] Demobilized on August 6, 1940, Jolivet and his family move from the "free zone" back to Paris (and the occupied zone), where he resumes his work as schoolteacher and composer.

Having written experimental, avant-garde works before the war, the pieces Jolivet composed between 1940 and 1945, including the *Pastorales de Noël* (flute, bassoon, and harp) of 1943, reflect his desire "to prove to myself that I was capable of writing music in a sense more conforming with tradition, music that was meant to be nothing more than a relaxation and escape."[12] He wanted to write pieces that people as war weary as he would enjoy.

In the summer of 1942, Jolivet was awarded a 40,000 franc grant from the Association for the Advancement of French Culture; it allowed him to forgo teaching for a year and devote himself entirely to his musical career. Approaching the four grand musical institutions of Paris, the Opéra, the Comédie-Française, the Conservatoire, and the Radio nationale (he was already well established at Radio Vichy), he worked on many projects simultaneously. At one point, the communist sympathizer and fellow traveler of the 1930s found himself composing and conducting incidental music for the Comédie-Française's 1943 production of Gerhart Hauptmann's play *Iphigenie in Delphi*, a production instigated by the Nazi occupiers' Propaganda Bureau.[13]

For the conservatory, Jolivet judged the fugue and counterpoint exams in the summer of 1942 and the following spring the cello, flute, and woodwind competitions.

In 1943 he received the first of several commissions to write a concours piece for the conservatory. Thus was born *Chant de Linos* for flute and piano.

Claude Delvincourt, the conservatory's director, required only that the piece be "difficult." Certainly *Chant de Linos*, written between January 26 and March 23, 1944,[14] satisfied that criterion. Its style and depth must have pleased Gaston Crunelle who, as flute professor since 1941, sought profound, contemporary pieces for the concours in contrast to those his predecessors had selected.

Jolivet had been interested in rituals and magic from early childhood, when he spent vacations a few miles southeast of Paris at the home of his "uncle," Louis Tauxier (actually his mother's second cousin), a colonial administrator in French West Africa. Young Jolivet was fascinated by an immense map of West Africa that hung in the room where he stayed. This map featured the names not only of countries, rivers, mountains, and towns but also of the indigenous peoples. "How could I not daydream, tracing the routes from Dakar to Conakry, from Bamako to Ouagadougou, encountering different tribes along the way," he later wrote.[15]

Uncle Louis not only gave him masks, weapons, and musical instruments but captivated him with stories of ceremonial customs. Certainly, this fueled Jolivet's lifelong fascination with ancient and non-Western cultures and led him to want "to give back to music its original ancient meaning, when it was the magical, incantatory expression of the religious beliefs of human groups."[16]

In a short preface to the printed score, Jolivet explained that the "Song of Linos" was, in Greek antiquity, a kind of threnody, a funeral lament, interrupted by cries and dances. The three contrasting elements of lament, cries, and dance are delineated in Chart 25.1. Chart 25.2 shows how the nine sections can be subdivided and thematically related to each other.

Several myths are associated with Linos, two of which describe a music teacher who meets a premature and pitiable death. In one version of the legend, Linos was killed by Apollo because the beauty of Linos's singing rivaled that of the god's. In a more often told story, Linos served as teacher of the musically inept Heracles (Hercules). Linos became so exasperated by the slowness of his student's progress that he lost patience and struck him. His young pupil struck back in anger with his lyre, killing Linos. The muses, who dearly loved Linos, joined in lamenting his untimely death and later, at funerals, such a lament became known as "the Song of Linos."

Jolivet featured the flute in many of his chamber and orchestral compositions, regarding it as the "musical instrument par excellence in that—enlivened by breath, by this deepest outstreaming of the human being—it fills its notes with both that which is corporeal and cosmic within us."[17] In ancient cultures, the flute was an

m #s	Section		# of mm	% of 229 mm
1-16	**Intro**	Introduction	16	7%
17-33	**A**	Lament 1	17	7%
34-46	**B**	Cries 1	13	6%
47-58	**A**[1]	Lament 2	12	4%
59-80	**B**[1]	Cries 2*	22	10%
81-175	**C**	Dance 1 (in two parts)	95	**41%**
176-187	**A**[2]	Lament 3*	12	5%
188-196	**B**[2]	Cries 3	9	4%
197-229	**C**[1]	Dance 2 (including coda)*	33	14%
* Jolivet designates mm. 73-80 as cadenza, mm. 176-187 as reminiscence (*rappel*) of the first lament, and mm. 197-229 as final dance. (Kayas, 340)				

CHART 25.1 Jolivet, *Chant de Linos*: Analysis of primary formal elements.

instrument of primitive magic and ritual; Jolivet believed that the ancient threnody could be effectively expressed in this, his first composition for flute and piano.

Chant de Linos opens dramatically: octave Gs in the piano immediately proceeding to half- and whole-step dissonances; syncopation contributes to the tension and the powerful forward drive. Jolivet's strict use of distinct pitch sets ("modes") helps to define and delineate the sections of the piece. For example, the mode of the introduction employs G (the "final"), A♭, B, C, C♯, D, and F. His small- and large-scale manipulations of these pitches highlight the mode's half-step (G–A♭, B–C–C♯–D) and tritone (G–C♯, A♭–D, B–F) relationships, as exemplified in m. 5, where the flute's second entrance begins on C♯, a tritone higher than the first. Following the introduction's three outbursts, each ending on G, the music calms, and the section concludes on F, a modal leading tone one whole step below the final.

For the first lament, Jolivet uses the same mode plus E♭. Above the piano's one-measure ostinato (with its prominent tritone on the second beat), the flute sounds the lament, three rhythmically supple phrases, each one louder than the last. Jolivet ends this lament on the final (G) in the flute and then the piano. Thus, whereas the introduction, ending on the leading tone, led on to the lament, the lament's ending settles on the final and so is more emphatic.

The calm of the first lament's close is followed by the first shrieks of the mourners (mm. 34–46). The change of tempo, dynamic level, meter signature, and mode could hardly be more dramatic. With respect to mode, Jolivet organizes the pitches of this section in four successive six-note sets, achieving the full aggregate of chromatic pitch types in the section as a whole. The mode in mm. 34–37 retains only the G and C♯ of the preceding lament, marking the work's first decisive change in pitch material. In the final measures of this section, repeated C♯s in the flute again

section	**Introduction**		**Lament 1**	**Cries 1**		**Lament 2**			
m #s	1-16		17-33	34-46		47-58			
sub-section	**shrieks**	**trans**		**a**	**b**				
m #s	1-10	11-16		34-38	39-46				
section	**Cries 2**				**Dance 1a (frenzied)**				
m #s	59-80				81-125				
sub-section	**c**	**d**	**e**	**f**	**intro**	**w**	**w¹**	**x**	**w²**
piano m #s	59-61	62-66	67-73	80	81-84	85-96	97-104	105-111	112-125
flute m #s	60-62	63-67	68-75	76-80					
section					**Dance 1b (cantando/marcato)**				**Lament 3**
m #s					126-175				176-187
sub-section					**intro¹**	**y**	**z**	**y¹**	
m #s					126-129	130-144	145-161	162-175	derived from mm. 18-32
section	**Cries 3**		**Dance 2**				**(coda)**		
m #s	188-196		197-215				216-229		
sub-section	**g**		**intro**	**w**	**w¹**	**w**	**w¹**	**w¹**	**w¹**
m #s	188-196		197-199	200-203	204-209	210-215	216-218	219-222	223-229
	elements of c, d, & e derived from mm 59-80								

CHART 25.2 Jolivet, *Chant de Linos*: Thematic analysis.

emphasize the tritone polarity with the preceding lament's final, G. After another lament, the shrieks resume: "c" and "e" use one mode, "d" and "f" a different one, though the two sets are both built on C♯ and share four other tones.

The first set of cries consists of shrieks "a" and "b," the second set, shrieks "c–f," and the third set, shriek "g." One pattern underlies these seven shrieks: a "rocket," a flute arabesque ornamenting the atmosphere near the rocket's apex, and a fall. Shriek "a" in the flute illustrates this pattern: rocket, m. 34; arabesque, mm. 35–36; fall, mm. 37–38. The piano participates with its own rockets, m. 34 and mm. 35–36, and fall, mm. 37–38.

The rest of the shrieks vary the pattern in subtle ways. For example, in shriek "c," the flute rockets "canonically" one measure after the piano, sustains the high tessitura for two measures (61–62), but does not fall. Rather, the flute, again following the piano's lead a measure earlier, launches its shriek "d" with a rocket (m. 63), followed by an arabesque (m. 64) and another rocket (m. 65), before falling for two measures. The flute in shriek "f" rises first gradually, then precipitously to the highest pitch Jolivet employs, an unsustained, unornamented d^4. The line then falls quickly to $e\flat^2$, which resolves down to d^2, the final of the subsequent dance, whose pitch set is simply a transposition of the piece's first collection on G down a perfect fourth to D. Shriek "g" (mm. 188–196) occurs just before the final dance and is composed of elements of shrieks "c" (mm. 59–61), "d" (mm. 65–66), "e" (mm. 73 and 75), and "f" (mm. 79–80).

The two dances make up well over half of the work's 229 measures. Even at its lively tempi, the first dance's duration, according to Jolivet's metronome markings, is over three times that of the next longest section. Formally, the dance is divided by character, tempi, and thematic material into halves: the first frenzied, almost chaotic; the second lyrical and slightly slower.

The principal characteristics of the subsection labeled "w" on Chart 25.2 are the piano accompaniment in m. 85 (carried over from mm. 81–84), which will be identified as "H," and the flute pattern in m. 85, identified as "I." "I" may be analyzed as a repeated pitch on the first dotted quarter, usually an eighth note and four sixteenths, followed by an "excursion" of eight sixteenth notes. After six measures of this, the flute extends its excursion for two measures. At m. 93, the piano forgoes "H" and takes over "I," which a measure later it relinquishes to the flute before reclaiming it in mm. 95–96.

The primary characteristics of "w^1" (mm. 97–99 and 101–103) are "I" back in the flute and a new accompaniment figure, "J," in the piano. In mm. 100 and 104 the piano extends the excursion of the flute's preceding "I" while the flute takes over "J."

Starting in m. 105, "x" is a seven-measure interlude, a break from "H," "I," and "J." The piano's first three measures are imitated by the flute, with a one-measure extension leading to a variant of "w."

The return of "w" at m. 112 is mostly a transposition up a major third of m. 85. The passage from mm. 120–126 corresponds to 93–96 plus an extension of two measures in which the flute, accompanied by "J," sweeps down from b^3 to arrive, at m. 126, on $E\flat^2$ and the beginning of dance 1b.

Like dance 1a, 1b is in ternary form. Its first element is characterized by "K," the two-measure accompaniment pattern starting at m. 126 (a pattern that is extended by a measure starting at mm. 130 and 133 and by two measures at m. 136), and by "L," the lyrical melody of mm. 130–132, 133–135, and, extended by a measure, 136–139. New material is introduced at m. 140: "M," a one-measure figure in the piano ("M^1," melodically reversed and extended at m. 143), and "N" in the flute, likewise one measure long, likewise reversed and extended at m. 143.

Dance 1b's contrasting middle section, "z," is dominated by "O" (piano, m. 145) and its closely related variant in the flute, "P" (m. 153). These are both single-measure figures, often extended by a falling measure in the flute (mm. 147, 150, 156) or rising in both instruments (m. 161). This section can be seen as (1) an eight-measure introduction in which the flute first functions as an extension of "O" and then participates in it, followed by (2) a four-measure passage in which both instruments offer their versions of "O," and (3) a five-measure passage in which both instruments offer slight variations of what they did in the preceding four measures.

At m. 162, we return to a variant of "y" with "K" in the piano, joined a measure later by, not "L" as at m. 130, but an equally lyrical four-measure "Q," followed at m. 167 by "Q^1," which ascends to c^4 and then falls as the piano rises. The first dance dissolves in mm. 172–175, with only a hint of the formerly hard-driving "K" in the piano.

Subsection "w" returns in the final dance (mm. 197ff.) and coda. A three-measure introduction sets up the familiar "H" and "I" at m. 200, then "w^1" with "I" and "J" at m. 204, returning to "w" at m. 210. Beginning on a grand unison D at m. 216, the coda consists of three-, four-, and seven-measure versions of "w^1." The last of these, with "J" back in the piano, hammers home D, the final of the ancient Phrygian mode. Jolivet chose this mode for the coda, knowing that it "was once condemned by Plato because of its Dionysiac passion."[18]

Performing *Chant de Linos*, five conservatory students, including the twenty-two-year-old Jean-Pierre Rampal, were awarded the *premier prix* in 1944. Rampal reported that he and Pol Mule were "the only candidates to master the difficulties of the piece to the point of performing it from memory."[19] A short time later, Jolivet felt that the piece needed a richer setting and prepared a second version for flute, string trio, and harp, which was premiered on June 1, 1945.

Jolivet later wrote four other works for the flute: Concerto for Flute and Strings, 1949; Sonata for Flute and Piano, 1958; *Suite en concert* for flute and four percussion,

1965; and *Ascènes* for Alto Flute, 1967. And beginning in January 1945, he was also able to realize his childhood dream, becoming a member of the Comédie-Française—as its music director.

Notes

1. Lucie Kayas, *André Jolivet* (Paris: Fayard, 2005), 23, 25, trans. William Wilsen.
2. Kayas, 33.
3. Hilda Jolivet, *Avec . . . André Jolivet* (Paris: Flammarion, 1978), 60.
4. Jane F. Fulcher, *The Composer as Intellectual: Music and Ideology in France 1914–1940* (New York: Oxford University Press, 2005), 302.
5. Martine Cadieu, "A Conversation with André Jolivet," *Tempo* 59 (Autumn 1961): 3.
6. Robert Sherlaw Johnson, *Messiaen* (Berkeley: University of California Press, 1989), 10.
7. Kayas, 200.
8. Kayas, 269.
9. Kayas, 271.
10. Kayas, 274.
11. Kayas, 287.
12. Benjamin Tucker, "Atonality, Modality, and Incantation in Two Works for Trumpet by André Jolivet" (DMA diss., University of Arizona, 1994), 18, quoted in Bryan Arthur Guarnuccio, "André Jolivet's Chant de Linos (1944): A Sentential Analysis" (master's thesis, Bowling Green State University, 2006), 3.
13. Kayas, 320.
14. Kayas, 339.
15. Kayas, 133.
16. Lucie Kayas, Association "Les amis d'André Jolivet." "Biography, Introduction" http://www.jolivet.asso.fr, accessed July 28, 2011.
17. P. G. Bergfors, liner notes for André Jolivet, *Chant de Linos*, trans. Linda Schenck. Goran Marcussen, flute, Joakim Kallhed, piano, Intim Musik, IMCD 040.
18. Written by André Jolivet and copied into correspondence between Mrs. André Jolivet and Joan Butterfield, Oct. 3, 1975. Quoted in Joan Butterfield, "André Jolivet: His Life, Musical Style, and an Analysis of his Composition Chant de Linos for Flute, Violin, Viola, Violoncello and Harp" (master's thesis, California State University, San José, 1976), 25.
19. Kayas, 342.

26 Bohuslav Martinů—First Sonata for Flute and Piano

BOHUSLAV MARTINŮ (1890–1959) grew up in a church tower 193 steps above the small Bohemian town of Polička. A devastating fire a half-century earlier had destroyed much of the town and convinced the citizens and church authorities that the rebuilt St. James tower should include an apartment whose occupant would alert people to fires and, in addition, wind the clock and toll the bell. Ferdinand Martinů, a humble, hardworking cobbler, accepted the position in 1889. A year later, on December 8, he excitedly rang the church bell and with a handheld megaphone shouted to the townspeople below, "It's a boy!"[1]

For eleven years, Bohuslav lived with his family in the cramped quarters of the tower. At age seven, he began violin lessons, regarded in the culture as "almost . . . a requirement for the proper education of a boy."[2] He practiced diligently and progressed rapidly, leading the people of Polička to raise money to support his attendance at the Prague Conservatory. Passing the entrance exams in September 1906, he moved to Prague the following January, just after his seventeenth birthday. Though Martinů found Prague's cultural life captivating and developed a lifelong friendship with violinist Stanislav Novák, he struggled with the strict and, for him, stultifying demands of the school. On June 4, 1910, he was expelled for "incorrigible negligence." A second attempt, encouraged by Novák in 1922—this time to study composition under Josef Suk—was also unsuccessful.

During the years following his first expulsion, Martinů was at loose ends, dividing his time between Polička and Prague.[3] He passed the state teachers' examination in 1912 but was unable to secure a position in Polička until 1916. He composed assiduously (over thirty works in 1912 alone) and, thanks to Novák's influence, began to play in the Czech Philharmonic. In 1919 he was selected for the ensemble's tour of London, Paris, and Geneva. Tantalized by his first glimpse of life in foreign lands, he longed to return to Paris. When in 1923 the Czech Ministry of Education offered a three-month travel scholarship for study in the French capital, he packed his manuscripts and boarded a train, determined to meet Albert Roussel, explore new, unfettered compositional styles, and develop his own distinctly personal voice.

Martinů lived in poverty during his first years in the city, a situation that eased only gradually after he met and, in 1931, married Charlotte Quennehen. A seamstress who devoted her life to him, she worked long hours so that he would be free to compose. Meanwhile, Martinů's work was encouraged by Roussel, in whom Martinů found "all that I came to look for in Paris."[4] Roussel reciprocated this admiration, declaring on the occasion of his sixtieth-birthday celebration in 1930, "My glory—that will be Martinů."[5]

In 1932 Martinů's string sextet won the Elizabeth Sprague Coolidge Prize for chamber music, and two years later his ballet *Špalíček* won the Bedřich Smetana Prize. He was developing both a distinctive style and a growing reputation. He composed prolifically, writing as many as twenty pieces in a single year.

During his years in Prague, Martinů had begun the lifelong habit of taking long solitary evening walks. He used this time to reflect on music he had just heard and to work out new compositions in his head. His ability to create pieces in this way—sometimes more than one at a time—contributed to his being able to write out compositions quickly and, at least on paper, to revise them only rarely. David Diamond recalled that Martinů, after his arrival in New York, walked down Sixth Avenue one day hearing an entire piece that he wanted to compose. When he got back to his apartment, he wrote the whole thing down, completing it in a day.[6]

Martinů returned to his homeland for several weeks in July 1938, having no idea that it would be his last visit. On March 15 of the following year, German troops invaded and took over Bohemia. From Prague Castle, Hitler proclaimed Bohemia and Moravia a German protectorate; Czechoslovakia ceased to exist. By June 1940, Paris had begun to fall. The Martinůs' good friend, pianist Rudolf Firkušný, telephoned to say that he was about to flee. Firkušný was so alarmed by Martinů's weary reply

> that he went to see him and found him in a trance-like state, without any protective plan. He had to yell at him in Czech and then to Charlotte in French.

After he got their attention, he ordered them to pack quickly and find a train to the south. It took this violent command to get Martinů moving.[7]

Thus began an arduous nine-month journey—to Rançon, then on to Aix-en-Provence, Marseilles, Madrid, Lisbon, and, finally, to freedom in America. The Martinůs learned later that the day after their departure from Paris, the Gestapo had visited their apartment looking for the composer.[8]

With little money, four manuscripts, and only a few other belongings, the Martinůs finally arrived in New York on March 31, 1941. Greeted by Miloš Šafránek and other old friends, they began the long process of assimilating into their new environment: "English is difficult, but I'll get it," Martinů wrote to his family.[9]

In time, he recovered from the ordeal of his escape and acculturation and resumed his work. In 1942, Boston Symphony Orchestra music director Serge Koussevitzky offered a commission for an orchestral work (which became Martinů's First Symphony) and a summer teaching position at the Berkshire Music Center at Tanglewood, both of which helped immensely. The following year he had major works premiered by the Cleveland Orchestra (under Erich Leinsdorf), the New York Philharmonic (Artur Rodzinski), the Philadelphia Orchestra (Eugene Ormandy), and the Boston Symphony (Koussevitzky).

Martinů lived in New York City and the surrounding area during his years in the United States but spent summers in other places along the east coast. In 1945, the war having ended, he thought of moving back to his homeland, but on the recommendation of Nadia Boulanger,[10] he decided to spend the summer in South Orleans, on Cape Cod, to get his thoughts in order. Here at the height of his career, he composed his First Sonata for Flute and Piano. (He never wrote another.) He dedicated the piece to Georges Laurent, principal flutist of the Boston Symphony, whom he had gotten to know during his summers at the Berkshire Music Center.

Soaring from the tonic E♭ in the lowest register of the piano, a bold series of arpeggios introduces the first theme of the work. The rhythmic vitality of this theme suggests the influence of Czech folk music, which often colored Martinů's compositions.[11] A modulatory passage redolent of Debussy (mm. 12–15) leads to a restatement of the theme, now in A♭ major but returning to E♭ just before the flute enters.

Martinů often spun expansive melodies from cells (a process known as *Fortspinnung*).[12] The flute's initial line is an example of this. The character then changes suddenly to a playful sixteenth-note passage that begins in contrary motion between flute and piano and builds to a *forte* cantabile restatement of the first theme, this time accompanied by murmuring sixteenth notes (mm. 40ff.). With this statement Martinů begins the large-scale "A^1" section, an inventively varied presentation of earlier material, including, in mm. 60–67, a lively figure derived from the movement's first theme (mm. 3ff.).

Like Debussy, Martinů believed that "every work produces its own form"[13]: he did not adhere to traditional structures. A constantly modulating "B" section, the second part of which is a rhythmically and metrically sophisticated (but simply notated) piano solo, concludes with a long descending passage (mm. 126ff.) leading to the same low E♭ that opened the work. A reprise of the second half of "A" (mm. 15–39) begins at m. 133, followed by a complete, literal restatement of "A^1." A short coda moves from F major to B♭, concluding the movement in one of the keys in which Martinů seemed to feel most at home.[14]

While Martinů's formal designs in this sonata elude facile classification, he does return at the end of each movement to a full, exact restatement of the principal section in its original key: "A–A^1–B–A^2–A^1–coda" in the first movement, "A–B–C–D–A–coda" in the second, and "A–B–C–C–D–A" in the third.

The middle movement also begins on a low E♭, but in contrast to the first, here the two instruments outline a minor chord. The subsequent measures (4–13) reveal a continuously evolving tonality, eventually settling on B♭ major to conclude the section.

With the beginning of the central portion of the movement, one hears the same ominous sound, again back in E♭ minor and beginning with a variation of the movement's opening. Divided into three sections, "B," "C," and "D" (mm. 16–28, 29–41, and 42–55), the whole of this central portion includes sixteenth-note subdivisions that animate the movement. Only at the end of sections does the motion slow before Martinů unleashes renewed animation.

After "A" and "B," each beginning in E♭ minor and modulating to B♭ major in mm. 13 and 20, respectively, Martinů, in m. 27, hints at E♭ major but instead, by means of a deceptive cadence, moves on to F minor. As is often the case in his music, pedal points underpin this sometimes dissonant piano solo, giving the passage a sense of F and B♭ as pitch centers,[15] interrupted by a moment of atonality (m. 33) before returning to B♭ major and moving on to B♭ minor and F minor. A new section, "D," begins with the flute playing delicate arabesques. This section builds to a climax in m. 50, then gradually subsides into the reprise of the movement's opening and a coda, which, from m. 72 on, is in E♭ major, colored in mm. 74–78 by the G♭s and C♭s of the parallel minor in which the movement began.

The third movement opens with a cell (two sixteenth-note pickups followed by an eighth) from which Martinů builds a longer theme. Between the three versions of this melody (at mm. 1, 12, and 23), Martinů introduces a new gesture, beginning at the end of m. 5 and revealing itself as a canon with the lower voice imitating the upper an octave lower and one beat later. From these two elements, Martinů creates a rhythmically masterful, energetic introduction, near the end of which this figure appears:

EXAMPLE 26.1 Martinů, First Sonata for Flute and Piano, Mvt. 3, mm. 25-27.

Charlotte Martinů explains the origin of this motive in her book *My Life with Bohuslav Martinů*:

> We found a small injured bird which was black with a bluish belly. We took care of it and when it had recovered, Bohuš taught it to fly. It sang under our window which is why in Bohuš's *Sonata for Flute and Piano*, the theme of this song by the bird, called 'Whippoorwill,' has been repeated.[16]

Following the call of the whippoorwill, the flute enters with the principal theme, built on the movement's opening motive.

As he had done in the first two movements, Martinů creates a soaring, expressive melody (mm. 59ff.) accompanied by energizing sixteenth notes. The flute joins the rhythmic frenzy, which leads to a short reprise of the principal theme (mm. 79–82), followed by a reminder of the whippoorwill (mm. 85–90).

New contrasting sections begin in measures 91, 109, 124 (essentially identical to 109), and 139, a development of the movement's principal theme (mm. 30ff.). While not notated in a slower tempo, fewer rhythmic subdivisions and softer dynamics create a different mood for the first three of these sections.

The whippoorwill's song begins the retransition, the latter part of which (mm. 165–170) can be construed to function in any of four keys: B♭ or F minor, D♭ or A♭ major. As in the other movements, Martinů reprises the entire fifty-three-measure "A" section. In the codetta, the flute and piano once more remind one of the whippoorwill that made such an impression on the man who gently guided it back to health.

In September 1945, the Martinůs returned to New York City, where Bohuslav taught one day a week at the Mannes School. The war now over, Charlotte wanted to move back to Europe; Bohuslav was ambivalent. The growing rift between them deepened when, a week before their departure on a trip to Europe in the spring of

1946, Koussevitzky again invited Bohuslav to teach at the Berkshire Music School. Charlotte was crushed by her husband's decision to accept the offer. As she left to visit her family in Paris, he went to Tanglewood, where he developed a relationship with the young composer Roe Barstow.

Suddenly, on July 25, the Martinůs' world was further upended when Bohuslav fell from the balcony outside the second-floor room where he was staying. He was in a coma for several days, and in addition to four broken ribs, he suffered serious head and ear injuries that caused disruption of balance, partial deafness, and buzzing noises in his head.[17] He was hospitalized for five weeks, after which he endured a long, painful recuperation at the home of his dear friend Frank Rybka. When Charlotte returned in November, she found her husband withdrawn, irritable, and unable to cope with even the slightest noise.[18] Just as he was experiencing his greatest professional success, this accident caused a devastating setback. He found it difficult to compose, and with medical bills mounting, the couple's financial circumstances deteriorated rapidly to the point where Charlotte had to go back to work as a seamstress in a garment factory.[19]

For several years, Martinů struggled to compose and remained indecisive about a return to Europe. Finally, in 1953 he and Charlotte returned to Paris, then moved to Nice. After a brief return to New York in 1955, the couple moved to Switzerland, where in 1959, at the age of sixty-eight, the composer died and was buried. On the twentieth anniversary of his death, his remains were reinterred in his family's grave in Polička.

Notes

1. F. James Rybka, *Bohuslav Martinů: The Compulsion to Compose* (Lanham, MD: Scarecrow Press, 2011), 1–2.
2. Rybka, 7.
3. Rybka, 26.
4. Bohuslav Martinů, "Albert Roussel," *La Revue musicale*, Paris, 1937, quoted in Brian Large, *Martinů* (London: Duckworth, 1975), 37.
5. Miloš Šafránek, *Bohuslav Martinů: His Life and Works*, trans. Roberta Finlayson-Samsourová (London: Allan Wingate, 1962), 95.
6. Rybka, 134.
7. Rybka, 91–92.
8. Rybka, 92.
9. Martinů to his family, August 27, 1941, Martinů Center letters, quoted in Rybka, 107.
10. Charlotte Martinů, *My Life with Bohuslav Martinů* (Prague: Orbis, 1978), 86.
11. Olivier Messiaen, broadcast interview on WABC radio station, New York, August 4, 1942, quoted in Large, 140.

12. Kimberly Walter-Clark, "Bohuslav Martinů's Three Works for Flute, Violin and Keyboard" (DMA document, University of Houston, 1999), 23.

13. Walter-Clark, 22.

14. Large, 144.

15. Walter-Clark, 55.

16. Charlotte Martinů, 86.

17. Large, 95.

18. Large, 96.

19. Šafránek, 256.

27 Olivier Messiaen—*Le merle noir*

OLIVIER MESSIAEN (1908–1992) was five years old when, in July 1914, the world went to war. His father, Pierre, a translator, English teacher, and scholar who produced a complete French translation of Shakespeare's works, joined the French army while his mother, poet Cécile Sauvage, took their two sons to Grenoble, where the three lived with Cécile's mother for the duration of the war. It was here, at the foot of the Alps, that the sights and sounds of the countryside made profound, lifelong impressions on the young Olivier. Many years later, he recalled:

> Here I spent the formative years of my life. . . . I have never forgotten Grenoble with its marvelous mountain landscape, and every year, during the three months of the summer, I come to one of the loveliest places in the region [Petichet], simply to compose music. . . . It was in Grenoble that I realized I was a musician. I was seven-and-a-half and had just been bought, from Deshairs [Grenoble's largest music shop], [a score of] Gluck's *Orphée*.[1]

The Messiaen family was reunited following the armistice in November 1918. After six months in Nantes, where Olivier had his first lessons in piano and harmony, they moved to Paris: Pierre Messiaen had accepted a teaching position at the

Lycée-Charlemagne. Olivier dates that year, 1919, as the start of his studies at the Paris Conservatory.[2] He was ten.

Among his professors, Maurice Emmanuel, Marcel Dupré, and Paul Dukas made lasting impressions. Emmanuel taught music history and sparked Messiaen's interest in ancient modes and non-Western music[3]; Dupré, his organ professor, recommended him for the position of organist at "La Trinité" (église de la Sainte-Trinité), in the ninth arrondissement, a post he won at the surprisingly young age of twenty-two and held for sixty-one years, until his death in 1992; and Dukas reminded him, "Listen to the birds. They are great masters."[4]

Messiaen's conservatory studies ended in 1930, a year after he won the coveted Diplôme d'études musicales supérieures, awarded in recognition of multiple first prizes—in Messiaen's case, organ, fugue, music history, and piano accompaniment, including score reading and improvisation.[5] During the course of his studies, he won ten other conservatory prizes, including the *premier prix* in composition.[6] Only the Prix de Rome eluded him.

Messiaen married violinist Claire Delbos in 1932 and launched his career as organist and composer. Also that year he was elected to the selection committee of the Société nationale de musique, the leading forum for contemporary French chamber and piano music. In 1934, as he was reviewing hundreds of scores for the society, he discovered an outstanding string quartet. Writing to its composer, André Jolivet, three years Messiaen's senior, he declared: "Monsieur, you write the music I would like to write. Can we meet?"[7] The two formed a close friendship, joining forces in the contemporary music group La Spirale and shortly thereafter as two of the four members of La Jeune France.

Also during the 1930s, Messiaen began teaching at the École normale de musique and the Schola Cantorum and completed *La nativité du Seigneur*, a set of nine meditations for organ. Through this seminal composition and the Boston Symphony's American premiere of *Les offrandes oubliées* under Serge Koussevitzky, Messiaen began to draw international recognition.

In the midst of his developing career and happy domestic life with Claire and their son Pascal (born in 1937), Messiaen was called to war in September 1939, serving as a manual laborer and then a medical orderly.[8] His unit surrendered to German forces at Verdun in June 1940, and in July he was transported to a camp in Silesia where he spent nearly nine months. As described by Charles Jourdanet:

> This Stalag [prisoner of war camp], like many others in Germany, was no holiday camp. [. . .] But these were not concentration camps either. Protected by the Geneva Convention and visited by the International Red Cross, the

> prisoners of war were often able to benefit from better living conditions, particularly in the areas of sport and culture.[9]

Messiaen clung to a small collection of miniature scores—Bach, Berg, Stravinsky, Debussy, Ravel, and Honegger—that he kept with his few belongings, and a German officer gave him pencils and manuscript paper. It was here at Stalag 8A that Messiaen composed and, in January 1941, performed in the premiere of one of his most revered works, the *Quatuor pour la fin du temps* for clarinet, violin, cello, and piano.

In March 1941 he sent a jubilant message to his friend Claude Arrieu: "I am free!" Returning to Paris and his position at the Trinité, he was soon appointed by the new director of the Paris Conservatory, Claude Delvincourt, to a position teaching harmony.

Messiaen recalled the 1940s as a period when his creative powers seemed invincible.[10] He was surrounded by a group of extraordinarily gifted students, including Pierre Boulez, Karlheinz Stockhausen, and the pianist Yvonne Loriod; he wrote *Technique de mon langage musical*, a treatise detailing his compositional methods; he began teaching a class in aesthetics and analysis that Delvincourt created especially for him; and in 1949 Koussevitzky, whose foundation had commissioned the *Turangalîla-symphonie* four years earlier, invited him to Tanglewood to teach alongside Aaron Copland.

Following the completion of *Turangalîla*, Messiaen entered a period of experimentation and self-doubt. He told his class at the conservatory, "We are all in a profound night, and I don't know where I'm going; I'm as lost as you."[11] His aesthetic uncertainty paralleled turmoil and tragedy in his personal life as Claire, his wife and the mother of his young son, suffered the progressively debilitating signs of early dementia. An unsuccessful operation in 1949 aggravated her condition, and in 1953 she was placed in a nursing home;[12] Messiaen took over all aspects of running the household and caring for his teenaged son.

From early childhood, Messiaen, a devout Catholic, had always looked to "God's musicians" as his inspiration:

> Nature, Birdsong! These are my passions. They are also my refuge. In melancholy moments, when my uselessness is brutally revealed to me . . . What else is there to do except search for the true face of nature, forgotten somewhere in the forest, in the fields, in the mountains, on the seashore, among the birds: For me, it is here that music lives: music that is free, anonymous, improvised.[13]

When Delvincourt commissioned Messiaen to compose a work for the conservatory's 1952 flute concours, Messiaen fused the inspiration he found in nature with another concept he had contemplated for years. As early as 1944, he had shown scores of *Pierrot lunaire* and the *Lyric Suite* to his class and expressed his regret that Schoenberg and Berg had not serialized timbres, dynamics, and durations as they had pitches.[14] In 1946, he noted in his diary, "Develop timbres, durations and nuances along serial principles,"[15] and by 1949 he had put this idea into practice in one of his *Quatre études de rythme*, the short piano piece "Mode de valeurs et d'intensités" ("Organization of durations and dynamics"). The final section of *Le merle noir* ("The Blackbird"), written in March 1952,[16] continues along these lines.

The work is in three large sections (A-A¹-B). Each "A" is divided into three subsections, those in "A¹" being slightly extended variations of those in "A."

A: mm. 1–8: Modéré & cadenza;
mm. 9–35: Presque lent;
mm. 36–43: Un peu vif
A¹: mm. 44–53: Modéré & cadenza;
mm. 54–82: Presque lent;
mm. 83–90: Un peu vif
B: mm. 91–125: Vif

In the "B" section Messiaen serializes both pitch and duration.

The piano plays a blurred chromatic gesture, *pianissimo*, in the instrument's lowest octave to open the piece. A mood of quiet, nocturnal mystery is established. The blackbird introduces itself in m. 3, featuring abrupt changes of dynamics and short melodic fragments, each of which begins with a quick note or burst of notes and ends with a longer one. Messiaen strives to reproduce the blackbird's song as precisely as possible, though he acknowledged that, when transcribed for a standard musical instrument like the flute, the birdsong is necessarily compromised: the bird's pitches have to be lowered, the pace slowed, and the original song's microintervals expanded to a half-step, the smallest interval available on the instrument. He also admitted that, though he was proud of the accuracy of his work, "those who are truly familiar with birds cannot recognize them in my music. Evidently . . . I introduce something of my own style, my own way of listening, when interpreting the bird songs."[17]

Messiaen said that the blackbird's song is "at once solemn and mocking" and mentions the tritone as one of the intervals on which its song is based. Here, in the first cadenza (mm. 3–8), he emphasizes, through frequent use, four pitch classes, A, E♭, D, and G♯, which, when paired, produce two tritones. These same four pitches are also the most prominent notes in the second cadenza (mm. 46–53), a unifying feature.

Messiaen excludes one pitch, B♭, from the first cadenza, believing that "colour comes from a choice of chromaticism. If you play a cluster, you play all the notes at once and there are no colours. You get grey or black—colours are absent. To produce colours you must suppress something. . . . [I]f you have eleven notes out of the twelve or ten notes out of the twelve, that produces a colour."[18] B♭ appears in the piano at the beginning of the second subsection of "A" (m. 9) but does not appear in the birdsong until near the end of the second cadenza (m. 52). The B♭ in m. 53, a *f* < *ff* > *ppp* flutter tongue, is the longest note of either cadenza. The chromatic completion thus achieved is a technique Messiaen and other composers used as a means of unifying and concluding a section of music.

The beginning and end of each cadenza contribute another unifying element. The first cadenza ends with the same five notes that the piano played to open the work, now four octaves higher. This time, however, the descending portion of the line is omitted, leaving the phrase "open" and suggesting that the birdsong is not complete. The second cadenza, more active than the first, is preceded by the same gesture with which the piece began, but this cadenza's penultimate moment has a chromatic figure descending to E, suggesting closure. It is followed by a two-note "quizzical" farewell.

Messiaen had strong ideas about rhythm, once declaring, "I totally despise even beats and even tempos. I not only hate military music, I also detest jazz because it depends on even beats. My music depends on uneven beats as in nature."[19] During his student days at the Paris Conservatory, he had studied Indian and ancient Greek music, and he adopts rhythmic concepts from these sources, using multiples of the shortest note value in much of his music, including *Le merle noir*. Through the principal of additive rhythm, Messiaen achieves an independence of rhythm from meter. This is in keeping with the asymmetry of birdsong. It is clear then that Messiaen's use of bar lines delineates not regular metrical groupings but rather phrasing within the birdsong.

The second subsection of "A" (mm. 9ff.), with a fixed dynamic of *mf* until its final measures, begins with a melody used in "Jardin du sommeil d'amour" of Messiaen's *Turangalîla-symphonie* and is perhaps an attempt to suggest the bird's habitat or may be Messiaen's "way of presenting the emotion which birdsong produces when recollected in tranquility."[20] Underpinning the long, lyrical phrases of this melody is a series of chromatically moving tritones, one of Messiaen's preferred intervals (and one of the blackbird's, too, he tells us). Two of the tritones use the pitch classes prominent in the preceding section (E♭ to A and D to A♭).

At the return of this second subsection (m. 54), Messiaen creates a canon between the flute and the right hand of the piano at a distance of ten sixteenth notes. There is another canon at m. 72, this time in three parts at the distance of an eighth.

In the final section of the piece, "B," Messiaen serializes pitch and rhythm in the piano part. He manipulates a series of four rhythmic values: sixteenth note (here designated "1"), eighth note ("2"), dotted eighth ("3"), and quarter ("4"), ordering these durations to create twenty-four different (nonrecurring) presentations of them. If one of four elements appears always in the first position, then a total of only six permutations of the four elements is possible: 1234, 1243, 1324, 1342, 1432, 1423. Placing "2" in the first position creates six more possibilities, likewise "3" and "4," for a total of twenty-four possible sets.

The two hands of the piano present two different permutations of the same four note values. The right hand begins with a sixteenth note ("1"), followed by an eighth, dotted eighth, and quarter. Messiaen then progresses, in mm. 92–98, through the five other permutations possible when starting with the sixteenth note, and he does so in the same order as in the example given above: 1234, 1243, etc. When this cycle is complete, in the middle of m. 98, he begins a second cycle in the right hand, this time starting with the dotted eighth note ("3").

At the same time that the right hand begins its first series of permutations (m. 91), the left hand begins a cycle using the eighth note ("2") to start each of its six permutations after which (m. 98) the quarter note ("4") begins the second cycle in the left hand. In mm. 106–120, the right and left hands exchange the durational sets presented in mm. 91–105. In this way, each hand completes the thirteenth through twenty-fourth permutations of the four-note rhythmic cell. The flute does not participate in this rhythmic ordering.

With regard to pitch, the prime form of the twelve-tone row (P0) occurs initially in the piano's right hand (mm. 91–94). This is followed by three more complete statements of the prime version of the row, each a half-step higher (P1, P2, P3) than the previous occurrence: B♭ in m. 94, B in m. 98, and C in m. 102. At the same time that the right hand is presenting P0, the left begins with a retrograde inversion of the same row (RI5). In the same way as the right hand, its three subsequent appearances are presented one half-step higher (RI6, RI7, RI8) in mm. 94, 98, and 102.

In mm. 106–120 the hands exchange pitch sets just as they exchange durational sets. The right hand, through the middle of m. 113, now presents pitch sets RI5 and RI6, while the left hand offers pitch sets P0 and P1. From the middle of m. 113 through m. 120, the right hand presents pitch sets RI7 and RI8, the left hand, sets P2 and P3.

Meanwhile, the flute chatters away, not participating in the serialism but instead displaying a tendency toward ostinato. Messiaen also "colors" the flute line by avoiding B♮ throughout the "B" section. As in the cadenzas, the flute focuses on several pitches (A, G♯, G) and adds others to develop each fragment. The piece ends with three resonant piano crashes spanning d^4 to A_2 and a flute flourish culminating on g^3 followed by the flute's only *fff* on its only c^4 (surely not V-I!).

In contrast to his many lengthy works with huge orchestrations, *Le merle noir*, lasting just over five minutes, is Messiaen's shortest composition. It is also one of only three published chamber works in his oeuvre, the others being the *Quatuor pour la fin du temps* and the *Thème et variations* for violin and piano, which he wrote for Claire Delbos in 1932, the year of their marriage.

Through his daring commission, Claude Delvincourt, who had already been responsible for inviting Eugène Bozza, Henri Dutilleux, and André Jolivet to contribute flute concours pieces, showed that he was serious about "testing not only the students' technique but also their sympathy with avant-garde musical ideas."[21] Meanwhile, Messiaen, in the weeks after completing the commission, embarked on studies with ornithologist Jacques Delamain; during the course of the decade, he composed *Réveil des oiseaux* (1953), *Oiseaux exotiques* (1956), and *Catalogue d'oiseaux* (1958).

Notes

1. Olivier Messiaen, "Discours pour la céremonie du 20 janvier 1984 à Grenoble," typescript of Messiaen's speech when he was made an honorary citizen of the city, quoted in Peter Hill and Nigel Simeone, *Messiaen* (New Haven, CT: Yale University Press, 2005), 12.

2. Hill and Simeone, 16.

3. Hill and Simeone, 19.

4. Olivier Messiaen, *Technique de mon langage musical*, 2 vols. (Paris: Leduc, 1944), vol. 1, 27.

5. Roger Nichols, *The Harlequin Years: Music in Paris, 1917–1929* (London: Thames and Hudson, 2002), 187.

6. Hill and Simeone, 16–17.

7. Hilda Jolivet, *Avec André Jolivet* (Paris: Flammarion, 1978), 83.

8. Antoine Goléa, *Rencontres avec Olivier Messiaen* (Paris: Julliard, 1960), 59, quoted in Christopher Dingle, *The Life of Messiaen* (Cambridge: Cambridge University Press, 2007), 68.

9. Hill and Simeone, 102.

10. Peter Hill, ed. *The Messiaen Companion* (London: Faber and Faber, 1995), 7.

11. Alex Ross, *The Rest Is Noise: Listening to the Twentieth Century* (New York: Farrar, Straus and Giroux, 2007), 451.

12. Hill and Simeone, 209.

13. Olivier Messiaen, quoted in Peter Hill, *Réveil des oiseaux*, Philharmonia Orchestra, http://www.philharmonia.co.uk/messiaen/music/reveil.html, accessed December 26, 2012.

14. Goléa, 247, quoted in Paul Griffiths, *Olivier Messiaen and the Music of Time* (Ithaca, NY: Cornell University Press, 1985), 143.

15. Peter Hill, "The Performance History of Messiaen's *Quatre études de rythme*," paper presented at the 2002 Messiaen conference, Sheffield, June 20–23, 2002, quoted in Dingle, 124.

16. Hill and Simeone, 199.

17. Olivier Messiaen to Claude Samuel, *Entretiens avec Olivier Messiaen* (Paris: Pierre Belfond, 1967), 111–112.

18. Olivier Messiaen to Roger Nichols, quoted in "'Le merle noir': The Case of a Blackbird in a Historical Pie," *Musical Times* 129 (Dec. 1988): 649.

19. Harold C. Schonberg, *The Lives of the Great Composers*, 3rd ed. (New York: Norton, 1997), 608–609.

20. Hill and Simeone, 200.

21. Nichols, "'Le merle noir': The Case of a Blackbird in a Historical Pie," 648.

28 Francis Poulenc—Sonata for Flute and Piano

BORN IN THE HEART of Paris to affluent parents who appreciated literature and the arts, Francis Poulenc (1899–1963) lived his life stimulated by the rich cultural offerings of his native city. His parents entertained leading artists at their Paris apartment and cultivated their son's interest in music, visual art, ballet, and the cinema. With his uncle, the young boy enjoyed concerts, plays, and art galleries.

Poulenc's mother, a well-educated, sophisticated woman and a gifted amateur pianist, encouraged her son's early musical training, and he began piano lessons with her at the age of five. She wanted him to study at the conservatory, but his father, believing in the importance of a general education, thought it better to send him to a lycée.[1]

At fifteen, Poulenc met Ricardo Viñes (1875–1943), a Spanish pianist who had come to Paris years earlier to attend the conservatory and then stayed on for the whole of his successful career. Viñes took the young Poulenc under his wing, nurturing his talent and encouraging his first forays into composition. "I owe him everything,"[2] Poulenc later declared. Viñes was a leading advocate of modern Parisian music and premiered many works of Debussy, Ravel, Satie, and Albéniz. He introduced Poulenc to important Parisian artists, including Georges Auric, who became a lifelong friend.

It was the premiere of the ballet *Parade* (book, Jean Cocteau; music, Erik Satie; costumes and sets, Pablo Picasso) by Serge Diaghilev's Ballets russes on May 18, 1917, that provided the sparks that ignited Poulenc's career. The ballet, which Cocteau called "the greatest battle of the war,"[3] caused infighting among the participants and an uproar among the Montparnasse intellectuals. A group of young French composers rallied around Satie in admiration of his score, Poulenc asserting that "*Parade* is to Paris what *Petrushka* is to St. Petersburg."[4] Satie called them (Darius Milhaud, Louis Durey, Georges Auric, Arthur Honegger, and slightly later Francis Poulenc and Germaine Tailleferre) Les Nouveaux Jeunes. By the end of 1919, they had become a group of artistic consequence.[5]

Unfortunately for Poulenc, he was drafted into the military just as his career was beginning to take off. On January 17, 1918, ten days after his nineteenth birthday, he began three years of service. It "could not have come at a worse time" for the reluctant soldier.[6] Through connections, he was transferred after a year and a half to Paris, where he continued his military service as a typist for the ministry of aviation. This allowed him time to compose and also to gather socially with the other Nouveaux Jeunes composers.

On January 16, 1920, the Parisian critic Henri Collet wrote an article comparing Rimsky-Korsakov's *Ma vie musicale* to Cocteau's *Le coq et l'arlequin: notes autour de la musique* and the work of the Russian Five to Les Nouveaux Jeunes. Collet's subsequent article, "Les Six Français," focused on the six young French composers, forever changing their name from Satie's Les Nouveaux Jeunes to Collet's Les Six.[7] Though their music was dissimilar and their association lasted only a year (Durey leaving Paris for St. Tropez in 1921), the name stuck and public renown grew.

Just after his military discharge, Poulenc began composition studies with Charles Koechlin. The following year Diaghilev commissioned the twenty-two-year-old composer to write *Les biches*, the ballet that became his first triumph.

The success of his family's pharmaceutical firm, Rhône-Poulenc, allowed the composer to devote his attention wholly to music, never having the burden of financial concerns. He kept an apartment in Paris and in 1927 bought a sixteenth-century house in Noizay, a small village in the Loire valley. It was in this quiet, peaceful environment that he composed: "Being wildly visual, everything distracts me, causing me to fritter away my time. I must, therefore, retire into my shell and work in solitude. That is why I cannot work in Paris."[8] At Noizay, he awoke early, composed until noon, and then enjoyed the remainder of the day.[9] He believed music to be more a craft than an art and, as such, "must be an everyday task, devoid of pretention."[10]

Poulenc spent the World War II years in Noizay, interrupted by a brief tour of duty in 1939. Between 1935 and 1959, he toured extensively with the eminent baritone Pierre Bernac, performing at the piano and writing nearly one hundred songs.

In 1953 he began work on his first serious opera. Guido Valcarenghi, director of the Italian publisher Ricordi, had first offered a commission for a ballet to be premiered at La Scala in Milan, but when Poulenc confessed his lack of interest, Valcarenghi suggested instead that Poulenc compose an opera based on Georges Bernanos's *Dialogues des Carmélites*. Poulenc immersed himself in rereading the drama and, convinced that it was written for him, accepted the commission. He launched into the project with great intensity, writing, "I am working like a madman—I don't go out. I see no one . . . I am so obsessed with my subject I am beginning to believe that I know these women."

Composition of the opera occupied him until June 1956. He coped with bouts of depression and later a nervous breakdown as he engaged in a legal struggle to obtain performing rights for the text. The three and a half years he spent on *Dialogues* were monumental, and "the impact would be felt on much of the music he composed in the remaining eight years of his life."[11] *Dialogues des Carmélites* premiered at La Scala on January 26, 1957.

Poulenc had always been attracted to woodwind instruments, this predilection no doubt encouraged by the long-standing tradition of high-quality teaching and playing in Paris. He had begun work on a flute sonata in 1952, but other projects soon claimed his attention. It was not until after he completed *Dialogues* that he returned to the sonata. Keith Daniel, author of *Francis Poulenc: His Artistic Development and Musical Style*, suggests that "given the impact that the opera had on Poulenc's life and style, we should not be surprised that many of the musical motives in the sonata can be traced back to *Dialogues*. . . . Rarely has a [twentieth-century] composer . . . unblushingly used so many common motives in two of his works."[12]

Harold Spivacke, chief of the Music Division of the Library of Congress and representative for the Coolidge Foundation, offered a chamber music commission in April 1956; when Poulenc declined because of work on *Dialogues*, he offered it again a month later. Poulenc accepted the commission in August and composed the piece in Cannes between December 1956 and March 1957. As allowed by the contract, the sonata was premiered at the Strasbourg Festival in June 1957, with Jean-Pierre Rampal, flutist, and the composer at the piano. Rampal and pianist Robert Veyron-Lacroix then gave the American premiere at Coolidge Auditorium at the Library of Congress on February 14, 1958.[13]

The sonata opens in E minor with a descending chromatic line woven into the first theme; thus is the Allegro malincolico ("with melancholy") subtly introduced. With the ascending scale into m. 5, the chromaticism and minor mode give way to two measures in diatonic C major before A♯ and a V/V chord lead back to the tonic key and a variant of the opening theme. At m. 34 (See Chart 28.1), the mood is momentarily lightened by a new theme with new expression and articulation: light and

section	A																					
phrase	a	b	a	c	a	b	a^1	a^2	d	d^1												
# of mm	4	4	4	4 + 2	4	4	4	3	4	3												
starts m#	1	5	9	13	19	23	27	31	34	38												
tonal center	e			C (c)	e	C	a	c#	F													
section	(A continued)												B									
phrase	a^3	a^3	a^4		a	b	a				trans		e	f	e	f^1	g		e^1	g^1		
# of mm	4	4	4		4	4	4+2				3 + 3		3	2+2	3	3	4 + 2		4	3		
starts m#	41	45	49	51	53	57 59	61				67	72	73	76	80	83	86	90	92	96	97	
tonal center	f	e^b	(b^b)	a		(F) (a)					f#	F			D^b	b^b	A	C			a	
section	A^1																			Coda		
phrase	a	b	a	c							trans						g^2			x	(a)	(a)
# of mm	4	4	4	4 + 2							3 + 2						4 + 3			3	2.5	2.5
starts m#	99	103	107	111							117	120					122	126	127	129	132	134.5
tonal center	(a cont'd)		e	C (c)							e	modulation (whole-tone)					E	G	mod	e		

CHART 28.1 Poulenc, Sonata for Flute and Piano: Analysis of the first movement.

"biting," piano without pedal, staccato flute introducing the piece's first accented notes. After seven measures, however, F major turns to F minor, and the opening theme returns, first in the flute, then echoed by a statement in the piano a whole step lower (mm. 45ff.). As heard here, Poulenc the melodist preferred to restate themes in different keys and with different scoring rather than to extract and develop their motives.[14]

Major-minor juxtaposition continues in the "B" section of this ternary-form movement, exemplified in mm. 78–79, where Poulenc echoes the F major material of the preceding measures in the minor mode. Throughout this section, the piano's persistent syncopation contributes an agitated quality. A pedal point on D♭ as the mediant of B♭ minor (mm. 83–85), then C♯ as the mediant of A major (mm. 86–89), adds another element of tension.

Poulenc injects Picardy thirds into the E minor cadential context of mm. 117 and 118, then modulates to E major in two measures that employ the notes of a whole-tone scale on C. Returning to E minor in m. 129, he again colors the final three measures with Picardy thirds in the piano and devilishly incorporates both minor and major thirds (G and G♯) in the final reminiscence of the thirty-second-note gesture that opened the movement.

The prolific composer of songs writes a beautiful Cantilena in B♭ minor as the middle movement of the sonata. (See Chart 28.2) The supple phrase rhythms, rich harmonic language, and original modulations (often simply the juxtaposition of two keys) demonstrate the master's touch behind this outwardly simple creation. When first performed by Rampal and Poulenc, the audience was so enthusiastic that the performers repeated this movement.[15]

Following a two-measure introduction, the first phrase moves through a prolongation of dominant harmony over a tonic pedal (mm. 4–5) to a resolution on the downbeat of m. 6 in the piano, the flute resolving its suspension one beat later. As Poulenc modulates from F minor to A minor in mm. 17 and 18, he makes use of a chromatically altered dominant chord (m. 18) to propel the harmony forward just when one might expect a moment of repose. Time and again, as the flute arrives on sustained notes at the ends of phrases, Poulenc directs the harmony toward the next bar. Approaching the *en animant* in m. 41, he accelerates the harmonic rhythm to eighth notes (mm. 37–39), though ever so light-handedly. Above a bass line that descends chromatically from F to C in mm. 49–51, parallel augmented triads on the third and first beats thwart the sense of key just before the final return to B♭ minor (m. 52) and the delicate coda (mm. 56ff.).

The final movement, Presto giocoso, is a delightful romp in A major. The bright tempo, syncopated jabs, disjointedness, and virtuosity of the opening run headlong into the lyrical "B" section, then on to a truncated "A" and "B." (See Chart 28.3)

section	**A**																		
phrase	**intro**	**a**	**b**	**a**^{1}		**c**		**a**^{2}		**d**	**e**	**e**		**a**^{2}					
# of mm	2	4	4	4		4		4		3	3	2		4					
starts m#	1	3	7	11	13	15	18	19	22	23	26	29	30	31	34				
tonal center	**b**^{b}				**f**		**a**		**g**				**e**^{b}		**f**				
section	**B**															**Coda**			
phrase	**f**	**f**^{1}		**g**	**g**^{1}		**f**^{2}		**trans**							**a**^{2}	**h**		
# of mm	2+2	2		2	3		3		2+5							4	2 +	1*	3
starts m#	35	39	40	41	43	44	46	47	49	52						56	60	62	63
tonal center	**(f cont'd)**		**C**^{b}**/B**			**A**	**f#**	**c**	**D**^{b}	**b**^{b}						**(b**^{b} **continued)**			
																		*elision	

CHART 28.2 Poulenc, Sonata for Flute and Piano: Analysis of the second movement.

section	A					A^1								B						A^2		B^1						A^3
phrase	a	b	c	a	d	a		c	a		d	a		e	e	f	e		(d)	a	b	e	e	(d)	transition			(a)
motive																									Δ †			
# of mm	4	4	4	4	3 +	1*	3	4	4		3 +	1*	3	3	3	3+	1*	2	4	4	4	3	3	2	4+4 + 4 + 4			2+2+2
starts m#	1	5	9	13	17	20	21	24	28	31.5	32	35	36	39	42	45	48	49	51	55	59	63	66	69	71	79	83	87
tonal center	A			E	A			e		E				a			c		A^b			a^b	c			b^b	a	D
					*elision						*elision						*elision								† upbeats to mm. 71, 73, 75, 79, 81			
section	C								(B)																			
phrase	g	h	transition						f																			
motive			Σ		μ	Ω	μ	μ																				
# of mm	4	3	4		2	2	2	2	3+4																			
starts m#	93	97	100	102	104	106	108	110	112																			
tonal center	G	A^b	A	C	e		f	a^b	f																			
section	D												E															
phrase	i	j	i^1		(h)	i	j^1	transition					intro	k §							transition							
motive								$\mu^{extended}$	μ^{ext}	μ	μ	Σ^{ext}	Π								Δ†	$\Sigma^{truncated}$						
# of mm	4	6	4 + 2		4+4	4	2	4	4	2	2	6	3	2+3							8+6	3						
starts m#	119	123	129	133	135	143	147	149	153	157	159	161	167	170	174						175	189						
tonal center	F		A	C	a^b	A^b		b		c	e^b	C	A^b	F#	mod						a							
														§ cf. "e"s & "e^1," mm. 73-95, in Mvt. 1.							† mm. 177, 183, 187							
section	A					C^1			D^1		Coda																	
phrase	a	b	c	a	d	g		(h)	i	j^2																		
motive											Π		$\Delta^{inverted}$															
# of mm	4	4	4	4	3 +	1*	3	2+4	4	2	4+2+4																	
starts m#	192	196	200	204	208	211	212	215	221	225	227	228	230.5	231.5	233													
tonal center	A			E	A				6-m. tonic pedal		d		e^b	C	A													
					*elision																							

CHART 28.3 Poulenc, Sonata for Flute and Piano: Analysis of the third movement.

A transition, beginning in m. 71, leads to an emphatic statement of new material at m. 93. Following four measures of intense trills, the listener is caught off guard when, suddenly, the dynamic softens and the mode changes to minor. A second presentation and expansion of this material (mm. 149–160) ends with a prolonged scream over a frenetic accompaniment. A pregnant pause. Then out of nowhere, a slow, lyrical phrase begins in unaccompanied flute and leads to a five-measure melancholy reminiscence of the "B" section of the first movement, a device Poulenc often employed in his multi-movement instrumental works. From there, he returns to Tempo presto, now in A minor, and featuring a seventeen-measure dominant pedal in the piano with brief interjections by the flute, each louder than the last. Anticipation builds until the dominant resolves to the tonic of the movement, A major, where Poulenc offers us a last *fortissimo* version of "A," along with snippets from other parts of the movement.

Poulenc accompanied several flutists in performances of his sonata and was anxious to have the work published. Clearly he thought well of it. Had he not, evidence suggests that he might have destroyed it, as he had earlier compositions. "After laboring over a string quartet, which he finally finished in 1945, he unceremoniously threw it down a Paris sewer after hearing it once."[16]

During the final five years of his life, Poulenc continued to compose solo woodwind sonatas: in 1962 he completed one for clarinet and one for oboe. He seems to have intended to complete the cycle with a bassoon sonata, but he died suddenly in January 1963 before he had begun work on it.

Notes

1. Keith W. Daniel, *Francis Poulenc: His Artistic Development and Musical Style* (Ann Arbor: UMI Research Press, 1980), 9.

2. Benjamin Ivry, *Francis Poulenc* (London: Phaidon, 1996), 17.

3. Carl B. Schmidt, *Entrancing Muse: A Documented Biography of Francis Poulenc* (Hillsdale, NY: Pendragon, 2001), 35.

4. Harold C. Schonberg, *The Lives of the Great Composers*, 3rd ed. (New York: Norton, 1997), 474.

5. Schmidt, 72.

6. Schmidt, 50–52.

7. Schmidt, 72.

8. Stéphane Audel, ed., *Moi et mes amis* (Paris: La Palatine, 1963), 76, quoted in Daniel, 28.

9. George R. Keck, *Francis Poulenc: A Bio-Bibliography* (Westport, CT: Greenwood Press, 1990), 7.

10. Daniel, 99.

11. Daniel, 51.

12. Daniel, 129–130.

13. Carl B. Schmidt and Patricia Harper, eds., "Historical Introduction" to Francis Poulenc, *Sonata for Flute and Piano*, rev. ed. (London: Chester Music, 1994), ii–iii.

14. Daniel, 59.

15. Ivry, 195.

16. Henri Hell, "Hommage à Francis Poulenc," *Musica* 109 (April 1963): 39, quoted in Daniel, 49.

29 Luciano Berio—*Sequenza*

LUCIANO BERIO'S UPBRINGING suggested that he would become a musician, but no one could have predicted his emergence as a pioneering figure in the avant-garde of the mid-twentieth century. Born in 1925 in Oneglia, on the Mediterranean coast midway between Genoa and Cannes, he grew up in a family of musicians: both his father and grandfather were organists, composers, and leading figures in the town's musical life. By the age of nine, the budding musician was performing as a pianist in his father's chamber music evenings. This was his "oasis of absolute musical happiness" and introduced him to the music of Mozart, Beethoven, Schubert, Schumann, Mendelssohn, Brahms, and Dvořák.[1]

It seemed that World War II might bypass Oneglia, but in the winter of 1944/45, Berio, then nineteen, was conscripted into the army of Mussolini's Italian Social Republic, a Nazi puppet state in the north of Italy, which, dominated by its German masters, was locked in combat with Rome-based, Allied-supported Italy proper (still a monarchy, under Victor Emmanuel III). Berio complied only reluctantly and entered a chaotic situation that would soon force him to give up aspirations of becoming a concert pianist: "on his first day, without any previous instruction, he was given a loaded gun. As he was trying to understand how it worked, it blew up, severely injuring his right hand."[2] He spent three months in a military hospital then faked a discharge, fled to Milan, and subsequently moved on to Como to join the antifascist partisan resistance.[3]

After the war ended, Berio entered the Milan Conservatory, where he studied for six years. (His fine musical background allowed him to begin the ten-year course as a fifth-year student.) In spite of the injury to his hand, he was still able to perform as an accompanist, but now turned primarily to composition. He embarked upon counterpoint studies with Giulio Cesare Paribèni and, in 1948, joined Giorgio Ghedini's composition class. He also studied conducting with Antonio Votto and Carlo Maria Giulini.

While he had performed works of the great classical and romantic masters during his youth in Oneglia, Berio had had no opportunity to become acquainted with the newest works of contemporary composers. Only in 1946, during his first year at the conservatory, did his musical world begin to expand: he was introduced to Schoenberg's *Pierrot lunaire* as well as compositions by Milhaud, Bartók, and Stravinsky.

At twenty-five, as he was completing his studies in Milan, Berio worked briefly as a conductor in provincial Italian opera houses and also as an accompanist. Accompanying put him in contact with Cathy Berberian, a gifted young singer whose virtuosity would inspire many of his early works, most notably the third in the *Sequenza* series. The two married in October 1950.

The following year, his schooling completed, Berio applied for and was awarded a scholarship from the Koussevitzky Foundation to study with Luigi Dallapiccola at the 1952 Berkshire Festival at Tanglewood. During his four-week visit to the United States, in addition to studying with the great composer of lyrical twelve-tone pieces, Berio also attended the first American concert ever to include electronic music (October 28, 1952, New York's Museum of Modern Art, music of Varèse, Luening, and Ussachevsky). Enthralled with the new genre, he contacted RAI, the Italian national radio and TV company, upon his return to Italy and in 1953 was commissioned to compose music for a series of TV films. It was also at this time that he created his first tape piece, *Mimusique* no. 1.

The 1950s, the first decade of Berio's professional career, proved an enormously productive time during which he thrust himself into the avant-garde of musical composition. He began to collaborate with Bruno Maderna, opening an electronic studio at RAI in 1955 with Maderna as codirector; together they held the first of a series of electronic music concerts in May 1956. As leading Berio scholar David Osmond-Smith relates, "Berio and Maderna were providing the musical complement to one of Milan's most adventurous decades."[4]

In 1958, having already written orchestral and electronic pieces, Berio turned to chamber and solo compositions, hoping to encourage more frequent performances of his music. He wrote the first of the *Sequenze* in Darmstadt that year for the great

Italian flutist Severino Gazzeloni. Like Berberian's, Gazzeloni's virtuosity inspired Berio to compose this series of fourteen extremely demanding works: thirteen for solo instruments and one for female voice.

Sequenza was originally published (Zerboni, 1958) using proportional rhythmic notation, the first and most famous example of the system. Here, tempo is indicated by demarcations in the score approximately one inch apart. Through most of the piece, each segment represents just less than one second (70 on a metronome), with rhythms indicated by their placement on the page. Notes that are close together are fast while notes that are far apart are of longer duration or have silence between them. "Small gaps between note clusters are little hiccups that momentarily interrupt the line."[5] Notes that are beamed are to be played legato but not slurred, while notes with a single flag are separated; slurred notes are indicated in the customary way.

Paul Roberts, Berio's assistant, relates that the composer originally notated the piece using standard notation. "It was written using very strict serial rhythms and was barred in 2/8 from start to end."[6] Berio then decided to change the notation, explaining: "I considered the piece so difficult for the instrument that I didn't want to impose on the player specific rhythmical patterns. I wanted the player to wear the music as a dress, not as a straitjacket." His new notation, however, was not without drawbacks: "[A]s a result, even good performers were taking liberties that didn't make any sense, taking the spatial notation almost as a pretext for improvisation."[7] Because of his disappointment with performances of the work, Berio asked Roberts to return to the original version and help him produce a score using standard notation. The revised edition was published by Universal in 1992.

Berio's original work on the piece in 1958 occurred as he and Maderna were searching for new sounds and ways of thinking about musical material. Berio began to explore new concepts of structure, considering comparative densities of texture and qualities of timbre as contributors to creating large-scale formal priorities.[8]

Some twenty-two years after composing the *Sequenza*, Berio discussed the piece in an extensive interview with Rossana Dalmonte. In addition to expressing his thoughts regarding virtuosity, Berio offered insights that provide a framework for analyzing *Sequenza*. He defined four dimensions—temporal, dynamic, pitch, and morphological [morphology involves, among other things, "the forms, relations, metamorphoses . . . of organs apart from their functions"][9]—and spoke of comparative densities of each, characterizing them in terms of "maximum, medium and minimum levels of tension."[10] He stated that at least two of the four dimensions are at their maximum level at any given moment in the composition.

With regard to the temporal (rhythmic) dimension, he defined maximum tension as being "produced by moments of maximum speed in articulation and moments of maximum duration of sounds."[11] Certainly, the middle staves of page 4

(Zerboni edition), the climax of the piece, exemplify maximum tension. In contrast, "the medium level is always established by a neutral distribution of fairly long notes and fairly rapid articulations, and the minimum level entails silence, or a tendency to silence."[12]

Regarding the second dimension, dynamics, Berio explained that "[t]he maximum level of the dynamic dimension is naturally produced by moments of maximum sound energy and maximum dynamic contrast."[13] When, as can be seen at the bottom of page 4, following the climax, the dynamic levels are soft and without pronounced contrasts, there is a minimal level of tension.

Pitch is the dimension that has been most thoroughly addressed in analyses of the work.[14] Berio himself never discussed the specific pitch content, commenting only that "[tension in t]he pitch dimension is at its maximum level when notes jump about within a wide gamut and establish the tensest intervals, or when they insist on extreme registers: the medium and minimum levels follow logically from this."[15] Theorists have identified a tone row and traced its varied repetitions through the course of the piece. The variations provide a sense of structure but also lead the melodic identity of the piece toward transformation,[16] a process Berio found most interesting.

The final dimension, the morphological, "seeks to define degrees of acoustic transformation relative to an inherited model [of how the flute produces sound] which in this case is the flute with all its historical and acoustic connotations. Thus a level of maximum tension within the morphological dimension is obtained when the image, *my* image of the flute, is drastically altered with flutter tongues, key clicks and double stops."[17] The flutter-tonguing and key clicks of the morphological dimension contribute to maximum tension on page 4. While the dynamic dimension is at the minimum level at the top of page 5, morphological tension continues with Berio's use of harmonics and multiphonics.

The multiphonics also represent Berio's "desperate search for polyphony with the most monodic instrument in history."[18] Indeed, in addition to the display of virtuosity and the changing densities of the temporal, dynamic, pitch, and morphological dimensions that produce and relieve tension, one of Berio's goals in writing the *Sequenze* was, through the use of dynamics, register, and multiphonics, to create the illusion of polyphony:

> All the . . . *Sequenzas* . . . for solo instruments are intended to set out and melodically develop an essentially harmonic discourse and to suggest, particularly in the case of the monodic instruments, a polyphonic mode of listening. . . . I wanted to establish a way of listening so strongly conditioned as to constantly suggest a latent, implicit counterpoint. The ideal was the "polyphonic" melodies of Bach.[19]

At the age of thirty, Berio created a worthy successor to the innovative solo flute works of Debussy and Varèse. In fact, some believe that the contour of *Sequenza*'s opening three-note motive pays homage to *Syrinx* and *Density 21.5*: all three pieces begin with a descending half-step followed by a melodic turn upward. Had Berio waited just one more year to write the piece, there would be an additional symmetry, each separated by twenty-three years: 1913, 1936, 1959. Over the course of forty-five years, music for solo flute had become a vital new genre of the avant-garde.

Notes

1. David Osmond-Smith, trans. and ed., *Luciano Berio: Two Interviews with Rossana Dalmonte and Bálint András Varga* (New York: Marion Boyars, 1985), 45–46.
2. David Osmond-Smith, *Berio* (Oxford: Oxford University Press, 1991), 3.
3. Osmond-Smith, *Berio*, 3.
4. Osmond-Smith, *Berio*, 14.
5. John Heiss, quoted in Vanessa Breault Mulvey, "Seven 20th-Century Pieces John Heiss Teaches Everyone." *Flute Talk* 22 (July/August 2003): 9.
6. Cynthia Folio and Alexander R. Brinkman, "Rhythm and Timing in the Two Versions of Berio's *Sequenza I* for Flute Solo: Psychological and Musical Differences in Performance," in *Berio's Sequenzas: Essays on Performance, Composition and Analysis*, ed. Janet K. Halfyard (Aldershot, UK: Ashgate, 2007), 15.
7. Theo Muller, "'Music Is Not a Solitary Act': Conversation with Luciano Berio," *Tempo* 199 (1997): 19, quoted in Janet K. Halfyard, ed. *Berio's Sequenzas: Essays on Performance, Composition and Analysis*, 15.
8. Osmond-Smith, *Berio*, 14.
9. *Webster's Third New International Dictionary of the English Language* (unabridged) (Springfield, MA: Merriam, 1981), 1471.
10. Osmond-Smith, *Two Interviews*, 97–98.
11. Osmond-Smith, *Two Interviews*, 98.
12. Osmond-Smith, *Two Interviews*, 98.
13. Osmond-Smith, *Two Interviews*, 98.
14. See, for example, Cynthia Folio, "Luciano Berio's *Sequenza* for Flute: A Performance Analysis," *Flutist Quarterly* 15 (Fall 1990): 18–21, and Irna Priore, "Vestiges of Twelve-Tone Practice as Compositional Process in Berio's *Sequenza I* for Solo Flute," in *Berio's Sequenzas: Essays on Performance, Composition and Analysis*, ed. Janet K. Halfyard, 191–208.
15. Osmond-Smith, *Two Interviews*, 98.
16. David Osmond-Smith, Introduction, in *Berio's Sequenzas: Essays on Performance, Composition and Analysis*, ed. Janet K. Halfyard, 2.
17. Osmond-Smith, *Two Interviews*, 98.
18. Osmond-Smith, *Two Interviews*, 98.
19. Osmond-Smith, *Two Interviews*, 97.

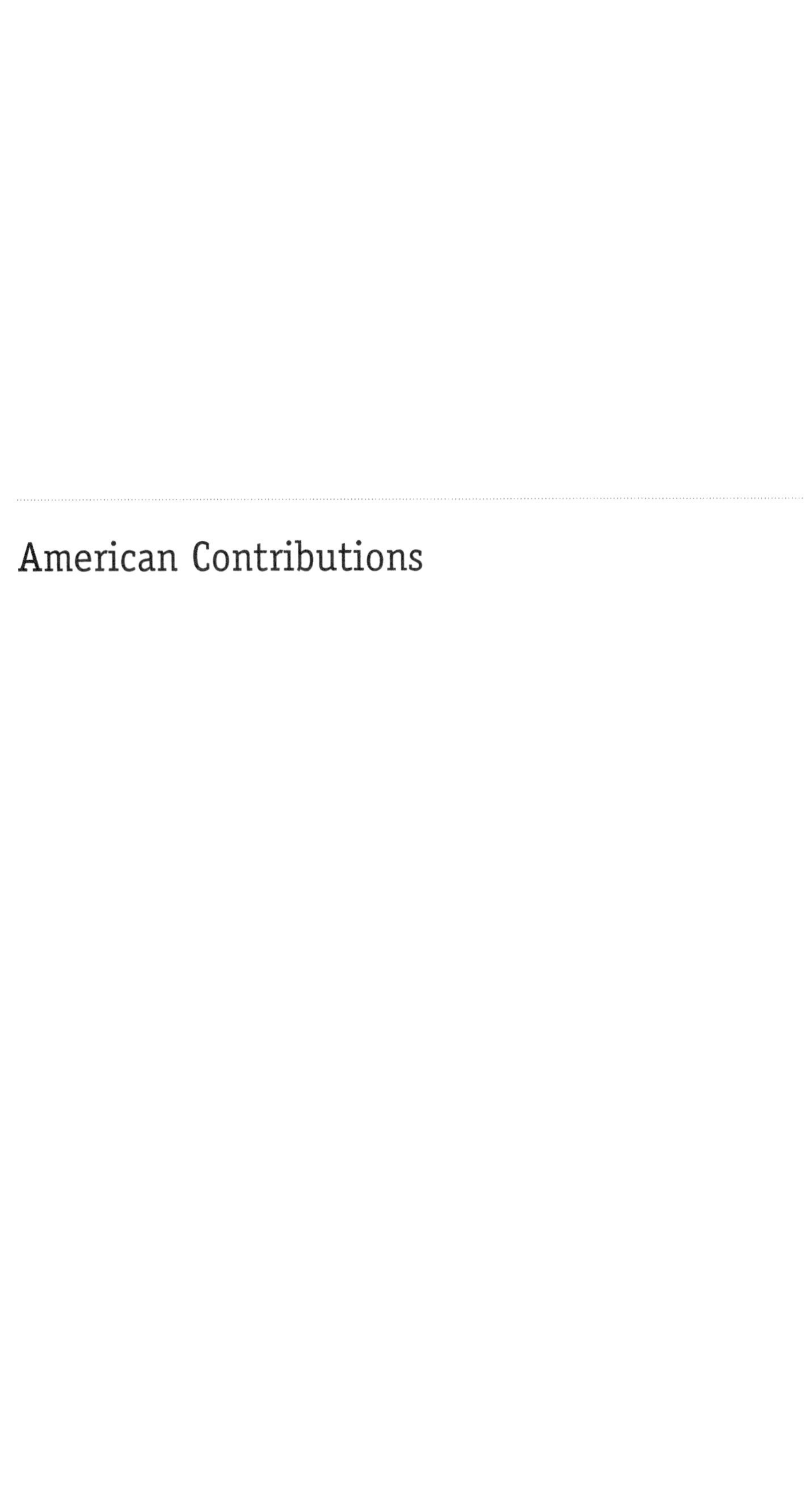

American Contributions

30 Charles Griffes—*Poem* for Flute and Orchestra

BORN THE THIRD of five children to hardworking, middle-class parents, Charles Griffes (1884–1920) grew up in the small town of Elmira, New York, 230 miles northwest of New York City. His older sister Katherine's piano studies prompted his initial interest in learning to play the instrument. She taught him what she could, after which he began lessons with her teacher, Mary Selena Broughton. The eccentric Miss Broughton, born in New Zealand and trained in Berlin as a piano student of Karl Klindworth, had come to America in 1891 to accept a position as professor of piano at Elmira College. It was 1899 when the teenaged Griffes began studies with her. They worked together for four years, Miss Broughton serving as a powerful musical and personal mentor. Griffes wrote his first compositions during these early studies and dedicated the works to her.

As Griffes's graduation from the Elmira Free Academy approached, he knew that he wanted to pursue advanced musical studies toward a career as a pianist and to delve further into composition as well. Like his teacher and many other budding American musicians at the time, he determined to move to Berlin. Miss Broughton offered to lend the money needed to finance his studies, and he departed for Germany in August 1903. Miss Broughton, on summer vacation in Europe, met him just after his arrival to help him get settled.[1]

Griffes entered Berlin's Stern Conservatory (the renowned school where conductor Otto Klemperer and pianist Claudio Arrau subsequently received musical training), studying piano, counterpoint, and composition. By the end of his first year, he had given up the idea of becoming a concert pianist and turned more decisively to composition. "My hands are a fearful nuisance," he would later write to Miss Broughton. "I should like to exchange them for a decent pair."[2]

Griffes loved life in Berlin, soaking up the rich intellectual and cultural atmosphere and enjoying a close relationship with German engineering student Emil Jöel. In 1905, after two years there, he decided to leave the conservatory to pursue composition study with Engelbert Humperdinck while continuing piano lessons with one of his former conservatory teachers. As the third year progressed, he dreamed of a fourth in the cosmopolitan city. But Humperdinck, because of his hectic schedule, discontinued Griffes's lessons in April 1906, and by 1907 the twenty-two-year-old knew that it was time to return home and begin a career.

Shortly after his return to the United States in July 1907, Griffes secured a teaching position at a private boy's boarding school in Tarrytown, New York. Situated in the beautiful Hudson River Valley an hour north of New York City, the town was a favorite summer getaway for the wealthy. Griffes's position at the Hackley School proved to be both a blessing and a burden. His duties included teaching piano lessons, directing the choir, playing hymns at morning chapel services, and giving informal recitals for faculty and students on Sunday evenings. Because music was not a required course, he never knew how many singers he would have in the choir, and he complained that the work was a "deadly bore."[3] Still, the position offered financial security—his salary modest but steady—and proximity to New York City, where he worked hard to advance his career. Griffes wanted a studio in New York, but in spite of scrupulous management of his finances,[4] he was never able to achieve this goal. Instead, he would teach at Hackley until a few months before his death thirteen years later.

During his years at the school, he continued to compose, and he made the hour-long trip into New York City as often as possible to perform, visit musicians, and call on his publisher, G. Schirmer. In 1909 Schirmer published five German songs by Griffes, but the composer then endured much frustration as the company rejected the subsequent works he submitted. "Apparently, Schirmer did not like the direction his music was taking. But to Griffes's credit, he continued on his own path, undeterred by Schirmer's criticism."[5] Gradually he moved away from the influence of his German training and developed his own musical identity. In a letter dated November 30, 1911, he wrote, "One cannot possibly play the new composers much without being influenced by them in one's own compositions. But I do have a deathly fear of becoming one of the dull imitators of the innovators. There are already enough of those."[6]

Things moved ahead slowly as the hardworking Griffes soldiered on for years. In 1917 he began work on his piano sonata and completed *The Pleasure-Dome of Kubla Khan*. Likewise, 1918 proved a productive year during which he composed the *Poem* for flute and orchestra, a piece that would play no small part in his escalating success.

French flutist Georges Barrère had come to the United States in 1905 to serve as principal flutist of the New York Symphony Orchestra under Walter Damrosch. Griffes had arranged several pieces for the Barrère Ensemble of Wind Instruments,[7] and Barrère's favorable impressions led him to request a new work from the young composer.

Griffes was not interested in writing the type of technical showpiece that constituted so much of the flutist's repertoire. A talented painter who was keenly sensitive to color and adored delicate aquarelles,[8] he was inspired by Barrère's sound. Indeed, Barrère had enjoyed renown for the beauty of his tone since his performance as solo flutist in the premiere of Debussy's *Prélude à l'après-midi d'un faune* years earlier. Griffes, striving to showcase the instrument's unique tonal spectrum, which Barrère brought out so eloquently, provided an accompaniment of strings, two horns, harp, and percussion to augment the timbral palette. (This was one of only three orchestral works that he did not arrange from a preexisting piano composition.)[9] He took great care in writing the piece, working closely with Barrère from its early stages through its premiere.

Griffes completed *Poem* in July 1918, and the New York Symphony's premiere was set for November 16 of the following year in Aeolian Hall, an 1,100-seat auditorium in mid-Manhattan that the orchestra used (along with Carnegie Hall) until 1924. After Barrère sent Griffes a postcard on September 16, 1919 ("I am working hard on the *Poem* . . . Help! Am back in town."),[10] the two continued rehearsing, Griffes playing from the orchestral score. Later, Griffes attended rehearsals with Damrosch and the orchestra, listening attentively and conferring with Barrère about cuts, revisions, and rescoring.[11]

By this time, Griffes was beginning to emerge as one of the most imaginative American composers of his time. *Poem* brought together his remarkable gift for lyricism, his rich harmonic palette, his sophisticated handling of instrumental color and texture, and his ability "to assimilate the best around him and stamp it with his own power of expression and individuality."[12] It is the mature composition of a thirty-four-year-old.

The piece, in C♯ minor, is elusive in form but achieves coherence through the recurrence of a motive, Ω (See Example 30.1), that dominates the first part of each of the work's five sections and the refrain that closes all but the third section. Overall, the design may be viewed as outlined in Chart 30.1.

At the start, cellos and basses announce, unadorned, the important Ω motive.

section	**1**								
theme	**Intro**	**A**						**Refrain**	
starts m#	1	9						30	
key	**c#**		**a (A)**						**D^{b}/C#/c#**
starts m#	1		20						41
section		**2**							
theme		**A (tr)**		**B (dev)**				**Refrain**	
starts m#		49		53				75	
key		**(D^{b}/C#/c#)**		**b/d#/e**	**a/A**				
starts m#		(49)		53	66				
section		**3**							
theme		**A (tr)**		**Intro**	**C**				
starts m#		84		94	116				
key		**c#**	**b^{b}/a#**			**C#**	**a#**	**C#/c#**	
starts m#		84	88			132	150	167	
section		**4**							
theme		**A**		**D (Codetta)**				**Refrain**	
starts m#		195		209				259	
key		**(C#/c#)**		**g#**	**atonal/D#/mod**			**a→A**	
starts m#		195		209	241			259	
section		**5**							
theme		**A**						**"Refrain"**	
starts m#		268						281	
key		**c#**							
starts m#		268							

CHART 30.1 Griffes, *Poem* for Flute and Orchestra: Analysis.

EXAMPLE 30.1 Griffes, *Poem* for Flute and Orchestra, Ω motive (m. 1).

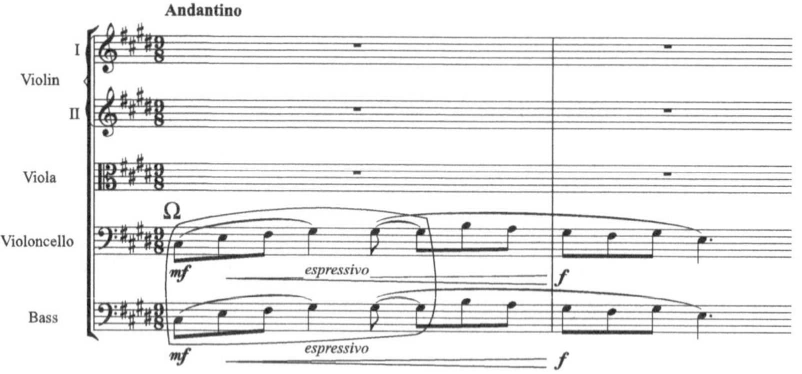

Already in the fifth measure of the introduction, one hears an augmented version of Ω moving from the fifth through the sharp sixth scale degree (A♯, m. 7) directly to the tonic, fresh in its omission of scale degree seven. The flute's presentation of the motive in its original form ushers in the "A" section. The motive, expanded into a lyrical theme, is presented over a tonic pedal point. Griffes uses pedal points throughout the work to establish or reinforce tonal centers.

When the opening melody returns in m. 22, it is introduced by syncopated repetition of the tonic chord (now A minor seventh), just as it had been in m. 8. Variants of the same syncopated figure will be used to effect the transition (mm. 48ff.) to "B," to introduce the second occurrence of the refrain (m. 74), and three times during the "C" section. Here, in m. 21, it signals the return of Ω with a new harmonization. A tonic pedal again underlies this passage and its shift between minor and major modes.

Griffes develops two closely related motives in the tranquil refrain: a variant of Δ, a six-note motive first heard starting on the pickup to m. 18, and then, π, an inversion of Ω, first heard in m. 17. (See Example 30.2) Both are developed sequentially, the first surging toward its apex, the second attenuating through mm. 36–42. After a short-lived acceleration, π returns in C♯ minor to conclude the refrain.

EXAMPLE 30.2 Griffes, *Poem* for Flute and Orchestra, π motive, m. 17; Δ motive, mm. 17-18; π, mm. 32-33; Δ^1, mm. 33-34 (Variant because, while the contour is the same, the second interval is a descending second instead of a third).

A transition, built on a spinning out of Ω accompanied by the syncopated figure introduced in m. 8 now extended into a hemiola, leads to a developmental passage followed by a second presentation of the refrain. This passage begins in B minor (m. 53) and modulates to D♯ minor three measures later, all over a ten-measure E♯ pedal point that contributes to the tension. Also feeding the tension are the constantly accelerating motion, increasing dynamic level, and pounding accompaniment. Throughout this section, we hear development of the Δ motive, again with Griffes's frequent employment of sequences (e.g., mm. 53–55, 56–58; 63, 64, 66, 67; 68, 69). Deceptive cadences (V –> VI of D♯ minor in mm. 60–61; V of D♯ minor –> E minor in mm. 62–63) surprise the listener but do nothing to reduce the tension. The flute's *forte* and *fortissimo* dynamics in the upper register, the rapidly changing tremolo chords, and a modulation beginning in m. 68 lead inexorably to a climax in

m. 73. Syncopated rhythm, again reminiscent of mm. 8, 21, and 48–52, usher in the relaxation of the refrain.

Beginning in m. 84, Griffes builds a transition, again using the Ω motive. This is followed by a portentous introduction to "C." Through sequences, Griffes leads the listener forward, each statement louder than the last. The underlying tremolos, punctuated in mm. 100–101 with the interjection of a bold descending bass line, the bitonality with pedal C major over F♯, and the accelerando, give way to a brilliant outburst by the solo flute.

The introduction accomplished, a scherzando begins at m. 116, the flute in 6/8 meter, the orchestra in 2/4. Its form, in mostly regular periods, is:

a (8 mm.) b (8) c (8) c^1 (10) a (8) b (8) tr (5) d (12) d^1 (12)

Long pedal points (A♯, mm. 116–131; G♯, mm. 132–146) underlie the changing harmony. A syncopated measure (m. 149) stalls the motion before a repetition of "a" and "b" over a more active accompaniment, now including the color of a snare drum without snares, *ppp*.

In the transition to "d," Griffes changes the orchestra's meter to 6/8, aligning with the flute, and as has been heard before, a syncopated measure leads to a new melody, presented first by the flute (mm. 171–182), then by the solo horn, with the soloist adding figuration around it. This poco meno mosso/più mosso moves from C♯ major to its parallel minor, preparing the way for a forceful return to "A" (in the tonic key) in m. 195. Here, the flute plays Ω as a 2+2+2 hemiola over 3+3 groupings of eighth notes in the orchestra. The voices begin to align rhythmically in m. 201 before the accompaniment subsides, and the flute questions its direction (m. 208) before the two rekindle for the codetta.

For the Vivace and Presto, Griffes adds tambourine and, once again, demonstrates his mastery at building a climax and then relinquishing energy for the return of the refrain (m. 259) over a long pedal on A. A solo viola brings back the Ω motive of the opening and simultaneously returns to the home key of C♯ minor. With final, nostalgic references to Δ (m. 277) and π (mm. 281–2), the piece comes to a quiet close.

The premiere of *Poem* on November 19, 1919, was to be followed by the Boston Symphony's premiere of *The Pleasure-Dome of Kubla Khan* on November 28 (with additional performances in Boston on the 29th and in Carnegie Hall on December 4 and 6) and the Philadelphia Orchestra's premiere of *Bacchanale, The White Peacock, Clouds,* and *Nocturne for Orchestra* on December 19. It was exactly what Griffes wanted, but it came with tremendous pressure and strain, as he described in a letter to his old piano teacher and patron, Miss Broughton, on October 15, 1919:

> I haven't been feeling well for the last few days and just managed to keep the necessary things going. . . . I am rushed to death now. Everything comes with

> me at once. . . . All these things have to be put in final shape and parts prepared. Also I am finishing up my music for the Neighborhood Playhouse production in January, which is a tremendous job. Then in addition I have just signed a five years' contract with the Duo-Art Reproducing Piano to make records only for them. I am to make six of my own pieces the first year and must start in a couple days.[13]

In the midst of all of these projects, Griffes had returned to his teaching at the Hackley School for another year. For months he juggled his responsibilities at the school with composing, rehearsing, and preparing scores for publication.

The premiere of *Poem* met with laudatory reviews, and Griffes's sister, Charlotte, recalled that he was so thrilled by the BSO's performance of *Kubla Khan* that he telephoned his family from Boston.[14] Then it was off to New York for the Carnegie Hall performances. Writing to his dear friend John Meyer, he declared, "this New York performance is the event of which I spoke to you some time ago as the greatest concert honor which can come to a composer in America (at least in my opinion)."[15]

He was elated with his successes, but the months of accumulated pressure and work had left Griffes drained of energy: "He could barely stand to acknowledge the applause"[16] in Carnegie Hall. Within days of the BSO performances, Griffes collapsed from exhaustion and was diagnosed with empyema (pleurisy with infection). From his sickbed at Hackley, he completed work on the four scores that the Philadelphia Orchestra was scheduled to perform in mid-December but was too ill to travel to Philadelphia for the performances. Just as acclaim finally came to him, Griffes was lying in bed, near death.

Meanwhile, Schirmer was anxious to publish a flute-and-piano reduction of *Poem*. So ill that he found it impossible to work, Griffes wrote to his publisher pledging that it would be among his first projects upon his recovery. On January 28, 1920, he signed a royalty agreement—his last—for publication of the piece.[17] His condition worsened, and he was unable to complete the task. Following his death on April 8, Barrère was engaged to prepare the publication. Using the composer's sketches and his own memories of their rehearsals together, Barrère prepared the score, which was published in 1922. The original orchestral version was finally published in 1951.

Notes

1. Donna K. Anderson, *Charles T. Griffes: A Life in Music* (Washington, DC: Smithsonian Institution Press, 1993), 49.

2. Anderson, *Charles T. Griffes*, 71.

3. Edward M. Maisel, *Charles T. Griffes: The Life of an American Composer* (New York: Knopf, 1943), 225.

4. Maisel, 270.

5. Anderson, *Charles T. Griffes*, 122.

6. Edward M. Maisel, "Piano Music of Charles Tomlinson Griffes," http://www.newworldrecords.org/linernotes/80310, accessed May 28, 2013.

7. Maisel, 161.

8. Anderson, "Charles Tomlinson Griffes," http://www.newworldrecords.org/linernotes/80273, accessed July 8, 2013.

9. Anderson, *Charles T. Griffes*, 217.

10. Maisel, 289.

11. Maisel, 194.

12. Anderson, "Charles Tomlinson Griffes."

13. Maisel, 291–292.

14. Anderson, *Charles T. Griffes*, 161.

15. Anderson, *Charles T. Griffes*, 161.

16. Anderson, *Charles T. Griffes*, 163.

17. Anderson, *Charles T. Griffes*, 168.

31 Eldin Burton—Sonatina for Flute and Piano

(THOMAS) ELDIN BURTON was born in Fitzgerald, Georgia, two hundred miles southeast of Atlanta, on October 26, 1913. He studied piano and composition with George Lindner at the Atlanta Conservatory of Music and, in 1940, became director of a conservatory in Georgia for a year. Wishing to further his training in composition, he later moved to New York and enrolled in a class in small forms at the Juilliard School. The class was taught by the Dutch-American composer, conductor, and violinist Bernard Wagenaar (1894–1971).[1] Wagenaar, a neoclassical composer, wrote "tonal and polytonal pieces demonstrating lyrical melodic grace, finely wrought counterpoint, and pungent harmonies."[2] For the class, Burton composed a piano piece that his classmate, flutist Samuel Baron, suggested he convert to a work for flute and piano. Burton agreed with the suggestion, and the piece, Sonatina for Flute and Piano, won the New York Flute Club's 1948 composition contest. First prize came with an offer of publication by G. Schirmer, and with this, the sonatina secured a solid place in the flute repertoire.

The three-movement sonatina is written in a romantic style with standard formal structures and a modal, tonal, and occasionally bitonal harmonic language. The opening movement, Allegretto grazioso, begins in E Aeolian mode; that is, E minor with a flat seventh scale degree. (This mode results in triads on the fifth and seventh scale degrees that are minor and major, respectively, instead of major and diminished.) In m. 8, Burton introduces a G♯ that creates the sound of a bright Picardy third to end the first phrase. Beginning in m. 10, the opening eight-measure phrase is repeated, now with the flute performing the melody *forte* and an octave higher. A four-measure transition presents the first half of the same melody in the pianist's right hand while the left hand sounds a dominant pedal of F, which resolves deceptively to E major on the downbeat of m. 22. Here, Burton presents the "a" material again, this time expanding each half of the phrase from four to five measures and, in the second half, adding a syncopated, rising line in the flute (mm. 28ff.) to propel the music toward the second part of the exposition.

The Più mosso ("b") introduces a distinctive rhythmic motive that will be heard in each measure of this section. The motive (Δ), two successive dotted eighth–sixteenth figures (first appearing at the end of m. 32 and the beginning of 33), changes in rhythm and contour, but each presentation remains forceful and recognizable. With its increasing dynamic level and successively higher range (from f^3 through F♯ to G♯ in m. 34 to F♯ rising through G♯ to A♯ in m. 35), the motive leads the music to a climax on b^3 in m. 36. At the end of this measure and the beginning of the next, the motive descends, as it did in mm. 32–33. Burton varies the contour again in m. 38 and both the contour and rhythm in m. 39 on the way to a second climax, *sff*, on the downbeat of m. 40.

A deceptive cadence (mm. 41–42) introduces a three-measure transition to "c" (mm. 45ff.) Burton launches this third section of the exposition with the Δ motive of "b," now presented bitonally. While the piano's right hand performs the melody in C major, the left hand accompanies in C♯ minor for three measures before acquiescing to C major halfway through m. 48. A "hammered" four-measure interlude over a tonic pedal (mm. 50–53), leads to three variations of "c" (mm. 54–66), this time with the flute in C major throughout, the piano in G minor for two measures, then on V of A minor for three, in A Aeolian for four, and finally in C major and D♭ major.

After a closing flourish, Burton forgoes development and returns at the beginning of m. 71 to "a" material with E as tonal center. However, the mode is not the Aeolian with which the piece began, but instead E Mixolydian. Indeed, m. 71 is the beginning not of the reprise but rather of a retransition leading to an abbreviated reprise beginning in m. 76. Following a single statement of "a," intimations of "b" and "c," featuring the Δ motive, are heard in B♭ minor. The movement concludes with a final ten-measure statement of "a," similar to mm. 22–31, followed by a four-measure elaboration of the tonic.

The second movement, a dreamy Andantino, is set in ternary form. It begins in E Aeolian mode, as the first movement did, with two four-measure phrases moving briefly through B Dorian and B minor. A repetition of the first phrase, back in

E Aeolian, begins with the pickup to m. 9. This time, however, the melody ascends into the second measure of the phrase with further alterations immediately following, leading to a new five-measure phrase (mm. 12–16) and a two-measure cadential tag. The piano picks up this two-measure tag and makes of it a heavy modulating transition to the "B" section of the movement.

This stormy middle section achieves its affect through complex cross rhythms, increasing dynamics, a faster tempo with faster rhythmic subdivisions, explorations of the instruments' extreme registers, a rising bass line (G♯ to A to B♭ to B♮) and modulations that occur every two measures, from G♯ minor in mm. 21 and 22 to A minor to F minor to E Phrygian (flute in D Dorian) and finally to a dominant seventh chord of E major leading to a triumphant authentic cadence and the return of "A" in m. 31.

Just as the first movement began in E Aeolian and ended in the brighter E major, so, too, the second concludes with nineteen measures in this key. Here, however, Burton allows the triplet motion that was established in the "B" section to continue in the right hand of the piano during the first measures of the return. Gradually, this rhythmic tension eases. The imitation between the piano and flute during the Quieto produces a lovely moment of counterpoint before the chordal accompaniment returns below the flute's lyrical melody to conclude the movement.

Burton labels the finale Allegro giocoso; quasi fandango, a fandango being a traditional Spanish couples' dance with a quick triple meter (often 3/8) and modal harmony. The sonatina's version of this dance opens with a vigorous introduction that presents the ostinato rhythm that will underlie much of the "A" section. With a pitch center of D, the movement opens in Lydian mode, including its raised fourth scale degree (G♯). The stepwise descending bass line in mm. 4–6 leads the listener through a modulation, arriving at a bitonal passage beginning in m. 6, where the flute and right-hand piano are in B minor while the bass is in F♯. Hemiola, a metric device that Burton will use throughout the movement, is introduced in the piano in m. 7 and the flute in m. 8. An abrupt move to C major in m. 10 (confirmed by an authentic cadence into m. 12) with a resolute scale passage in the flute heralds a varied repetition of the opening theme, now with a newly composed accompaniment.

Hemiolas in mm. 23 and 24 lead to a transition (mm. 25ff.), which borrows the opening motive of the principal theme (dotted quarter tied to eighth plus two eighth notes) and presents it in sequence. This ten-measure transition (in F♯ Aeolian) is followed by the "B" section, a short, brilliant staccato perpetual-motion-inspired passage in B minor. The flutist abandons sixteenth notes in mm. 41–42 to present hemiolas against the accompaniment, then resumes its virtuoso passagework.

A retransition in D Mixolydian mode begins in m. 53 with a seven-measure pedal point on the seventh degree of the mode (C♮). Burton then turns to E minor, now with an eleven-measure dominant pedal point that continues to the silence following

m. 70. This sudden stop is one of the distinctive features of a fandango. Following the pause, the introduction and "A" return in the mode of the opening (D Lydian). After a reprise of the movement's first twenty-four measures, Burton assures a brilliant conclusion to the sonatina by means of a codetta (mm. 98ff.) featuring a rising piano flourish in D major that mirrors the flute's descending line in D Phrygian. He then makes the flute change direction and rocket to its highest note. The piano, now also in D Phrygian, accents the approach to d^4 with a iv–V^7–I cadence, the F♯ of the final *sff* triad acting as a Picardy third.

Eldin Burton composed this showpiece, the only piece for which he is known today, as a thirty-five-year-old composer. In subsequent years, he composed a flute concerto and some small-scale pieces and performed as a pianist in New York, but his principal occupation was as an employee of G. Schirmer Publishing, where he worked until 1979. He then returned to the South, living in Sarasota, Florida, until his death on March 18, 1981.

Notes

1. P. G. Bergfors, program booklet for *American Sonatas*, trans. Linda Schenck. Göran Marcusson, flute, Joakim Kallhed, piano (Olofstorp, Sweden: IntimMusik, 1994).

2. Herbert Antcliffe and Barbara A. Renton, "Wagenaar, Bernard," *New Grove Dictionary of Music and Musicians*, ed. Stanley Sadie, 2nd ed., vol. 26 (London: Macmillan, 2001), 926.

32 Ernest Bloch—*Suite modale*

BORN IN GENEVA, Switzerland, Ernest Bloch (1880–1959) was the child of a small-business owner who envisioned his son as a participant in L'industrie suisse, the family's thriving clock and tourist shop. When Ernest was six, his mother bought him a toy flute, and he amused himself by learning to play the instrument and composing melodies for it. Three years later, he began violin studies. Though his father made it clear that Ernest's priority must be the family's business, by the age of eleven he had decided to devote his life to music.[1] At fourteen, he began composition studies with Émile Jaques-Dalcroze, a faculty member at the Geneva Conservatory and the founder of Dalcroze Eurhythmics.

In 1896, Belgian violinist Martin Marsick, a professor at the Paris Conservatory, arrived in Geneva on tour. The sixteen-year-old Bloch summoned his courage and went to the virtuoso's hotel, performing and showing him the string quartet he had recently composed. Recognizing the youth's talent, Marsick persuaded Bloch's wary parents to allow their son to travel to Brussels to study with the famous violinist, Eugène Ysaÿe.[2] Bloch later recounted the day his father took him to the train station, "a figure 'small and bent' with his face 'behind a veil of tears.' "[3] On that day, Ernest Bloch began the nomadic existence that would take him to a new city (and often a new country) every few years for the next forty.

Ysaÿe, believing the young musician to be more gifted as a composer, encouraged him in that direction.[4] After three years in Brussels, Bloch continued his training and composition work in Frankfurt, Munich, and then briefly in Paris. Financial difficulties caused him to return to Geneva in 1904, working in the family business as salesman and bookkeeper and composing at night. During the same year, he married Marguerite Schneider, a pianist who had been his classmate at the Hoch Conservatory in Frankfurt. Their three children were born in 1905, 1907, and 1909.

Bloch scored an early success in 1910, when the Opéra Comique in Paris accepted and produced his opera *Macbeth*. During subsequent years, he "shouldered the major responsibility of running the family business as his father's health began to fail."[5] The burden became all the greater with the onset of World War I. Still, the period 1912 to 1916 was an enormously productive time during which Bloch composed his self-proclaimed Jewish Cycle: *Israel*, a symphony with voices; *Three Jewish Poems; Prelude and Two Psalms* for soprano and orchestra; *Psalm 22* for baritone and orchestra; and *Schelomo*.

Knowing of his friend's musical frustrations, Alfred Pochon, second violinist of the Flonzaley Quartet, suggested that Bloch apply for the position of conductor for a US tour that modern dancer Maud Allan was planning. Obtaining the appointment, Bloch set sail for New York on July 30, 1916. The tour began in October but was aborted six weeks later; Bloch found himself in New York without family and without income. Ironically, it was this failed tour that led to recognition for the thirty-six-year-old composer. He persevered, and within six months his career in America had been launched with the successful premiere of his String Quartet no. 1 by the Flonzaley Quartet, an invitation from Karl Muck to conduct *Three Jewish Poems* with the Boston Symphony, and a performance of *Schelomo* on an all-Bloch concert in New York.

Returning to Europe and to his family in 1917, Bloch received a telegram offering a position as head of the theory department at the new Mannes School of Music. He was thrilled with the offer, and after a family vacation, the Blochs crossed the ocean and settled into a Lexington Avenue apartment. Ernest had given many lectures at the Geneva Conservatory, but this new position marked the beginning of his long, successful teaching and administrative career in the United States.

While teaching at both Mannes and the Hartt School of Music in Hartford, Connecticut, Bloch was awarded a publishing contract with G. Schirmer and the Elizabeth Sprague Coolidge Prize for his Suite for Viola and Piano. He was then invited to Ohio to serve as founding director of the Cleveland Institute of Music. Within two years, the school enrolled more than four hundred students,[6] its success paralleling Bloch's own blossoming career as composer and pedagogue. His pedagogical ideas, however, including the abandonment of textbooks in favor of score study, led to disagreements with the school's trustees and, in 1925, to his resignation. When the founders of the San Francisco Conservatory (where he had taught a five-week course during the summer of 1924) offered him a position a short time later, he accepted. Composing continued during these years, including three prize-winning pieces: *Four Episodes* for Chamber Orchestra (Carolyn Beebe Prize), *America: An Epic Rhapsody* (*Musical America* Prize), and a tribute to his homeland, *Helvetia* (one of five winners of the RCA Victor Prize).

A series of events, commencing with Cantor Reuben Rinder's invitation to join an advisory board for the Society for the Advancement of Synagogue Music, led to Bloch's resignation from duties at the San Francisco Conservatory in 1930 and, with financial support from the Rosa and Jacob Stern Fund, to return to Switzerland to write his *Sacred Service*. After nearly nine years away, Bloch returned to the United States in spring 1939. He resumed his teaching career, now at the University of California at Berkeley, "in accordance with the arrangement he had made with the Stern family and the university before he left San Francisco."[7]

His return to California at the age of fifty-eight led to the purchase of his first home, the place where he later composed *Suite modale*. As biographer David Kuscher relates:

> During a spring day in 1941, while Bloch was driving his Buick coupe to Portland, he was detained by a roadblock the cause of which was an inordinately high water level. He decided to spend the night at the nearby resort village of Agate Beach. Two days later he was still in this coastal community, not because of the water levels on the roads, but because, after walking among the mushrooms and investigating other scenic delights, ranging from the Pacific Ocean and the agates along the beach to the nearby mountains, he made a decision he had avoided making his entire life. He arranged to purchase a roomy house for sale on Agate Beach. Thus it was that Ernest and Marguerite Bloch, after a lifetime of wandering, settled in a place.[8]

Bloch retired from UC Berkeley in 1952, ending the distinguished teaching career that provided "training to some of the strongest musical minds of the younger generation,"[9] including Roger Sessions, Randall Thompson, and Henry Cowell. During the last seven years of his life, he composed a remarkable body of music. He also enjoyed long daily walks, taking along his miniature scores of Bach's *Well-Tempered Clavier*, which he had long taught and admired. "During these daily excursions, he would often stop to write a Bach fugue from memory. At seventy, he had increased his speed to the point where, as he humorously indicated, '. . . 32 minutes is my record, and I am trying to reduce the time to 28!' "[10]

During the summer of 1956, inspired by the beautiful sound of flutist Elaine Shaffer, Bloch composed the four-movement *Suite modale*. Never one to follow compositional trends, Bloch created a unique, largely contemplative work that eschews the flashy brilliance of other compositions written for the instrument. On the flute-and-piano manuscript, dated August 31, 1956, he added instrumental indications in ink for a version with string orchestra.[11]

As with other pieces written during this final Agate Beach period, Bloch turned to absolute music, writing a suite based on classical forms. The first movement follows a two-part sonatina structure (A-B-A-B); that is, an abridged sonata form with no development. Opening in E Phrygian, the free-flowing first theme is accompanied by open fourths and fifths, typical of Bloch. The piano's turn with this melody leads to a second theme, now in F Lydian (m. 14).

The "B" section, beginning in m. 20, introduces the *Kernmotiv* (core or basic motive), a descending fifth followed by an ascending second, that pervades the work. (See Example 32.1) The descent occasionally outlines a minor sixth, dimin-

EXAMPLE 32.1 Bloch, *Suite Modale*, Mvt. 1, mm. 20-22. Notes of *Kernmotiv* shown with x's.

ished fifth, augmented fourth, or perfect fourth, and the ascending second may be major or minor. The motive may also appear in inversion, rising a fifth (or fourth) before falling a second. This eight-measure section features two themes (elided in m. 24). It begins in D Dorian and moves to G Mixolydian for the second theme. The piano returns to the movement's opening theme in m. 28, accompanied by the flute playing a version of the *Kernmotiv* introduced in m. 20. (See Example 32.2)

EXAMPLE 32.2 Bloch, *Suite Modale*, Mvt. 1, mm. 28-29. Theme 1, piano right hand; *Kernmotiv*, flute.

section	A	B	A	B	C	A
m#	1	15	23	27	33	39
meter	3/4	2/4	3/4	2/4	4/4	3/4
mode	**A** dorian to **B** phrygian (m 8)	**G** lydian	**E** dorian	**D** lydian	**D** dorian to **D** minor (m 33) and **A** minor (m 37)	**A** dorian

CHART 32.1 Bloch, *Suite Modale*: Analysis of the second movement.

The returns of both "A" and "B" (m. 34) are in E Phrygian, as they would be in the reprise of a sonata form. While the tonal center of "B's" recurrence is transposed up a second, from D to E, the melody is a perfect fifth higher than it was in m. 20 and is now four octaves (rather than three octaves and a fifth) above the bass. The concluding three-measure phrase, borrowed from m. 18, confirms the cadence in E Phrygian.

The second movement, in which Bloch introduces more interplay between the flute and piano lines, is cast in rondo form and outlined in Chart 32.1. Bloch had often used cyclical procedures to unify his compositions, and in this movement there are two melodic links to the previous one. Harking back subtly are the *Kernmotiv* and its inversion, primarily in the movement's "B" and "C" sections (mm. 18–19, 19–20, 31–33, 33–34, 34–35, 35, 37–38, 38; inverted: mm. 15, 16, 18–19, 27, 28, 31) but also in the second and third iterations of "A" (mm. 40–41, 44–46, 47–48, and inverted, mm. 25–26). More overtly, one hears the theme of the first movement's "B" section (first movement, m. 20) as a theme in the second movement's "C" section. First heard in the flute in m. 33, it passes to the piano in m. 34 and is repeated, entirely in the piano, in mm. 37–38.

After the lyrical, moderately paced opening movements, the bright, gigue-like character of the third offers a welcome change of mood. As he had in the first two movements, Bloch here delineates the formal sections, in this case, A-B-A, by metrical change.

The first theme, introduced in the flute, consists of two iterations of the *Kernmotiv* in C Mixolydian, then Lydian: c^3 to g^2 in mm. 3–4; g^2 to d^2 in mm. 5–6. The next four-measure phrase, in A Dorian, begins with an inversion of the *Kernmotiv* (mm. 7–8). The "A" section's second theme, first presented in mm. 25–27 in E Dorian, is repeated sequentially. As it continues, first in one-measure, then in half-measure sequences in mm. 29–34, the modality disintegrates. The tempo slows, and buoyancy gives way to lyricism as the piano and flute lines descend. A tonal cadence—V/G → G (Dorian)—is the gateway to "B."

The folklike melody of "B" brings back the suite's pervasive mood of tranquility. Melodically, however, this theme parallels, in augmentation, the first theme of the "A" section (middle of m. 3 to middle of m. 6). Such motivic transformation is characteristic of much of Bloch's writing[12] and is exemplified again in the flute's "new" theme (mm. 46–49). Both aforementioned themes (beginning at mm. 36 [piano] / 41 [flute] and 46 [flute] / 54 [piano]) are actually augmented and extended versions of the *Kernmotiv*. Through most of this section (mm. 41–61), one hears the stability of a single mode (D Dorian), which resumes at m. 65 with the return of "A." Interestingly, the sustained bass notes from as far back as m. 46 outline the mode of D minor. Bloch truncates the second "A" section and "modulates" to a new mode (G Dorian at m. 70), before writing a coda that returns to the C Mixolydian → Lydian modality of the movement's opening.

Suite modale's last movement (See Chart 32.2) opens with a quiet but stately adagio, the dotted rhythms redolent of a French overture. In mm. 5–6, one hears a presentation of the *Kernmotiv* (appearing in each preceding movement but here most obviously linked to mm. 40 and 41 of the second). Measures 6 and 7 recall the first two measures of the piece, mm. 8 and 9, the first movement's conclusion. Together these cyclical elements serve as a strong unifying force.

Bloch uses one of his favorite markings, allegro deciso, for the vibrant "B" section, in which he spins out his ideas using imitation and sequence. "C" follows (beginning in C Mixolydian, m. 24) with a majestic theme first in the flute, then, two measures later, in the pianist's left, then right hand. A one-measure extension, prolonged sequentially, leads to another statement of the section's principal theme (mm. 31–35) and a varied repetition of the adagio opening, now a fifth higher. In m. 44, the allegro tempo returns as "D" is launched with an inversion of the first measure of the preceding allegro, "B." Ornamenting the *Kernmotiv* in mm. 45–46 (flute and treble piano) and mm. 50–51 (treble piano), Bloch adds the rhythmic spark of mixed meters while the treble piano in mm. 49 and 54 interjects the scale patterns that opened both allegros. The flute follows suit in m. 59. Like the "A" sections, the return of "C" in m. 62 is transposed up a fifth to G Mixolydian.

With the beginning of the coda (m. 72), Bloch ingeniously recalls themes from each movement: mm. 72–78 = first movement; 79–82 = third movement; mm. 83–87 = fourth movement; mm. 88–97 = second movement. The integration is all the more compelling because the *Kernmotiv* that pervades all four movements is included in the third-movement and (in mm. 86–87) fourth-movement recollections.

When Elaine Shaffer sent Bloch a taped recording of her performance of *Suite modale*, the composer was so pleased that he decided to write another work for her. Stricken with cancer and admitted to a hospital while composing the work, he convinced the doctors to delay surgery and release him so that he could complete the piece. "On the day he finished copying the orchestral score [for this piece (titled *Two Last Poems*)], he called his family in to see the manuscript,"[13] and as his daughter Suzanne recounts: "Then with his everlasting sense of irony, having not too much

Overview: A B C A^1 D C^1 B^1 Coda							
section	**A**		**B**			**C**	
theme	**a (French Overture)**	**b**	**c**	**d**	**c^1**	**e**	**e^1**
source (MVT: mm)		IV: mm 6-7 = I: mm 1-2; IV: mm 8-10 ≈ I mm 39-41					
# of mm	5	5	2+2	3	3+3	2+2+2+1	3+2
starts m#	1	6	11	15	18	24	31 35
mode	**A** minor **A** dorian	**E** minor (**B** phrygian)	**E** dorian		**B** dorian	**C** mixolydian **A** aeolian	**A** minor: V VI^6
starts m#	1 4	6	11		18	24 28	31
		e: V - iv^6 - v^{b3}					
section	**A^1**		**D**				
theme	**a**	**b^1**	**f ***	**f^1 ***	**f^2 ***		**f^3 ***
# of mm	5	3	5	5	3 + 2		3
starts m#	36	41	44	49	54		59
mode	**E** minor **E** dorian	**B** minor	**B** aeolian	**F#** aeolian	**C#** aeolian	**E** mixolydian	
starts m#	36 39	41	44	49	54	57	
		b: V - iv^6 - V	* "f"s begin with 1st m. of "c" (m. 11) or its inversion.				

CHART 32.2 Bloch, *Suite Modale*: Analysis of the fourth movement.

section	**C**[1]		**B**[1]				
theme	**e**		**d**[1]				
# of mm	2+2+2+1		3				
starts m#	62		69				
mode	**G** mixolydian **E** aeolian		**A** dorian				
starts m#	62 66		69				
section	**Coda**						
theme	**from Movement 1**	**from Movement 3**	**from Mvt 4**	**from Mvt 4 (and Mvt 1)**		**from Movement 2**	
source (MVT: mm)	I: mm 1-4; also, from IV, piano l.h. m 72 = flute m 24	III: mm 3-5 (*Kernmotiv*); also IV: mm 5-6; II: 40-41; I: 20-21	IV: mm 1-4	IV: mm 9-10 (≈ I: mm 40-41)		II: mm 1-6	II: mm 45-48 (IV: m 94 = II: 45, ≠ II: 7)
# of mm	7	4	5			10	
starts m#	72	79	83	86.5		88	94
mode	**E** minor					**E** dorian	
starts m#	72					88	
	in e: V-$ii^{4/3}$-V-$\mathbf{ii^{4/3}}$ *	V^{2}-VI^{2}-$v^{7/b3}$-i^{6}-iv-i^{6}-$\mathbf{iv^{6}}$ *	$ii^{6/5}$-V-$VI^{4/3}$-$V^{4/3}$-VI^{6}-iv^{6}-v^{b3}-iv^{6}-$\mathbf{ii^{6/5}}$ *				
	* In E minor, the iv chord is A minor, the ii^{7} is A minor above F#; both chords have subdominant function.						

CHART 32.2 Continued

faith in the pronouncements of the medical profession, he ceremoniously added to the title the word "maybe" and meticulously put three dots after it."[14] Bloch did, in fact, live to finish *Two Last Poems* (*Maybe* ...) and two other compositions before succumbing to the cancer on July 15, 1959, nine days before his seventy-ninth birthday.

Notes

1. David Z. Kushner, *The Ernest Bloch Companion* (Westport, CT: Greenwood Press, 2002), 14.
2. Kushner, 15.
3. Mary Tibaldi Chiesa, *Ernest Bloch* (Turin: Paravia, 1933), 18, quoted in Kushner, 16.
4. Kushner, 16.
5. Kushner, 29.
6. "'À Bas Formalism!' ['Down with Formalism'] Is Device of Cleveland Institute," *Musical America* (July 8, 1922): 9, quoted in Robert Strassburg, *Ernest Bloch: Voice in the Wilderness* (Los Angeles: Trident Shop, 1977), 55.
7. Kushner, 110.
8. Kushner, 110.
9. Michael David Nott, "Ernest Bloch's Pedagogical Writings: A Didactic Legacy of Twentieth-Century America" (PhD diss., Eastman School of Music, 1985), 6.
10. Ernest Bloch, "Thoughts at Seventy," *Étude* (February 1951): 10, quoted in Robert Strassburg, 90.
11. David L. Sills, "Bloch Manuscripts at the Library of Congress," *Notes: Quarterly Journal of the Music Library Association* 42 (June 1986): 749.
12. Kushner, 97.
13. Wendy Isaac Bergin, "Ernest Bloch's Works with Solo Flute: An Analytical Study" (master's thesis, University of Houston, 1993), 7.
14. Suzanne Bloch, *Ernest Bloch: Creative Spirit: A Program Source Book*, with the collaboration of Irene Heskes (New York: Jewish Music Council of the National Jewish Welfare Board, 1976), 4, quoted in Bergin, 7.

33 John La Montaine—Sonata for Flute Solo, op. 24

JOHN LA MONTAINE (1920–2013) was thirty-seven and on the cusp of the greatest successes of his career when, in 1957, he composed his Sonata for Flute Solo, op. 24. His dream had always been to live his life as a full-time composer, but having barely sustained himself for the first three years of this endeavor, he was uncertain that he would be able to continue to realize his dream.

He hadn't had an easy start: his father died while he was still a baby, and his mother had to raise her three children on the small salary she earned as a secretary. At eighteen, he left Oak Park, Illinois, for the Eastman School of Music, in Rochester, New York, with tuition money for only one semester. That winter, just as he received a letter from the school saying that he would not be allowed to return because he couldn't pay the bill, another letter arrived, this one from his home town,

> from this algebra teacher. It said something like, "when you were my student, I was writing a book and the book is now published. By law, I'm not allowed to accept any royalties from books sold in my own school, so I'm sending you $125. I want to thank you for your part in making my book."[1]

With that gift, La Montaine was able to continue his education at Eastman, studying composition with Bernard Rogers and Howard Hanson. He cited Hanson's symposiums as the most important part of his education, for they allowed him to have all of his orchestral compositions performed. "It was the most critical thing. For four years, we heard everything. Everything was tested out under actual conditions."[2] One of his first pieces, written during his freshman year, was selected for national broadcast. "It was wonderful. You just don't breathe,"[3] he later recalled.

Following graduation in 1942, he served in the naval reserve for four years, during which time he began work on a piano concerto: "My first sketches were from the day I went into the Navy. That was cooking in my head throughout the war."[4] He would complete the concerto, his opus 9, subtitled "In Time of War," in 1958, winning the Pulitzer Prize for it the following year.

La Montaine was also a talented pianist and early in his career earned income by accompanying opera stars Mary Garden, Maggie Teyte, and Leontyne Price while continuing his composition studies at Juilliard. In 1950, he became pianist of the NBC Symphony, a position he held for four years, coinciding with Toscanini's final years as conductor. In a 2003 interview, La Montaine described his appointment:

> I had a telephone call from someone I didn't know who said I'd been recommended to them and wanted to know if I'd care to go with Toscanini about the country. I said, "Would you please repeat that?" I said I certainly would and he said, "Have you played *La Mer*?" I said, "No I haven't played *La Mer*." He hadn't asked me if I'd played the celesta, and I'm glad he didn't because I never had. He said, "Get out the score and look at it, come to the rehearsal on Thursday, play the performance on Saturday and, if you're still in the orchestra on Monday, you're hired."[5]

With that, La Montaine won the position. Paul Renzi was a colleague in the orchestra's flute section. While La Montaine wasn't "deeply acquainted" with Renzi, he composed his solo sonata as "a thank-you note for all I learned from him in the four years I sat in front of him [when playing celesta]."[6]

The sonata has a traditional four-movement structure (moderate, fast, slow, fast), but each movement is a rondo. Movement 1, "Questioning," is cast as a-b-a-c-a-d-a, with each of the four "a" sections introduced by a simple yet defining two-note gesture, a descending minor third, "t" (mm. 1, 10, 19, 38). This gesture then becomes part of a four-note *Kernmotiv* (core or basic motive) "u," the range of which is expanded in "v," as shown in Example 33.1. The tonal center is G, with both major and minor modes expressed through the use of both B♮ and B♭. This bimodality, employing what are often called "split thirds," in which the use of thirds is "split" between major thirds and minor thirds, is related to the major-minor chord: a tetrad in which, in root

EXAMPLE 33.1 John La Montaine, Sonata for Flute Solo, Op. 24, Mvt. 1, mm. 1-4, motives "t," "u," (*Kernmotiv*) and "v."

position, an encompassing perfect fifth contains both a major and a minor third, e.g., C–E♭–E♮–G.

Kernmotiv "u" or one of its five variants, "v," "w," "x," "y," "z" (See Example 33.2), accounts for twenty-nine of the movement's forty-four measures. The motives each contain four pitches, begin with an ascending minor third (except "z"), and end with a descending minor third (except "v"). They are differentiated by their range, defined by the ascending interval between their first and third notes.

EXAMPLE 33.2 John La Montaine, Sonata for Flute Solo, Op. 24, Mvt. 1, four more variants of the *Kernmotiv* ("u"): "w" (m. 5), "x" (m. 6), "y" (m. 8), and "z" (m. 38–39).

The second section ("b," mm. 5–9) is a spinning out and intensification emanating from the initial ascending minor third of motive "w." In an interview more than thirty-five years after writing this piece, La Montaine recalled:

> I'm very involved with the significance of intervals. All of the intervals have a very special meaning, and that seems to be quite universal in human experience. . . . Whether they go up or down, what they're preceded with and what follows them. . . . At the time, I was interested in writing a series of works which would make the maximum use of a particular interval. . . . The flute sonata was based on the minor third.[7]

With a large-scale crescendo and accelerando, "b" leads to a forceful return of "t" (m. 10), which reintroduces "a," now *forte* and a fourth higher, in C major/minor.

Section "c" follows (mm. 14–19), its first motive (immediately repeated) beginning with the all-important descending minor third, "t." The next motive (starting with the second note in m. 16) opens with that interval's inversion, a major sixth. As with "b," this section begins *pianissimo* and intensifies as La Montaine spins out the material leading to a forceful presentation of "t" in F♯ minor, which signals the return of "a."

Following the first presentation of *Kernmotiv* "u" in F♯ major/minor (mm. 20–21), this basic motive, in B♭, is inverted (mm. 21–22), as is "v" (mm. 22–23). There follow four more inversions of "u" passing through G and D to C, all in their major/minor guises. The six presentations of these inverted motives (mm. 21–27) limn a descending tessitura and a gradual dissipation of energy and close with a quiet ascending minor third.

In a surprise move, La Montaine begins the new section ("d") with an ascending *major* third, *pianissimo*. From this soft beginning, he builds momentum for the longest, most intense section of the movement. Beginning in the low register and climbing, the music modulates, crescendos, and accelerates while the rhythmic motion becomes more frenzied and unpredictable. A series of hemiolas (mm. 31–36, in this case two dotted quarter notes in the second half of the measure replacing the three quarter notes in the first half) exploits the contrast between 6/4 and 12/8 meters, contributes to the excitement, and builds to the movement's ultimate climax: the return of "t" *fortissimo* (m. 38) and of G major/minor. Then, as he had in the preceding "a," La Montaine dissolves the material upon which he has based the movement before a final version of the *Kernmotiv* brings it to a close with a haunting, lingering, descending minor third.

"Jaunty," the sonata's second movement, is also cast in rondo form, with each "A" section anchored in G major/minor. (See Chart 33.1)

While the opening measures present symmetrical phrasing (4 + 4), an unexpected third-beat accent in m. 8 introduces the second phrase one beat early and hints at the rhythmic game playing that will characterize this movement. The period that this unexpected accent introduces upsets the expected symmetry of antecedent-consequent phrasing with its sequence of 4 + 5 measures.

Hemiola, a classic feature of scherzos, spices up the metric structure of "B" (in mm. 31–32) before "A" returns to reestablish, at least momentarily, metric stability and tonic key. However, new slurs and accents strengthen the hemiola (mm. 43–44) that was previously implied by the melodic contour of mm. 10–11. In fact, each "A" offers a fresh take on the recurring material.

A softer, lyrical section, beginning in E♭ Lydian (characterized by the raised fourth, A♮) follows. This "C" section, in two eight-bar periods, will modulate to B♭ major through common pitches (mm 61–62). The entire section recurs at m. 152 starting in A♭ Lydian, modulating to E♭ major.

Between the "C" sections are two "A" sections followed by developmental passages, the first of which plays on the three-note link (mm. 84–85) that introduces it. The link's two repeated notes followed by a descending interval set off this

section	**A**					**B**															
phrase rhythm (# of mm)	4	4	4	5		4	4	4	4												
starts m#	1					18															
key	**G/g**					**D**															
starts m#	1					18															
section	**A^{1}**																**C**				
phrase rhythm (# of mm)	4	4	4	5													4	4	4		4
starts m#	34																51	55	59		63
key	**G/g**																**E^{b}** lydian			**→B^{b}**	**B^{b}**
starts m#	34																51			61	63
section	**A^{2}**				link	development						trans									
phrase rhythm (# of mm)	4	4	4	5	2	6			6+4			3									
starts m#	67				84	86			92			102									
key	**G/g**					**G/g**	**E**	**g/G**		**A**	**G/g**										
starts m#	67					86	88	90		94	96										
section	**A^{3}**				link	development											**C^{1}**				
phrase rhythm (# of mm)	4	4	4	3	2 +	1	+ 3	2	4	4	2	4	3	3	4		4	4	4		4
starts m#	105					122					136			145	148		152	156	160		164
key	**(G/g)**					**modulation**					**A**			**E**		**C**	**A^{b}** lydian			**→E^{b}**	**E^{b}**
starts m#	105 (ends on downbeat of m.122)					122					136			145		150	152			162	164
section	**A^{4}**					**Coda**															
phrase rhythm (# of mm)	4	4	4	4		4	4	5													
starts m#	168					184	188														
key	**G/g**					**a/A**	**g/G**														
starts m#	168					184	188														

CHART 33.1 John La Montaine, Sonata for Flute Solo, Op. 24: Analysis of the second movement.

section, which is marked by abruptly juxtaposed dynamics, quickly changing keys, and La Montaine's masterful development of intervallic relationships. A transition (mm. 102–104), the thrice-stated link motive, leads back to "A," the last two measures of which (120–121; cf. mm. 16–17) constitute a link that provides the thematic material for the beginning of the second and longer foray into development. This second development is the most dense, technically challenging section of the piece, its intensity marked not only by rapid sixteenth-note motion, quickly juxtaposed register changes, and unflagging *forte* dynamics but also by the intensified conflict between major and minor thirds. This conflict, explored from the first measures of movement 1 is the essence of the sonata's tonality; its emphasis here is a hallmark of this climactic section of movement 2.

"Introspective"—again, a rondo—is framed by a prologue and epilogue, perhaps in D major/minor but probably more properly characterized as tonally ambiguous, even atonal. The primary theme begins with the two pickups to m. 4 and, varied and truncated, is repeated. The next phrase ("b"), leading into m. 13, appears at first to be a spinning out of "a" (cf. its first two notes and the rhythmic similarity of its first four measures). However, it has a very different contour and may therefore be viewed as a contrasting section that leads back to two more varied statements of "a" (pickups to mm. 20 and 25). The second of these, *forte* and up an octave, leads forcefully to the climax of the movement. This climactic section ("c") is an elaboration of two diminished seventh chords (mm. 28–34, Example 33.3): one in the treble, descending from b$\flat^3$ to g^3 to e^3 to c$\sharp^3$ (the vii^{o7} of D minor); and one in the bass, the final and lowest notes of descending groups of two, three, and four notes, from a$\flat^1$ (the last note of m. 29) to f^1 to d^2 to f^2 to d^2 to b^1 to d^2 to b^1 (the vii^{o7} of C minor).[8] This passage is an example of La Montaine's elevating the minor third (which figures so prominently in the melodic identity of the composition and three of which, stacked, create a diminished seventh chord) to structural importance.

EXAMPLE 33.3 John La Montaine, Sonata for Flute Solo, Op. 24, Mvt. 3, mm. 28–34.

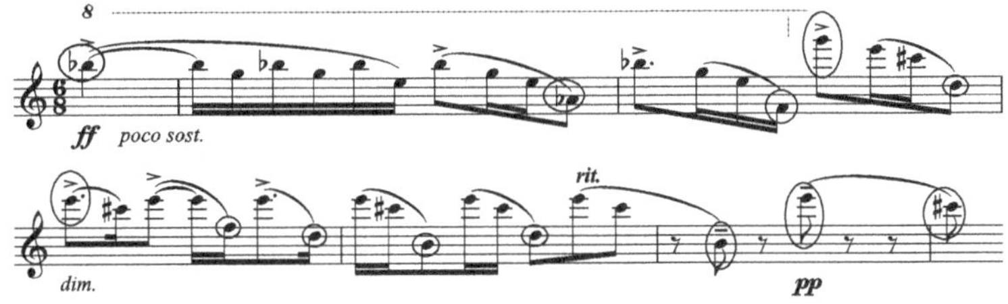

After the tonally ambiguous third movement, the finale, "Rakish," returns to the G major/minor tonality of the first and second movements, again juxtaposing major and minor thirds right from the start. Four motives, labeled "u," "v," "w," and "x" on

section	**Theme**				**Episode**	**Theme**		**Episode**	
motive	u	v	w	x		u	v		
starts m#	1	3	5	7	8½	12½	15	18	
tonal center	**G**				**A**	**C**		**modulation**	
section	**Theme**		**Episode**			**Theme**		**Episode**	
motive	u	v^1				u	v		
starts m#	25	27	29			34	36	38	43½
tonal center	**B^b**		**modulation**			**E^b**		**C**	**D (vii^{o7}/d)**
section	**Theme**				**Episode**				
motive	u	v	w^1	x^1					
starts m#	49	51	53	55	57				
tonal center	**E**			**D**					
section	**Theme**							**Episode**	
motive	$u^{truncated}$	v	v	u	$v^{extended}$	w^2	x^2		
starts m#	57¾	58½	60½	62½	64½	67	69	70¾	
tonal center	**G#**		**modulation (F)**	**D**			**modulation**	**e^b**	
section	**Theme**							**Episode**	
motive	$u^{truncated}$	$u^{truncated}$	v	$u^{truncated}$	$u^{extended}$	$v^{extended}$			
starts m#	77½	78¼	79	81	81¾	84½		86¾	89¾
tonal center	**F#**				**A**			**D**	**modulation**
section	**Theme**								
motive	u^1	v^2	½v	½v	⅜v	⅜v	⅜v	⅜v	u^2
starts m#	95¾	98	100	101	102	102¾	103½	104¼	105½
tonal center	**G**								

CHART 33.2 John La Montaine, Sonata for Flute Solo, Op. 24: Analysis of the fourth movement.

Chart 33.2, constitute the primary thematic material. Each motive contains one or both cells of "u" (ascending arpeggiated minor tenth, descending arpeggiated diminished octave), which contributes to the movement's tight construction. While the motives are first presented in two-measure segments, subsequent presentations begin in different parts of the measure, continuing the metric asymmetries that have characterized this piece from the start. Presentations of the theme in different tonalities alternate with episodes (th-ep-th-ep-th-ep-th-ep-th-ep-th-ep-th-ep-th), a procedure akin to that of the Baroque ritornello.

In the episodes beginning in mm. 38, 70, and 86, La Montaine first presents the material in augmentation before compressing it into the sixteenth notes that prevail in the rest of the movement. He begins the final thematic section in the same way, augmenting the first cell of the "u" motive. These examples of augmentation stand in contrast to the latter part of these sections, as well as to the episode beginning in m. 17, where virtuosic sixteenth-note passages with syncopations created by dynamic accents, articulation patterns, and melodic contour drive the movement and make it a dazzling tour de force.

In 1957, the precarious year when La Montaine composed the Sonata for Flute Solo, he thought it necessary to develop an alternative plan for earning a living: he decided to study for and take the New York examination required to become a licensed stockbroker, an occupation that would allow him to earn "the most money in the least amount of time" and then return to writing music. Success came in the nick of time, when, to critical acclaim, Leontyne Price premiered his ten-year-old cycle *Songs of the Rose of Sharon* with the National Symphony Orchestra under Howard Mitchell. A year later (1958) came the premiere of his First Piano Concerto (with Jorge Bolet, Mitchell, and the National Symphony); in 1959, the Pulitzer Prize and a Guggenheim Fellowship; and in 1961, a commission for a work to be performed at the inauguration of President John F. Kennedy (*Overture: From Sea to Shining Sea*). For more than thirty years, he would never be without a commission, including one in 1993 from the National Flute Association for the Sonata for Piccolo and Piano, op. 61. He never needed to broker stocks.

Notes

1. John La Montaine, "Rediscovering John La Montaine," interview by Frank J. Oteri. May 20, 2003, American Music Center, transcript by Randy Nordschow. http://www.newmusicbox.org/assets/53/interview_lamontaine.pdf, accessed March 23, 2014.

2. Erica Beth Weintraub, "John La Montaine: Life on the Edge," *Music Educator's Journal* 69 (March 1983): 41–43.

3. Weintraub, 42.

4. John La Montaine, "Rediscovering John La Montaine."

5. John La Montaine, "Rediscovering John La Montaine."

6. Paula C. Hutchinson, interview with John La Montaine, transcribed in "Structure and Style in Three Flute Works of John La Montaine, with Three Recitals of Selected Works by Bach, Prokofiev, Messiaen, Reinecke, and Others" (DMA diss., University of North Texas, 1994), 104.

7. Paula C. Hutchinson, interview with John La Montaine, 16.

8. Hutchinson, 38.

34 Robert Muczynski—Sonata for Flute and Piano, op. 14

THE CAREER OF Chicago-born composer and pianist Robert Muczynski (1929–2010) got off to an impressive start. Within two years of completing his master's degree at DePaul University in 1952, he was commissioned by the Fromm Music Foundation to compose his First Symphony and by the Louisville Orchestra to compose (and then perform) his First Piano Concerto. He also played the concerto with the Chicago Symphony at Orchestra Hall in 1958. During these early years he taught at DePaul and Loras College (Dubuque, Iowa) and performed a debut recital of his piano works at Carnegie Recital Hall in March 1958.

In 1959 Muczynski was one of twelve composers selected to participate in a new program sponsored by the Ford Foundation. The Young Composers Project placed composers under the age of thirty-five (Muczynski was thirty) in public schools to serve as composers-in-residence and to help music educators who were ill prepared to teach students about contemporary music. Muczynski was placed in Oakland, California, for two years, and it was at this time, mostly during the spring of 1960, that he composed his Sonata for Flute and Piano, op. 14. The composer later recalled:

> I wanted to write music for the solo instrument devoid of frills and cascading swirls of notes which have become flute clichés in much of the early 20th

century literature for the flute. I tried to reveal the instrument as one that is capable of projecting music which is pungent in character rather than just serene and sweetly melodic.[1]

The work received its first two performances in France during the summer of 1961: Muczynski had been awarded a grant from the French government to study with Russian émigré Alexander Tcherepnin (his composition teacher at DePaul University) at the Académie de musique in Nice that summer. It was then that his flute sonata won the Concours Internationale Prize. G. Schirmer published it that same year.

Muczynski says the first movement, Allegro deciso, is in sonata-allegro form. Thematically, the outlines are clear as shown on Chart 34.1.

The first two measures in the flute make up theme "a," measures 40–43 in the piano, right hand, theme "b." In Chart 34.1, the "a" and "b" labels refer to passages that exploit these elements. Coincident with "b," there is a countermelody in the flute that, like "b," features four notes rising stepwise and a falling minor sixth. (In "b," the fall precedes the rise.) In fact, "b," after its first note, can be seen as an imitation of its countermelody one quarter note later.

Tonally, however, the relationship between Muczynski's movement and sonata form is harder to discern. The first measures of the flute part are strongly enough in F minor to dominate one's perception, even though the murky accompanying chords revolve around E♭. As one would expect, F minor is reasserted at the beginning of the reprise, m. 136, and, most emphatically, in the bass in the movement's final measures. But what about the vast space between these oases?

Moments of relative tonal stability begin in the exposition at mm. 23 (F♯ minor, over C at first), 40 (B minor), 44 (A♭ minor), 56 and 60 (B minor and A♭ minor again), and in the transition, 66 (F minor, over combined F minor and D minor

section	**Exposition**						**transition**					
theme	a	a	a^1	b	(a)	b	a					
starts m#	1	13	23	40	(46)	56	64					
section	**Development**											**retrans**
theme	a	b	a	b	a	(trans)	b	a	a	b	a	(b)
starts m#	73	79	81	88	92	96	104	106	114	119	127	132
section		**Reprise**				**Coda**						
theme		a	a^1	b	(a)	a	a					
starts m#		136	148	159	(165)	167	175					

CHART 34.1 Robert Muczynski, Sonata for Flute and Piano: Thematic analysis of the first movement.

triads; in other words, over an F major/minor tetrachord with an added major sixth).

The first section of the development concentrates on theme "a" but mentions "b" at mm. 79–80 and develops it in mm. 88–91. The development begins with flute in D minor over an E♭ minor triad with an added major seventh, a sonority that figures prominently throughout the sonata. This chord structure supports the melody at mm. 77 (F minor), 81 (D♭ minor, under C minor in the flute), and 88 (B minor, under first G minor and then B minor in the flute). Flute and piano unite in B minor at m. 92 with F♯ pedals in treble and bass. The transition between the development's two sections features, in m. 97 and mm. 99–103, an F minor triad with added major seventh and ninth in the piano.

The second section develops primarily theme "b," with interspersions of "a" at 106–107, 114–115, and 127–130. Many of the section's measures display a tonic-dominant succession, a half-measure of i followed by a half-measure of $V^{\#7}$: mm. 104–107 in E♭ minor; 108–111 in C♯ minor; 113, 116, 118–119, and 121 in F♯ minor; 122–123 in E minor; and 124–126 in C♯ minor. The final appearance of "a" material in this section is in G minor over an E minor accompaniment with added augmented fourth. The retransition, based on "b," is in B♭ minor.

As mentioned above, the abbreviated reprise begins in the opening key. Its first twelve measures parallel mm. 1–12. The next eleven (mm. 148–154 and 155–158) are a half-step lower than their counterparts (mm. 23–29 and 36–39) with the exception of the last four sixteenth notes, which lead to the reprise of "b" a whole step higher in mm. 159–162 and 163–166 (D♭ and B♭) than the B♮ and A♭ of mm. 40–43 and 44–47.

The coda recalls "a" in the flute (in F♯ minor, mm. 167 and 169-170, and E minor, m. 170) and bitonally in the piano (B♭ minor over F♯ minor, mm. 172-173). However, the coda's most interesting moments come in the rhythmic patterns that outline an alternation of C♯ minor and A minor triads (mm. 175–180) and then in its perverse insistence on "a" in E *major* instead of its customary minor, until the flute's last two notes, where E finally yields to F over a quiet reprise of m. 1 in the small and contra octaves.

The second movement is a fleet and fleeting scherzo (without trio) in ternary form with a development before the return of "A": "A-B-dev-A^1," like a sonata form with truncated reprise (if one ignores the essence of sonata form, tonality). As seen in Chart 34.2, there are two themes, "a" and "b," and a motive, "Ω," the second measure of "a," that plays an important role throughout the movement.

Closer examination of "A" reveals formal subtleties. While "a" consists of two halves that can be designated "x" and "y," "a^2" is constructed similarly but has a different second half (mm. 13–14), a sequence derived from m. 12 (Ω). The most interesting phenomenon in this regard is "a^1" (mm. 5–10), which is "a" expanded

section	**A**					
theme	a	**a**^{1}	a^{2}	**a**^{1} **contracted, then expanded**		transition
phrase rhythm (# of mm)	4	**3+2**+1	4	**2+4**+1		
starts m#	1	5	11	15	20	22
variants of motive Ω (Ω is *routinely* the 2nd m of "a")		Ω^{1} m 7; Ω^{2} & Ω^{3}s mm 9-10	Ω^{4}s mm 13-14		$\Omega^{\text{elaborated}}$	Ω^{extended}
section	**B**					
theme	b	b	b$^{\text{"inverted" \& extended}}$	b^{extended}	transition	
phrase rhythm (# of mm)	2+2+2	2+2+2	5 (3+2) + 9 (2+2+3+2)	2+2+2+2+2	2+2+4	
starts m#	27	33	39	53	63	
variants of motive Ω (Ω is *routinely* the 2nd m of "a")			Ω^{5}s mm 44, 48; Ω^{6} m50		$\Omega^{\text{elaborated}}$	
section	**Development**					
theme					retransition	
phrase rhythm (# of mm)	5 †	4+2+3	2 + 3	2+3	4+4	
starts m#	71	76	85	90	95	
variants of motive Ω (Ω is *routinely* the 2nd m of "a")		Ω^{extended}	Ω^{extended} + Ω^{extended}	two 2-m. sequences: 6, then 4 elements*		
	† repeating 5-note motive in 6/8 meter			* hemiola		
section	**A**^{1}					
theme	a	**a**^{1}	a^{2}	**a**^{1} contracted, then expanded		
phrase rhythm (# of mm)	4	**3+3**+0	4	**2+3**+1		
starts m#	103	107	113	117 ∞		
variants of motive Ω (Ω is *routinely* the 2nd m of "a")	Ω^{7} m 104	Ω^{1} m109, Ω^{2} & Ω^{3}s mm 111-12	Ωs mm 115 & 116			
				∞ m.1 developed into sequences: Pno/Fl in mm 117-18; Fl/Fl in mm 118-21		
section	**Coda**					
theme	a^{truncated}	a^{extended}				
phrase rhythm (# of mm)	2+2	3+2	4			
starts m#	123	127	132			
variants of motive Ω (Ω is *routinely* the 2nd m of "a")	Ω^{expanded} in mm 125-26 to echo m 124	Ω^{7} is basis of mm 128-131	Ω dominates m 132 to end			

CHART 34.2 Robert Muczynski, Sonata for Flute and Piano: Analysis of the second movement.

by two measures, 7 ("Ω^1") and 10, creating a phrase rhythm of 3 + 2 + 1 measures ("x" extended + "y" + 1 m.). In mm. 15–21, there is a different expansion: 2 + 4 + 1 ("x" + "y" extended by two measures + 1 m.). And while A¹, the reprise, is virtually the same as A, mm. 117–122 see "a¹" expanded differently yet again: 2 + 3 + 1 ("x" + "y" extended by one measure + 1 m.).

The scherzo starts in E, but the issue of tonality is cloudy: things don't always sound the way they look. Examining the first nine measures, the flute seems comfortable enough in E, and in the piano there are pillars of E every four measures, but in between, the piano is in E♭ until the jazzy cadence of mm. 8–9 reestablishes E. In fact, Muczynski's harmonic style in this movement is full of jazz chords and progressions.

The focus of "B," beginning in m. 27, is F♯, but it's F♯ Dorian with the same pitch material as E major. After a feint back toward E major / C♯ minor in mm. 33–34, the tonal center becomes D (Dorian) at m. 35 and modulates through A♭/G♯ (Phrygian), G♭/F♯ (Phrygian), D (Dorian), B (Aeolian), and C (major) at mm. 39, 42, 46, 48, and 50, respectively, before returning to F♯ at m. 53. Muczynski moves to the closely related C♯ at m. 57 and stays there until, in the transition (beginning at m. 63), he begins to flirt with C major, which then prevails in m. 71 where the development begins with a five-note ornamented arpeggiation of a C major triad for five measures. Four measures in B♭ lead to a passage in C♯ that features deceptive cadences: mm. 80–83 in C♯ minor, followed by a measure of A minor; m. 85 in C♯ (IV/IV–Neapolitan–V), resolving deceptively to $\mathrm{VI}^{\flat 3}$ (A minor); m. 87, like m. 85, with the V of C♯ this time resolving deceptively in m. 88 to D, a key the flute has been enjoying since m. 85 and the final stop before the reprise and coda in E.

Muczynski described his sonata's third movement, a sinuous and languorous Andante, as "a respite from the two [preceding] energetic movements."[2] The flute's opening measure, in its solo quality, its register, its descent and ascent, evokes Debussy's *Faune*, even though the descent is a diatonic third instead of a chromatic augmented fourth. Thematically, one recognizes an "A-B-A¹" structure in which "A" consists of "a–a¹ (mm. 11ff.)–a² (mm. 17ff.)." Though Muczynski did not have Roussel's Schola Cantorum background, his sonorities in this movement (like the Frenchman's in "Pan") are more the result of contrapuntal voice leading than of functional harmony.

Although the pitch B figures prominently in the first measure, by the second there is no sense of tonal center. The same is true of the first two measures of "a¹": B looks important here, but by m. 13 there is no focus. The G♯ minor triad and E minor seventh chords of mm. 15–16 could be construed as vi of B major and iv^7 of B minor, but does this support the idea that the movement has been "in B" from the beginning? With respect to section "a²," the bass begins on G♭ in m. 17 and ends on F♯ in m. 20, but how determining of the harmonies, and hence the tonality, is this in comparison to the stepwise motion bringing the two hands of the piano ever closer or in comparison to the Fs in the flute (mm. 17 and 19–22), which, in combination with the D♯s of mm. 20–21, steer the tonality toward a Neapolitan cadence on E in m. 22?

Section "B" is unified by the pedal points: E in "b" (mm. 23–29) and F in "b^1" (mm. 30–34) and by the persistent (rising and falling) fourths, their dotted eighth–sixteenth rhythm picked up by the piano from the last three measures of "a^2." (In "b^1," this rhythm is reversed to that of a Scotch snap.) Otherwise, the relationship of "b" and "b^1" may seem tenuous except for their flute openings: rising fourth–fifth, falling whole step of "b," rising fourth–fourth, falling whole step of "b^1," the latter beginning a half-step higher than "b," corresponding to the pedal tones supporting them. However, there are internal similarities between the two phrases. For example, m. 31 with its pickup is like m. 26, and the animation of m. 27 corresponds to the turbulence of mm. 32–33.

The retransition to "A^1" (mm. 35–38) is dominated by a fragment of the opening theme of the movement (beginning on the second half of the third beat and consisting of six notes). Then, after its third iteration (m. 38), it becomes the accompaniment for the first two measures of "a^3" in the flute. The last two measures of "a^3" (mm. 42–43) recall the dotted rhythms of "b" over a rising line in the piano that, at the start of the coda, culminates in a simultaneous I and vii^{o7} chord in F major (F–A–(C)–E–(G)–B♭–D♭), perhaps a dominant-thirteenth chord of the movement's final pungent B♭. Meanwhile, the flute continues in dotted rhythms as it ornaments the third of the V^{13} chord until m. 47, where the music begins to evanesce and finally vanishes.

The finale is a five-part rondo, "A-B-A-C-A," with a slender "B" and a final "A" ("a^3, $a^{dev/ext}$, a^4, a^5, a^6, a^7," coda) that occupies just under half (83) of the movement's 168 measures.

Chart 34.3 elucidates most of the important features of the movement, but the bitonality of mm. 51–72 (like that noted in the chart at mm. 9 and 73) is of special interest. At mm. 51, 53, and 57, respectively, the melody is in F major, C♯ minor, and F minor over accompanying triads in C♯ minor, G major, and B♭ minor, to which in m. 62 the flute adds a parallel descant a minor tenth above the piano's melody.

Except for their stable tonality, mm. 93–102 function as development, primarily by imitation, of the first five notes of "a" and the disjunct fourths and fifths of the flute's countermelody in mm. 5–6 and 8–9. The "cadenza," comprising "a^4, a^5, a^6," and a transition, is peppered with rhythmic directions (l'istesso tempo, ben ritmato, con precisione, non rubato) that deprive it of all the qualities of a cadenza (real or faux improvisation, recitative-like rhythm) except virtuosity, and considering the virtuosity required for the rest of the movement, that quality hardly sets the cadenza

section	**A**				**B**			
theme	a	a^1		transition	b			trans
phrase rhythm (# of mm)	2+2+2+2	2 + 4	2+4	2+2+2+2	4+5			3
starts m#	1	9	15	21	29			38
tonal center or key	**B^b**	**C** (rt hand) **D** (lt hand)	modulation	**D**		c minor	**B^b**	
starts m#	1	9	15	21		31	37	
Boldface capital letters standing alone designate tonal centers. Lower-case letters indicate minor keys. ("C major" & "D mixolydian" have customary meaning.)								
section	**A^1**	**C**			**A^2**			
theme	a^2	c	c^1	transition	a^3	$a^{developed/extended}$	transition	
phrase rhythm (# of mm)	2+3+2+3	3+3+2+3	3+4+3+1	3+2+4+2+2	2+2+3	2+2+2+4	2+4	
starts m#	41	51	62	73	86	93	103	
tonal center or key	**B**	c# minor (c#, G, c#, b^b)	c# minor (c#, G, c#, b^b)	flute: **a minor** piano: c, **a**, c, f#, **a**	piano modulates	d minor		
starts m#	41	51	62	73	86	93		
					flute ornaments f^3 & f^2			

CHART 34.3 Robert Muczynski, Sonata for Flute and Piano: Analysis of the fourth movement.

section	**A^3**							
theme	a^4			a^5	a^6	transition		
phrase rhythm (# of mm)	2+3+3			2+2+2	2+2+2	2+3+2+4		
starts m#	109			117	123	129		
tonal center or key	D mixolydian	b^b minor	modulation	e minor		modulation	e minor	
starts m#	109	111	114	117		129	133	
section	**A^4**	**Coda**						
theme	a^7	x	y	y^1	y^2			
phrase rhythm (# of mm)	2+5+2	2+2	4	3+3	4+2			
starts m#	140	149	153	157	163			
tonal center or key	e minor (continued)		C major					
starts m#	140		153					

CHART 34.3 Continued

apart. It's more a section for unaccompanied flute than a cadenza. The coda employs new thematic material and dwells in C from m. 153 on, the flute in C throughout while the piano outlines a Chopinesque cadence (like that of the Third Ballade): I (mm. 153–156), V^{11}/vi (E^{11} vice Chopin's V^7/vi, mm. 157–166), V^7 (m. 167), I.

In the fall of 1961, after returning from Nice, Muczynski began a second fellowship with the Young Composers Project, this time working for one year as composer-in-residence for the Tucson, Arizona, school system. Four years later he returned to that city to join the faculty of the University of Arizona as piano professor and head of the composition department. He remained at the university until his retirement in 1988. Muczynski lived his final years in Tucson with his partner Harry Atwood, the head of film production at the University of Arizona and the one to whom, decades earlier, Muczynski had dedicated the flute sonata.

While Muczynski launched his career with two major orchestral works, his focus later centered on solo piano and chamber music. He composed twelve works for woodwinds, among them an alto saxophone concerto that was nominated for the Pulitzer Prize and two later works for flute. None would ever surpass the earliest, however, the Sonata for Flute and Piano.

Notes

1. Robert Muczynski, liner notes for *Lurie and Baker play Muczynski*. Mitchell Lurie, clarinet; Julius Baker, flute; and Robert Muczynski, piano. Laurel Record, LR-131, 1984.

2. Robert Muczynski, liner notes for *Lurie and Baker play Muczynski*.

35 Aaron Copland—Duo for Flute and Piano

AARON COPLAND WAS born in Brooklyn in 1900, the youngest of five children of Jewish immigrants from Russian Lithuania: Sarah Mittenthal and Harris Copland (né Kaplan, but probably anglicized by a confused immigration official). The Coplands owned a successful department store, had little interest in music, and as the composer later recalled, "were of the opinion that enough money had been invested in the musical training of the four older children with meager results and had no intention of squandering further funds on me. But, despite the reasonableness of this argument, my persistence finally won them over."[1]

After his sister, Laurine, introduced him to the piano, ragtime, and opera, Aaron began piano lessons with Leopold Wolfsohn. In spite of limited musical experiences—he didn't attend his first concert until the age of fifteen—he decided to become a composer. And so in 1917, he embarked on the study of harmony and counterpoint with Rubin Goldmark, study that, along with piano and in lieu of college, continued for three years after his graduation from high school in 1918.

In 1919, a friend's enthusiastic letters about musical life in Paris fired Copland's imagination.[2] Sometime later he saw an ad in *Musical America* for a soon-to-be-established summer music school: the American Conservatory at Fontainebleau. Copland decided to enroll. He was awarded a scholarship that covered tuition for three months and set sail in June 1921.

After a brief period of study with Paul Vidal, he turned to Nadia Boulanger and studied with her for three years, first at Fontainebleau and then in Paris. It was a glorious time to be a musician in Paris, the world's musical center and home to Ravel, Stravinsky, Prokofiev, Satie, Les Six, and the Ballets russes. In addition to his studies there, Copland traveled extensively—to England, Belgium, Germany, Austria, and Italy—hearing new music, meeting composers, and studying scores. He later described his studies with Boulanger as the most important musical experience of his life.

The respect was mutual, and before he left Paris, Boulanger generously and astutely assisted the budding composer by providing two opportunities. First, in the spring of 1923, having learned that Russian-born conductor Serge Koussevitzky was to become music director of the Boston Symphony Orchestra beginning with the 1924/25 season, she arranged a meeting at his Paris apartment at which she introduced the young Copland.[3] This event had an enormous impact on Copland's career: Koussevitzky became an influential advocate whose repertoire embraced many of Copland's works, several of which he commissioned and premiered.[4] In 1940, when Koussevitzky founded the Berkshire Music Center, he appointed Copland assistant director. Copland held this summer position for twenty-five years.

The second of Boulanger's gestures on Copland's behalf began as an initiative of Koussevitzky on the day of their initial meeting: knowing that Boulanger was to make her American debut in 1924, Koussevitzky requested that Copland compose an organ concerto for Boulanger to perform with the Boston Symphony. It was a stunning invitation, and Copland accepted it, though he had little knowledge of the organ, had written only one large-scale piece, and had never heard a note of his own orchestration.[5] Boulanger then persuaded her friend Walter Damrosch to conduct Copland's work with the New York Symphony, thus securing two high-profile performances for her student.[6]

Throughout his career, Copland was determined to earn his living as a composer, rejecting the idea of a full-time university position. His decision led to many years of financial insecurity and austere living. Typically a slow, deliberate writer, he sometimes produced only one work a year, making it very difficult to rely solely on commissions and royalties. Through World War II, his income averaged only a few thousand dollars a year.[7]

Copland worked tirelessly to promote American music and dedicated himself to helping other composers. With Roger Sessions he organized the Copland-Sessions Concerts of contemporary American music (1928–1931) and, building on them, the Yaddo Festivals, held at the artists' retreat of the same name founded by financier Spencer Trask on his estate in Saratoga Springs. Copland was also cofounder and adviser of the not-for-profit Cos Cob Press, dedicated to publishing works by young American composers; an active member of New York's League of Composers; a lecturer; a writer of articles and music appreciation books; and a leading member of the American Composers Alliance.

During the 1930s, Copland, the modern, abstract composer, began to express doubts about the growing rift between the types of pieces composers were writing and the taste of the music-loving public: "It seemed to me that we composers were in danger of working in a vacuum. . . . I felt that it was worth the effort to see if I couldn't say what I had to say in the simplest possible terms."[8] Though he later considered his statements an "oversimplification" of his aims and intentions, there followed a string of more accessible pieces, including *El Salón México* (1936), *Billy the Kid* (1938), and *Rodeo* (1940). His World War II–era works, including *A Lincoln Portrait* (1942), *Fanfare for the Common Man* (1942), and the Pulitzer Prize–winning *Appalachian Spring* (1944), captured the patriotic fervor of the nation and established his music as the quintessential sound of America.

Although Copland didn't complete the Duo for Flute and Piano until March 1971, the piece shares characteristics with music he wrote during the 1940s. In fact, he is said to have "expressed disappointment that the work was so heavily influenced by his 1940s style."[9] The similarities are not surprising, however, given that he included music sketched at that time. Copland carefully preserved his sketches and manuscripts[10] and used them in many of his late works. Material in each of the three movements derives from 1940s sketches, one of which, dated September 26, 1944, includes, scribbled in parentheses, "Sonatina for Flute, Mvt. 2?"[11]

While he may have considered a sonatina at that time, it was not until almost three decades later that he composed his first work for flute and piano. Shortly after William Kincaid's death in 1967, a four-member committee (John Solum, John Krell, Kenton Terry, and Elaine Shaffer) initiated a commission for a composition in memory of the legendary teacher and performer, who had served as principal flutist of the Philadelphia Orchestra from 1921 until 1960 and as teacher at the Curtis Institute. Colleagues, friends, and seventy of Kincaid's former students contributed to the commissioning fund.

John Solum approached Samuel Barber, Leonard Bernstein, and Aaron Copland regarding the commission. Only Copland was willing to consider the idea.[12] The commission for a major work "to establish a 'living' memorial to perpetuate the name of William Kincaid" was offered in a letter dated August 16, 1967.[13] Copland agreed to compose the work for the sum of $2,500, with the caveat that a deadline for the work's completion not be specified. By this time, much of his attention had turned to conducting, and citing previous commitments, he was not sure when he might be able to produce the work. Nearly three years passed. Finally, with gentle prodding from Solum, Copland completed the second movement in late August 1970, the first movement in early December, and the final movement in March 1971.

The duo exhibits Copland's preference for three-movement designs.[14] The first movement, in arch form ("A-B-C-B-A"), opens with solo flute in B♭ major outlining I, IV, and V chords. Copland wrote this melody for the 1943 film *The North Star*.[15] Its mood and point of departure are, not surprisingly, much like the openings of both *Appalachian Spring* and *Billy the Kid*, written during the same period. The sound of *Appalachian Spring* continues after the entrance of the piano in m. 16.

The "B" section begins in m. 25 in D♭ major with two motives, shown in Example 35.1, interwoven in contrary motion.

EXAMPLE 35.1 Copland, Duo for Flute and Piano, Mvt. 1, mm. 25-28.

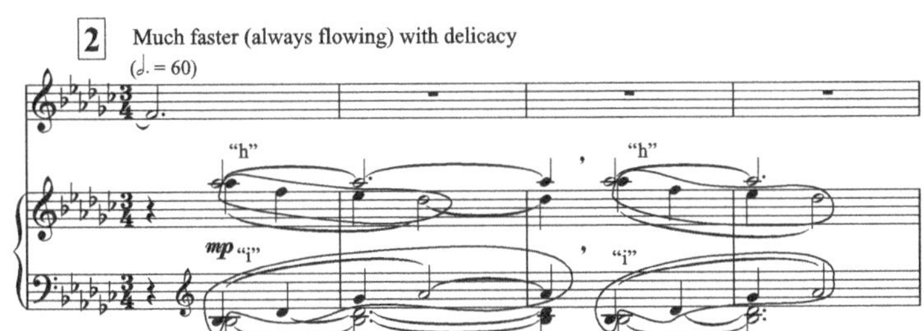

Measure 31 is compatible with both D♭ and C♭ major, the latter key prevailing in mm. 32–44, after which the center reverts to D♭, then, via the circle of fifths (mm. 53–56), to C♭ again (mm. 57ff.) leading into the sixteenth-note motion of "C." Here, modulations between key areas occur more rapidly:

m. 57	m. 61	m. 66	m. 70	m. 81	mm. 83–102
C♭ major	A♭ major	E Phrygian	E major	mod.	F major

Copland borrowed the final part of "C" (mm. 93–102) from his 1961 film score for *Something Wild*.[16] Following the return of "B" (m. 103) in its original keys of D♭ major modulating to C♭ major, Copland concludes the movement with the placid "A." The flute's melody is here a perfect fourth higher than in mm. 1–3 and 8–24. The movement closes in E♭ major after reminiscences of "B" material (mm. 147–152) in C♭ and D♭.

Copland considered the middle movement the least complex, both formally and melodically. "I think it came off well because it has a certain mood that I connect with myself—a rather sad and wistful mood, I suppose."[17]

As with the first movement, Copland incorporated into the second melodies that he had sketched earlier in his career. The first twenty-five measures of the movement (the "A" and "B" sections) are taken from a sketch dated September 26, 1944. Measures 51 to 62, which make up most of the "C" section, derive from undated sketches on another sheet of manuscript paper. Therefore, "very few of the movement's themes were actually conceived after Copland received the commission in 1967."[18]

The opening of the "A-B-A-C-A" movement is bitonal, the C major pedal of the piano's left hand contrasting with the C minor of the right hand, another example of the "split thirds" upon which the La Montaine Sonata for Flute Solo is based. (See Chapter 33) Embraced by the piano's tenor and treble, the flute unfolds in mm. 3–7 an expressive melody in A♭ Lydian continuing in A♭ Dorian, beginning with a motive that will recur many times.

Following a decisive arrival on a C major chord in all voices (m. 18), a faster tempo is introduced for the start of "B," whose louder, polyphonic, atonal, disjunct melodies with dotted rhythms contrast with the homophonic, tonal, conjunct, smoothly flowing melodies of "A." Also in contrast to "A," "B's" left–hand pedal expands from a major third to a dominant–seventh chord on C. A retransition, over a syncopated D♭ major chord, leads to the return of "A," now a half-step higher in A Lydian and Dorian, where the piano gets to share the melodic role.

The fourth section, "C," beginning with the upbeat to m. 46, is the emotional heart of the work, complex chords contributing to the intensity of expression as the flute soars into its upper register. Here again (mm. 53–58), the music recalls *Billy the Kid*'s "Open Prairie." In m. 63, Copland returns to music of the movement's opening.

The final movement begins attacca, with powerful tonic chords like those of Beethoven's *Eroica*. The melodies, texture, and energetic spirit again remind one of *Appalachian Spring*, also the "Hoe-down" from *Rodeo*: Copland had "fully explored" the flute's initial melody on manuscript pages dated May 8, 1945, and on other undated sketches.[19] After establishing D major, the composer visits an unpredictable series of keys: E major (mm. 13–14), B♭ major (mm. 15–16), D Mixolydian (m. 17), E major (mm. 18–20), D♭ major (mm. 21–23), then, after a modulatory passage, to B at m. 26, D♭ at m. 29, and F from m. 31 to the end of the "A" section.

The largely atonal "B" section of this ternary-form movement begins with a call-and-response passage between the two instruments. Later, measures 69–88 "resemble, but are not direct quotes from, the 'Gun Battle' movement of *Billy the Kid*."[20]

The return of "A" in m. 95 also marks a return to D major, followed by unpredictable juxtapositions of key areas and atonal passages:

m. 95	m. 99	m. 105	m. 107	m. 108	m. 109	m. 113	m. 117	m. 121	mm. 127
D	F	E♭	A	E	atonal	F	D♭	E♭	atonal

The meter changes in every bar of the first eight measures of the coda (mm. 131ff.), where, in the final seven measures, atonality finally gives way to D♯ major then, with a grandiose plagal cadence, its enharmonic equivalent. The tonal scheme of the composition is thus revealed: first movement B♭ major → E♭ major; second movement C major/minor → C major; third movement D major → E♭ major.

Immediately upon receiving Copland's letter announcing that he had completed the duo, John Solum replied with a proposal that the premiere of the work be scheduled for Sunday, October 3, 1971, as part of a benefit concert for the Settlement School of Philadelphia. Copland responded promptly that he would attend. Elaine Shaffer and Hephzibah Menuhin introduced the work, with Shaffer performing on Kincaid's platinum flute (Powell #365, made in 1939 for the New York World's Fair), which had been willed to her.[21] Shaffer later recorded the duo with Copland at the piano.

The duo, which Copland completed at the age of seventy, was his last large-scale composition. He composed very little between then and the end of his life at age ninety, saying, "It was exactly as if someone had simply turned off a faucet. [I was] lucky to have been given so long to be creative and resigned to the fact that it appears to be over."[22] By the time it *was* over, he had played a decisive role in the development of American music; to this day, Copland's music remains the sound of America.

Notes

1. Aaron Copland, *The New Music 1900–1960* (New York: Norton, 1968), 151.
2. Neil Butterworth, *The Music of Aaron Copland* (London: Toccata, 1985), 15.
3. Howard Pollack, *Aaron Copland: The Life and Work of an Uncommon Man* (New York: Henry Holt, 1999), 121.
4. Howard Pollack, "Copland, Aaron," *New Grove Dictionary of Music and Musicians*, ed. Stanley Sadie, 2nd ed., vol. 6 (London: Macmillan, 2001), 399.
5. Copland, 156.
6. Pollack, *Aaron Copland*, 121.
7. Pollack, *Aaron Copland*, 90.
8. Copland, 160.
9. Nina Perlove, "Ethereal Fluidity: The Late Flute Works of Aaron Copland" (DMA thesis, University of Cincinnati, 2003), v.
10. Pollack, *Aaron Copland*, 11.
11. Perlove, 18–19.
12. John Solum, "From Hindemith to Copland: Five Masterworks for Flute and Piano," *Flute Talk* 25 (March 2006): 15.
13. Richard Wyton, comp., "The Copland-Solum Correspondence, 1967–1975: The Duo for Flute and Piano Commission," *Flutist Quarterly* 17 (Winter 1992): 33.
14. Pollack, *Grove*, 403.

15. Perlove, 19–20.

16. Perlove, 50.

17. Aaron Copland, liner notes for "Copland Performs and Conducts Copland," Columbia Masterworks, M32737, 1974.

18. Perlove, 19.

19. Perlove, 23.

20. Perlove, 68.

21. Perlove, 25.

22. Pollack, *Grove*, 399.

Selected Bibliography

GEORG PHILIPP TELEMANN—SUITE IN A MINOR

Grove Music Online, s.v. "Telemann, Georg Philipp," by Steven Zohn, http://www.oxfordmusic-online.com.ezproxy.bradley.edu/.

Petzoldt, Richard. *Georg Philipp Telemann,* translated by Horace Fitzpatrick. New York: Oxford University Press, 1974.

Zohn, Steven. *Music for Mixed Taste*. New York: Oxford University Press, 2008.

GEORG FRIDERIC HANDEL—SONATA IN E MINOR, HWV 379

Best, Terence. "Handel's Chamber Music: Sources, Chronology, and Authenticity." *Early Music* 13 (Nov. 1985): 476–499.

Brown, Rachel. "Handel Flute and Recorder Sonatas." http://www.rachelbrownflute.com/_downloads/Handel%20Sonatas.pdf.

Burrows, Donald. *Handel*. New York: Schirmer, 1994.

Sawyer, John E. "Irony and Borrowing in Handel's 'Agrippina.'" *Music & Letters* 80 (Nov. 1999): 531–599.

ANTONIO VIVALDI—CONCERTO IN D MAJOR, *IL GARDELLINO*

Heller, Karl. *Antonio Vivaldi: The Red Priest of Venice*. Portland, OR: Amadeus Press, 1997.

Robbins Landon, H. C. *Vivaldi: Voice of the Baroque*. New York: Thames and Hudson, 1993.

Sardelli, Federico Maria. *Vivaldi's Music for Flute and Recorder*, translated by Michael Talbot. Aldershot, UK: Ashgate, 2007.

Talbot, Michael. *Vivaldi*. London: British Broadcasting Corporation, 1979.

JOHANN SEBASTIAN BACH—SONATA IN B MINOR, BWV 1030

Claypool, Richard David. "J. S. Bach's Sonatas for Melody Instrument and Cembalo Concertato: An Evaluation of All Related Manuscript Sources." PhD diss., Northwestern University, 1975.
Marshall, Robert L. *The Music of Johann Sebastian Bach*. New York: Schirmer, 1989.
Wolff, Christoph. *Bach: Essays on His Life and Music*. Cambridge, MA: Harvard University Press, 1991.
———. *Johann Sebastian Bach: The Learned Musician*. New York: Norton, 2000.

CARL PHILIPP EMANUEL BACH—SONATA IN A MINOR, WQ. 132

Helm, Eugene. "Carl Philipp Emanuel Bach." In *New Grove Bach Family*. New York: Norton, 1983.
Oleskiewicz, Mary. "The Flutist of Sanssouci: King Frederick 'the Great' as Performer and Composer." *Flutist Quarterly* 38 (Fall 2012): 18–26.
Ottenberg, Hans-Günter. *C. P. E. Bach*, translated by Philip J. Whitmore. Oxford: Oxford University Press, 1987.
Williams, Peter. "Towards a Close Reading of Carl Philipp Emanuel Bach." In *Eighteenth-Century Music in Theory and Practice: Essays in Honor of Alfred Mann*, edited by Mary Ann Parker. Stuyvesant, NY: Pendragon Press, 1994.

WOLFGANG AMADEUS MOZART—CONCERTO IN G MAJOR, K. 313

Anderson, Emily, trans. and ed. *The Letters of Mozart and His Family*. London: Macmillan, 1938.
Brook, Barry S. "The *Symphonie Concertante*: An Interim Report." *Musical Quarterly* 47 (1961): 493–516.
Küster, Konrad. *Mozart: A Musical Biography*. Oxford: Clarendon Press, 1996.
Levin, Robert D. *Who Wrote the Mozart Four-Wind Concertante?* Stuyvesant, NY: Pendragon Press, 1988.
Paumgartner, Bernhard. *Mozart*. Zurich: Atlantis, 1973.

FRANZ SCHUBERT—INTRODUCTION AND VARIATIONS, OP. POSTHUMOUS 160

Clements, Gretchen Rowe. "Situating Schubert: Early Nineteenth-Century Flute Culture and the 'Trockne Blumen' Variations, D. 802." PhD diss., State University of New York at Buffalo, 2007.
Erickson, Raymond, ed. *Schubert's Vienna*. New Haven, CT: Yale University Press, 1997.
Jackson, Stephen. *Franz Schubert: An Essential Guide to His Life and Works*. London: Pavilion, 1996.
McKay, Elizabeth Norman. *Franz Schubert: A Biography*. Oxford: Clarendon Press, 1996.
Newbould, Brian. *Schubert: The Music and the Man*. Berkeley: University of California Press, 1997.
Osborne, Charles. *Schubert and His Vienna*. New York: Knopf, 1985.

FRANZ DOPPLER—*FANTAISIE PASTORALE HONGROISE*, OP. 26

Adorján, András, and Lenz Meierott, eds. *Lexikon der Flöte*. Laaber, Germany: Laaber, 2009.
Stepper, Gernot. "Die Gebrüder Franz und Karl Doppler." *Tibia* 7 (1982): 88–95.

CARL REINECKE—SONATA, OP. 167, *UNDINE*

Bethea, Stephanie. "The Flute Music of Carl Reinecke." DMA diss., University of Washington, 2008.

Brown, Myrna. "Programmatic Elements in Carl Reinecke's Sonata, opus 167, 'Undine.'" *National Flute Association Newsletter* 7 (Winter 1982): 9–13.

Tomasone, Adeline. "A Fresh Look at Reinecke's Undine." *Flute Talk* 26 (Nov. 2006): 10–13, 29.

BENJAMIN GODARD—*SUITE DE TROIS MORCEAUX*, OP. 116

Blakeman, Edward. *Taffanel: Genius of the Flute*. New York: Oxford University Press, 2005.

Grove Music Online, s.v. "Godard, Benjamin (Louis Paul)," by Richard Langham Smith, http://www.oxfordmusiconline.com.ezproxy.bradley.edu/.

GABRIEL FAURÉ—*FANTAISIE*, OP. 79

Fauré-Fremiet, Philippe, ed. *Lettres intimes*. Paris: La Colombe, 1951.

Johnson, Graham. *Gabriel Fauré: The Songs and Their Poets*. London: Ashgate, 2009.

Nectoux, Jean-Michel. *Fauré: A Musical Life*, translated by Roger Nichols. Cambridge: Cambridge University Press, 1991.

———, ed. *Gabriel Fauré: His Life through His Letters*. London: Marion Boyars, 1984.

CÉCILE CHAMINADE—CONCERTINO, OP. 107

Citron, Marcia J. *Cécile Chaminade: A Bio-Bibliography*. Westport, CT: Greenwood Press, 1988.

Tardif, Cécile. "Cécile Chaminade and the Concertino, op. 107." *Flutist Quarterly* 15 (Spring 1990): 19–22.

———. *Portrait de Cécile Chaminade*. Montreal: Louise Courteau, 1993.

GEORGE ENESCU—*CANTABILE ET PRESTO*

Bentoiu, Pascal. *Masterworks of George Enescu: A Detailed Analysis*, translated by Lory Wallfisch. Lanham, MD: Scarecrow Press, 2010.

Malcolm, Noel. *George Enescu: His Life and Music*. London: Toccata Press, 1990.

Pincherle, Marc. *The World of the Virtuoso*. London: Gollancz, 1964.

PHILIPPE GAUBERT—*NOCTURNE ET ALLEGRO SCHERZANDO*

Dorgeuille, Claude. *The French Flute School (1860–1950)*, translated by Edward Blakeman. London: Tony Bingham, 1986.

Fischer, Penelope Peterson. "Philippe Gaubert (1879–1941): His Life and Contributions as Flutist, Editor, Teacher, Conductor and Composer." DMA diss., University of Maryland, 1982.

Grove Music Online, s.v. "Gaubert, Philippe," by Edward Blakeman, http://www.oxfordmusiconline.com.ezproxy.bradley.edu/.

GEORGES HÜE—*FANTAISIE*

Grove Music Online, s.v. "Hüe, Georges," by Richard Langham Smith, http://www.oxfordmusiconline.com.ezproxy.bradley.edu/.
Landormy, Paul. *La musique française: Après Debussy*. Paris: Gallimard, 1943.

CLAUDE DEBUSSY—*SYRINX*

Dietschy, Marcel. *A Portrait of Claude Debussy*. Oxford: Clarendon Press, 1990.
Fulcher, Jane F., ed. *Debussy and His World*. Princeton, NJ: Princeton University Press, 2001.
Nichols, Roger. *The Life of Debussy*. Cambridge: Cambridge University Press, 1998.
Orledge, Robert. *Debussy and the Theatre*. Cambridge: Cambridge University Press, 1982.
Stegemann, Michael, and Anders Ljungar-Chapelon, eds. *Debussy Syrinx La Flûte de Pan für Flöte solo*. Vienna: Wiener Urtext Edition, Schott / Universal Edition, 1996.
Wye, Trevor. *Marcel Moyse: An Extraordinary Man*. Cedar Falls, IA: Winzer Press, 1993.

ALBERT ROUSSEL—*JOUEURS DE FLÛTE*, OP. 27

Dobbs, Wendell. "Roussel: The Flute and Extramusical Reference." *Flutist Quarterly* 22 (Winter 1996/97): 51–57.
Follet, Robert. *Albert Roussel: A Bio-Bibliography*. Westport, CT: Greenwood Press, 1988.

CARL NIELSEN—CONCERTO FOR FLUTE AND ORCHESTRA

Lawson, Jack. *Carl Nielsen*. London: Phaidon, 1997.
Nelson, Amy Catherine. "The Flute Concerto by Carl Nielsen and the Contributions of Holger Gilbert-Jespersen." DMA diss., University of Colorado at Boulder, 2003.
Nielsen, Carl. *Living Music*, translated by Reginald Spink. London: Hutchinson, 1953.
———. *My Childhood*, translated by Reginald Spink. London: Hutchinson, 1953.
Petersen, Kirsten Flensborg. "Carl Nielsen's Flute Concerto: Form and Revision of the Ending." In *Carl Nielsen Studies* 2. Copenhagen: Royal Library, 2005.

JACQUES IBERT—CONCERTO FOR FLUTE AND ORCHESTRA

Huscher, Phillip. "Jacques Ibert: Flute Concerto, op. 37." Chicago Symphony Orchestra program book, Sept. 23–Oct. 8, 2011: 35–36A.
Macdonald, Hugh. "Jacques Ibert: Concerto for Flute and Orchestra." Boston Symphony Orchestra program book, Nov. 19–21, 2009: 43–49.
McCutchan, Ann. *Marcel Moyse: Voice of the Flute*. Portland, OR: Amadeus Press, 1994.
Michel, Gérard. *Jacques Ibert*. Paris: Seghers, 1967.

PAUL HINDEMITH—SONATA FOR FLUTE AND PIANO

Kater, Michael H. *Composers of the Nazi Era*. New York: Oxford University Press, 2000.
Kemp, Ian. *Hindemith*. London: Oxford University Press, 1970.
Luttmann, Stephen. *Paul Hindemith: A Research and Information Guide*, 2nd ed. New York: Routledge, 2009.

Noss, Luther. *Paul Hindemith in the United States*. Urbana: University of Illinois Press, 1989.
Rickards, Guy. *Hindemith, Hartmann, and Henze*. London: Phaidon, 1995.
Skelton, Geoffrey. *Paul Hindemith: The Man behind the Music*. London: Victor Gollancz, 1975.

EDGARD VARÈSE—*DENSITY 21.5*

Bernard, Jonathan W. *The Music of Edgard Varèse*. New Haven, CT: Yale University Press, 1987.
MacDonald, Malcolm. *Varèse: Astronomer in Sound*. London: Kahn and Averill, 2003.
Meyer, Felix, and Heidy Zimmermann, eds. *Edgard Varèse: Composer, Sound Sculptor, Visionary*. Woodbridge, UK: Boydell, 2006.
Rich, Alan. *American Pioneers: Ives to Cage and Beyond*. London: Phaidon, 1995.

FRANK MARTIN—*BALLADE* FOR FLUTE AND PIANO

King, Charles W. *Frank Martin: A Bio-Bibliography*. Westport, CT: Greenwood Press, 1990.
Shortall, Lori P. "Thematic, Harmonic, and Formal Aspects of Frank Martin's *Ballade* for Flute and Piano." Master's thesis, University of Western Ontario, 1996.
Soria, Dorle J. "Artist Life: Frank Martin, Master of All Trades." *High Fidelity / Musical America* 22 (March 1972): 11–13.
Vançon, Jean-Clair. "La Ballade pour flûte et piano de Frank Martin: Le style et l'écriture." *Traversières* 69 (2001): 9–19.

SERGEI PROKOFIEV—SONATA FOR FLUTE AND PIANO

Duke, Vernon. *Passport to Paris*. Boston: Little, Brown, 1955.
Gutman, David. *Prokofiev*. London: Alderman, 1988.
Nestyev, Israel V. *Prokofiev*. Stanford, CA: Stanford University Press, 1960.
Robinson, Harlow. *Sergei Prokofiev*. Boston: Northeastern University Press, 2002. First published New York: Viking, 1987.

HENRI DUTILLEUX—SONATINE FOR FLUTE AND PIANO

Mari, Pierrette. *Henri Dutilleux*. Paris: Hachette, 1973.
Nichols, Roger, trans. *Henri Dutilleux: Music—Mystery and Memory—Conversations with Claude Glayman*. Aldershot, UK: Ashgate, 2003.
Potter, Caroline. *Henri Dutilleux: His Life and Works*. Aldershot, UK: Ashgate, 1997.

ANDRÉ JOLIVET—*CHANT DE LINOS*

Fulcher, Jane F. *The Composer as Intellectual: Music and Ideology in France 1914–1940*. New York: Oxford University Press, 2005.
Grove Music Online, s.v. "Jolivet, André," by Barbara L. Kelly, http://www.oxfordmusiconline.com.ezproxy.bradley.edu/.
Kayas, Lucie. *André Jolivet*. Paris: Fayard, 2005.

BOHUSLAV MARTINŮ—FIRST SONATA FOR FLUTE AND PIANO

Large, Brian. *Martinů*. London: Duckworth, 1975.

Martinů, Charlotte. *My Life with Bohuslav Martinů*. Prague: Orbis, 1978.

Rybka, F. James. *Bohuslav Martinů: The Compulsion to Compose*. Lanham, MD: Scarecrow Press, 2011.

Šafránek, Miloš. *Bohuslav Martinů: His Life and Works*, translated by Roberta Finlayson-Samsourová. London: Allan Wingate, 1962.

Walter-Clark, Kimberly. "Bohuslav Martinů's Three Works for Flute, Violin and Keyboard." DMA document, University of Houston, 1999.

OLIVIER MESSIAEN—*LE MERLE NOIR*

Griffiths, Paul. *Olivier Messiaen and the Music of Time*. Ithaca, NY: Cornell University Press, 1985.

Hill, Peter, ed. *The Messiaen Companion*. London: Faber and Faber, 1995.

Hill, Peter, and Nigel Simeone. *Messiaen*. New Haven, CT: Yale University Press, 2005.

Nichols, Roger. *The Harlequin Years: Music in Paris, 1917–1929*. London: Thames and Hudson, 2002.

———. "Messiaen's 'Le merle noir': The Case of a Blackbird in a Historical Pie." *Musical Times* 129 (Dec. 1988): 648–650.

FRANCIS POULENC—SONATA FOR FLUTE AND PIANO

Daniel, Keith W. *Francis Poulenc: His Artistic Development and Musical Style*. Ann Arbor: UMI Research Press, 1980.

Ivry, Benjamin. *Francis Poulenc*. London: Phaidon, 1996.

Keck, George R. *Francis Poulenc: A Bio-Bibliography*. Westport, CT: Greenwood Press, 1990.

Schmidt, Carl B. *Entrancing Muse: A Documented Biography of Francis Poulenc*. Hillsdale, NY: Pendragon Press, 2001.

Schmidt, Carl B., and Patricia Harper, eds. "Historical Introduction" to Francis Poulenc *Sonata for Flute and Piano*, rev. ed. London: Chester Music, 1994.

LUCIANO BERIO—*SEQUENZA*

Folio, Cynthia. "Luciano Berio's *Sequenza* for Flute: A Performance Analysis." *Flutist Quarterly* 15 (Fall 1990): 18–21.

Halfyard, Janet K., ed. *Berio's Sequenzas: Essays on Performance, Composition and Analysis*. Aldershot, UK: Ashgate, 2007.

Osmond-Smith, David. *Berio*. Oxford: Oxford University Press, 1991.

———, trans. and ed. *Luciano Berio: Two Interviews with Rossana Dalmonte and Bálint András Varga*. New York: Marion Boyars, 1985.

CHARLES GRIFFES—*POEM* FOR FLUTE AND ORCHESTRA

Anderson, Donna K. "Charles Tomlinson Griffes," http://www.newworldrecords.org/linernotes/80273.pdf.

———. *Charles T. Griffes: A Life in Music*. Washington, DC: Smithsonian Institution Press, 1993.

Maisel, Edward M. *Charles T. Griffes: The Life of an American Composer*. New York: Knopf, 1943.

ELDIN BURTON—SONATINA FOR FLUTE AND PIANO

Bergfors, P. G. Program booklet for *American Sonatas*, translated by Linda Schenck. Göran Marcusson, flute; Joakim Kallhed, piano. Olofstorp, Sweden: IntimMusik, 1994.

ERNEST BLOCH—*SUITE MODALE*

Bergin, Wendy Isaac. "Ernest Bloch's Works with Solo Flute: An Analytical Study." Master's thesis, University of Houston, 1993.

Kushner, David Z. *The Ernest Bloch Companion*. Westport, CT: Greenwood Press, 2002.

Nott, Michael David. "Ernest Bloch's Pedagogical Writings: A Didactic Legacy of Twentieth-Century America." PhD diss., Eastman School of Music, 1985.

JOHN LA MONTAINE—SONATA FOR FLUTE SOLO, OP. 24

Hutchinson, Paula C. "Structure and Style in Three Flute Works of John La Montaine, with Three Recitals of Selected Works by Bach, Prokofiev, Messiaen, Reinecke, and Others." DMA diss., University of North Texas, 1994.

La Montaine, John, "Rediscovering John La Montaine." Interview with Frank J. Oteri. American Music Center, May 20, 2003. Transcribed by Randy Nordschow. http://www.newmusicbox.org/assets/53/interview_lamontaine.pdf.

ROBERT MUCZYNSKI—SONATA FOR FLUTE AND PIANO, OP. 14

Muczynski, Robert. Liner notes for *Lurie and Baker play Muczynski*. Mitchell Lurie, clarinet; Julius Baker, flute; and Robert Muczynski, piano. Laurel Records LR-131, 1984.

AARON COPLAND—DUO FOR FLUTE AND PIANO

Butterworth, Neil. *The Music of Aaron Copland*. London: Toccata, 1985.

Copland, Aaron. Liner notes for "Copland Performs and Conducts Copland," Columbia Masterworks M32737, 1974.

———. *The New Music 1900–1960*. New York: Norton, 1968.

Perlove, Nina. "Ethereal Fluidity: The Late Flute Works of Aaron Copland." DMA thesis, University of Cincinnati, 2003.

Pollack, Howard. *Aaron Copland: The Life and Work of an Uncommon Man*. New York: Henry Holt, 1999.

Wyton, Richard, comp. "The Copland-Solum Correspondence, 1967–1975: The Duo for Flute and Piano Commission." *Flutist Quarterly* 17 (Winter 1992): 33–43.

Index